TIN
DISINHERITED CHILDREN

Robin Young

TIME'S DISINHERITED CHILDREN

CHILDHOOD, REGRESSION AND SACRIFICE IN THE PLAYS OF HENRIK IBSEN

Norvik Press
1989

Other Norvik Press books:

Michael Robinson: *Strindberg and Autobiography*
Irene Scobbie (ed.): *Aspects of Modern Swedish Literature*
Sigbjørn Obstfelder: *A Priest's Diary,* edited and translated by James McFarlane
Annegret Heitmann (ed.): *No Man's Land* - An Anthology of Danish Women Writers
Bjørg Vik: *An Aquarium of Women,* translated by Janet Garton
Hjalmar Söderberg: *Short Stories,* selected and translated by Carl Lofmark
James McFarlane: *Ibsen and Meaning: Studies, essays and prefaces 1953–87*
Egil Törnqvist and Barry Jacobs: *Strindberg's Miss Julie*
P.C. Jersild: *A Living Soul,* translated by Rika Lesser

Our logo is based on a drawing by Egil Bakka (University of Bergen) of a Viking ornament in gold foil, paper thin, with impressed figures (size 16 x 21 mm). It was found in 1897 at Hauge, Klepp, Rogaland, and is now in the collection of the Historisk museum, University of Bergen (inv.no.5392). It depicts a love scene, possibly (according to Magnus Olsen) between the fertility god Freyr and the maiden Gerðr; the large penannular brooch of the man's cloak dates the work as being most likely 10th century.

British Library Cataloguing in Publication Data
Young, Robin
Time's disinherited children : childhood, regression and sacrifice in the plays of Henrik Ibsen
I. Title
839.8'226 PT8895

ISBN 1-870041-06-2

First published in 1989 by Norvik Press, University of East Anglia, Norwich, NR4 7TJ, England

Managing Editors: James McFarlane and Janet Garton

Norvik Press has been established with financial support from the University of East Anglia, the Danish Ministry for Cultural Affairs, the Norwegian Cultural Department, the Swedish Institute and Letterstedska föreningen, Sweden.

Printed in Great Britain by the University of East Anglia, Norwich.

CONTENTS

ACKNOWLEDGEMENTS.

The reader well-versed in such matters will recognize how much this study owes to the example of other critics; in particular, I have learned much from the work of Weigand, Stuyver, McFarlane and Durbach. To these and other critics, past and present, I gladly acknowledge my indebtedness.

I am also grateful to the Delegates of the Oxford University Press for permission to quote from *The Oxford Ibsen* (ed. J.W.McFarlane, 1960-77).

Much of the first draft of this study was written in the winter and spring of 1982, during a study-leave term at the Institutt for Nordisk språk og litteratur of the University of Oslo. For the hospitality of the Institutt then, and during a subsequent visit in 1986, I am most grateful. A special word of thanks must also be said to the Inter-library Loans staff of the University Library in Aberystwyth, without whose assistance it would have been difficult if not impossible to complete this book so far from the library resources of Scandinavia.

Amongst friends and colleagues in Aberystwyth, I am especially grateful to Maldwyn Mills, who has been an unfailing source of encouragement and shrewd advice during the writing of this book. I am also much indebted to James McFarlane and Janet Garton for reading and commenting on the book's final draft. Though I have not always followed their advice, I should like to place my gratitude on record, and to emphasize that whatever foolishness remains in the book is entirely my own responsibility.

Amongst those who have helped in the physical production of the book, special thanks must go to Morfydd Radford, who typed the whole of the final draft from manuscript. I am also grateful to Jean Cock for typing revisions and the Bibliography. That the book is so well produced is due in large part to Charlotte Carstairs, who transferred the text to disc, and to the ingenuity and professionalism of Norvik Press. I could not have wished for more helpful collaborators.

Robin Young
Aberystwyth, July 1988

TEXT AND TRANSLATION : A NOTE

The only proper basis for any serious critical study of Ibsen's work can be the authentic Norwegian text. Accordingly, all quotations are given first from the standard edition, the *Hundreårsutgave* (H), and then in an English translation based on *The Oxford Ibsen* (O). In some places (frequently in discussion of the verse dramas, more rarely elsewhere) I have altered the *Oxford Ibsen* translation to give a more literal reading or one that makes it easier for a reader with no knowledge of Norwegian to follow the sense of the original. Page-references to these altered translations are marked with an asterisk, thus:- O*. In such cases, the reader may go back to the *Oxford Ibsen* to see where and how the translations diverge.

Translations from Ibsen's poems and from the works of other Scandinavian authors are my own, unless otherwise stated.

For details of other editions used or consulted and for a list of abbreviations used in the footnotes, see section (i) of the Bibliography.

FOR MY MOTHER

Jede dumpfe Umkehr der Welt hat solche Enterbte,
denen das Frühere nicht und noch nicht das Nächste gehört.

Rilke, *Duineser Elegien*, VII.

Preface

HOMUNCULUS:
> Romantische Gespenster kennt ihr nur allein;
> Ein echt Gespenst, auch klassisch hat's zu sein.
>
> Goethe, *Faust, Zweiter Teil*

This study has a twofold purpose - to trace through Ibsen's work from *The Warriors at Helgeland* (1858) to *When We Dead Awaken* (1899) a complex of themes and motives relating to children, heredity, regression and sacrifice; and to use this thematic analysis as the basis for a reading of Ibsen's work as a whole.

Until comparatively recently, this aspect of the plays had not received much critical attention. Muriel Bradbrook in her *Ibsen the Norwegian* noted the presence of the Iphigenia theme in *The Wild Duck*, and suggested that it might have relevance for other plays, as well.[1] But it was only with James Kerans's essay of 1965 that any attempt was made to place the theme at the centre of Ibsen's creative work. Kerans claimed that 'beginning with *Brand*, it [*Kindermord*] unmistakably finds its place in the larger imaginative order of the play, and in every subsequent play it is fundamental to the dramatic action'.[2]

What Kerans does not really address himself to in his essay - let alone solve satisfactorily - is the *significance* of this pattern. His essay confines itself almost entirely to *Little Eyolf*; and even his comments on that play seem over-schematic both in the (over-)interpretation of detail and in his claim that the play as a whole (consciously?) enacts the re-living and transcending of childhood trauma. What misleads Kerans, I think, is the somewhat reductive assumption that the events depicted in a work of art can or should be explicitly translatable in terms of the sexual drives which (in some sense or other) these events 'represent', and that furthermore such a substitution can somehow explain or account for the work of art. Post-Freudian criticism shows here its usual difficulty in grasping that it is possible for a writer to use sexuality as a means to debate other and wider issues of human conduct. Yet that, I want to argue, is exactly what Ibsen is doing through his use of the *Kindermord* theme, not only in *Little Eyolf* but throughout his career as a creative writer.

For Ibsen did not write or think as a Freudian. To gain some understanding of the way in which his mind worked, it is necessary to go back to his early works and to the intellectual and cultural milieu in which they were created. Anglo-Saxon criticism - so ingrained are its imperial assumptions - can sometimes find it difficult to accept that so apparently familiar a writer as Ibsen could have written in a cultural context both unfamiliar and, to a large extent, inaccessible through translation. Even so perceptive and stimulating a study as Durbach's '*Ibsen the Romantic*' (1982) concentrates its discussion of Ibsen's affinities with other writers on those with Romantics in the English tradition, most of whom he probably had not read, even in translation.[3] Yet a study of Ibsen's early reading and literary loyalties would reveal that he wrote and thought as the heir to a very specific and in many ways *anti*-Romantic tradition in Norwegian and Danish literature, a tradition which had formed his literary taste, and some of whose preoccupations and attitudes (both intellectual and aesthetic) remained with him to the end of his life. The writer to whom Ibsen and his friends of the 50s and 60s looked back with the greatest affection and respect was the rationalist and sceptic Ludvig Holberg. A less Romantic soul never lived. As for more immediate literary ancestors, to mention (as Durbach does) Welhaven and Wergeland, Heiberg and Oehlenschläger in the same breath, is to miss the extent to which Ibsen himself, from the very beginning of his career, established a distance between himself and that Romanticism of transcendence and sacrifice which Durbach seeks to establish as an important element in his imaginative world. I am sure that Durbach is right when he says (speaking of Brand and Gregers) that 'the "murderer" of the Romantic child in Ibsen is the Romantic transcendentalist' and when he speaks of 'the neurotic basis of the idealistic impulse... and the catastrophic failure to locate transcendental value in a corresponding human reality'.[4] But his study seems to veer away from the implications of this perception for a reading of Ibsen's work as a whole.[5] I shall seek to establish that, far from seeking to balance Romantic and anti-Romantic elements, Ibsen builds throughout his work a consistent and devastating critique of just that Romantic idealism which Durbach (against much of the run of his own argument) seems to regard as an essential element of the author's creative personality. I shall argue that this attitude can be traced from the early poetry and the Viking dramas to the final plays; that it is absolutely congruent with that sceptical, anti-Idealist, anti-Romantic strain in Norwegian and Danish literature to which Ibsen was heir; and that in his revisions to the plays Ibsen stressed aspects which tend to alienate sympathy from those who would in some sense 'murder the future' in the name of their own ideals and in an attempt to preserve or resurrect their own past.

Yet if, on one level, Ibsen remained committed to what could be described as the classicism (moral as well as aesthetic) of the Welhaven-Heiberg tradition, in terms of artistic *innovation* he invoked that same sense of formal order and psychological scepticism to renew the artistic models of the past. *Brand* owes much both to the Nordic tragedies of Oehlenschläger and the neo-classic dramas of Paludan-Müller; *Peer Gynt* uses the form of Oehlenschläger's *Aladdin* yet often recalls the spirit of Heiberg's Vaudevilles. The early dramas of contemporary life, *A Doll's House* and *Ghosts* are indebted - sometimes too much so - to the theatre of melodrama and intrigue. Yet in each case Ibsen brought to his models not just a greater clarity and fastidiousness of formal design, but a much deeper awareness of the springs of human conduct.

One touchstone of this development is his creation within the characters on the stage of a sense of the dramatic past, colouring their personalities and actions, most of all when they are under the delusion that they are acting in freedom and alone. In evoking this sense of past-in-present, he came more and more to concentrate the focus of his dramas on the structures of the family.

There are important parallels here with developments in the European realist and naturalist novel. But whereas the great French and Russian realists explored the complexities of human and social relationships through broad panoramas, cycles of novels which trace the fictive histories of large groups of people, or of families through several generations, Ibsen tended to focus on a single family at a single point of dramatic time. Where Balzac and Zola can seem grand and diffuse, Ibsen's art is one of concentration, both in space and time. As if to compensate for the restrictions of outer scale imposed by the limitations of the conventional theatre of his day, he concentrates attention within the dramatic unities on the interplay of past and present in single characters or small groups of related characters. And he achieves this partly through intricately-woven *forhistorier*, partly through a depth of characterization in which we can always discern past in present, the child within the adult.

No playwright so consistently evokes the sense of the past which underlies present human behaviour; no playwright since Shakespeare has so imaginatively explored the inner space beneath the surface of dramatic action. Except for a brief period in the early 1880s, Ibsen had little truck with the mechanical, pseudo-scientific notions of heredity so beloved of the continental Naturalists. He had little to learn from such ideas; they were already a part of his dramatic world, from *Brand* and *Peer Gynt* onwards - and their conscious schematic formulation in *Ghosts* is rather a weakness in the play's structure. His characters are conceived as dramatic wholes, intensely imagined as theatrical presences precisely by virtue of those imagined pasts so cunningly revealed through their behaviour on stage.

And it is Ibsen's evocation of his characters' inner past that lends such significance and resonance to the fate of children, born and unborn, in the plays. For the title of this study does not only, or even principally, refer to such victims of parental selfishness as Alf, Hedvig and Eyolf - nor yet to the dead or unborn children of Ellida Wangel or Hedda Gabler. In a sense, the true 'disinherited children' are adults who are sealed by environment, heredity, chance or self-will into childish roles which they are incapable of outgrowing. In such characters - and every major Ibsen play after *Brand* contains at least one, usually more - the 'child within the man' has swollen to displace all possibilities of inner growth. Bøyg-like, it has the power to block, to forbid, to force the personality to 'go round', whatever the cost to itself or to others.

All Ibsen's greatest plays are concerned with that cost. So regularly, indeed, does the account of such sacrifice present itself for reckoning, that it is difficult not to suspect some direct and personal relevance. For Ibsen, judgement-day was, first and last, a settling of accounts with himself. Beneath the seemingly differing problems and destinies of apparently disparate characters, the plays are haunted by a sense of self-accusation, by suspicion of the way that the artist, too, distorts the life - and the lives - on which art is based. Perhaps it is this which gives the theme of the disinherited child its central place in Ibsen's work.

Introduction

> How to mediate a life of contradictions?
> How to tell beautiful lies
> or the perfect truth?
> (Gunnar Ekelöf, 'Monte Chronion')

(i)

In the last act of Ibsen's viking-drama, *The Warriors at Helgeland*, the chieftain-poet Ørnulf sits at the sea's edge, desolate at the loss of his favourite son. His daughter persuades him to put his grief into verse. Dolefully at first, then with rising enthusiasm, the old man transforms grief into song:-

Mine sønner tog hun;
men hun gav min tunge
evnen til i kvæder
ud min sorg at sjunge.

[H, IV, 89]

Of my sons she stripped me
yet also gave me speech,
the gift of lyric power
to voice in song my grief.

[O*, II, 86]

It is a moving moment, yet one which does not seem of particular relevance to the dominant themes of the play. As Koht remarked, even the provenance of this scene is markedly different from that of the rest of the play;[6] Ørnulf's lament is from first to last a paraphrase of the poem 'Son-burial' quoted in *Egil Skallagrimsson's Saga*. Koht remarks that this insertion of not apparently relevant material from a different literary source may seem puzzling. Yet with hindsight, it can be seen as a decisive moment in Ibsen's development, the first appearance of a motive which was to recur in many different forms throughout his literary production. What so interested Ibsen in the 'Son-burial' was not only the idea of freeing oneself from grief through song (as Koht surmises) but also, by implication, the sacrifices which poetry demands of the poet, and of those close to him. 'Son-burial' ends in a spirit of - at best - reconciliation to death. In Ibsen's adaptation, Ørnulf ends his poem by affirming the primacy of poetry, its power to transcend life and death:-

Hil jer, sønner gæve!
Hil jer, der I rider!
Gudegaven læger
verdens ve og kvider!

[H, IV, 89]

Hail, my doughty sons!
Hail to you where you ride!
Thus the gift, god-given
heals world's grief and pain!

[O*, II, 86]

Yet this affirmation is not to be taken at face value, at least in the context of Ibsen's later work. It marks the beginning, not the end of an argument. The price at which this 'gift god-given' must be purchased, the sacrifice necessary in order to create, and the human implications of that sacrifice, were to remain a recurrent and abiding preoccupation for the rest of Ibsen's creative life.

(ii)

Often a particular stage in the career of an imaginative artist can be identified as crucial to the development of an individual point of view, a personal style. The years between Ibsen's engagement to Suzannah Thoresen in 1856 and their departure for Italy in 1864 formed such a stage. The outward circumstances of the period - Ibsen's move to the new theatre at Christiania, his increasing unhappiness there - are not important except in so far as they may have aggravated that inner conflict between the claims of art and of life to which so many of the poems and plays refer. *Først da jeg var bleven gift fik mit liv et vægtigere indhold*, 'Only after I was married did my life acquire a weightier content', he wrote later; and the first fruit of this was the narrative/philosophical poem *'Paa Vidderne'*, 'On the Mountain Heights'. Critics have long recognized the significance of the poem in charting Ibsen's development. Yet *'Paa Vidderne'* remains an enigmatic work - a single, apparently uncompromising term in a much more complex argument, and a term, moreover, which seems to contradict most of the abiding beliefs which much of his later work was to express. Since the matters of which it treats are so crucial and since discussion of the poem, especially amongst critics writing in English, has been rather general, it may be useful to examine the work in some detail.[7]

As the poem opens, it is a moonlit summer night. The narrator leaves his mother's house in the village and goes out to woo his sweetheart. They spend the night together *i disigt måneskin*, 'in the mist-veiled moonlight'. Next morning, he justifies the night's proceedings by telling her that they will soon be married. No sooner has he said this, however, than he is afflicted by a different sort of longing (*længslen*); -

Her står jeg som pány besjælt,
så svalt er nu mit blod...
jeg er så frisk, jeg står så nær

mig selv og nær min Gud!

[H, XIV, 390]

Here I stand, inspired anew
So cool is now my blood...
I feel so well, I stand so near
myself and near my God.

It is the freedom of the mountain heights that now calls to him, in terms which - especially in the last two lines - seem to prefigure Brand's triumphant equation of self and God.[8] What the voices of the mountains seem to offer him is a world in which the compromises of domestic life are unnecessary or irrelevant. With the briefest of farewells, he sets off.

Already an elaborate play of dramatic irony is at work - for the narrator is perhaps the first in a long line of characters who, divided against themselves, contradict and deceive themselves at every turn. He now speaks of his night with the girl as having been provoked by

det trold, som heksebandt mit sind

[H, XIV, 391]

that troll who bewitched my mind.

Yet if only *she* were here, his soul would be purified in her gaze. All the contradictions of 19th century attitudes to women which Ibsen was later to explore and excoriate - the demand that they fulfil the roles of both madonna and whore, the tendency to *blame* them for provoking such feelings in men - are already present in this monologue. The narrator prays, from a distance, that his sweetheart's life be made easy - yet wishes, a moment later, that her life's path be hard, so that he can carry her along it.

At this point another character enters. He is never named, and it is not clear whether he really exists or is no more than a projection of the narrator's other self, summoned up to resolve his inner contradictions. Ambivalence is the leading-note of the stranger's character; *Gråden leger i hans latter*, 'Weeping sports within his laughter' and his eyes are compared to 'a blue-black tarn fed by the mountain snows' [H, XIV, 392]. The narrator is afraid yet fascinated - he would like to break away, but the encounter has robbed him of *selve evnen til at* ville, 'the very power to *will*'. Whoever the stranger is, his message is uncompromising. Like Gerd in *Brand* - and the trolls in *Peer Gynt* - he preaches a gospel of pure self-fulfilment amongst the mountain snows. Persuaded, or hypnotized, the narrator turns his back on life in the valley, and on the love and responsibility which go with it.

In the next section of the poem, autumn has come. It is his last chance to leave his mountain hut before it is cut off by the winter snows. But by now, rather like a precursor of the denizens of Thomas Mann's Magic Mountain, he has become unfitted for life below:-

her *blev mine tanker stærke,*
kun på vidden kan jeg trives.

[H, XIV, 394]

Here on the heights my thoughts
grew strong; here alone I can thrive.

Yet he still cannot reconcile himself to the isolation which this chosen path of life must imply. Even now he dreams of fetching his loved ones from the valley when spring comes, of teaching *them* his new-found (but unspecified) wisdom - thus foreshadowing both Brand's insistence on his wife and child remaining in a place which he knows will kill them, and Alfred Allmers's long treks over the mountains, reconstructing an idealized family life in his own mind.

Now the young man feels that he can bear the loneliness no more, that he must escape, if only for a day, to see his mother and his bride. But it is too late; all the paths are closed. And when, later, it does become possible to go out and look down again on the village, the stranger reappears, a sneer on his lips: - *ak ja, den hjemlige hytte!* - 'ah yes, the cosiness of home!'. At once, the narrator is cured of his momentary wish to spend Christmas with his family. Even when it becomes apparent that the cheerful glow of his mother's cottage is caused by the fact that it is burning down, the stranger is ready with words of consolation:-

han viste, hvor virksomt luens glød
over i månens strejflys flød
til en sammensat natbelysning.

he showed how effectively glow of the fire
and light of the moon were blending
to a luminous night-composition.

The scene has become aestheticized; the cold light of the moon (symbolizing impersonal inspiration) and the bright fire consuming his childhood home combine to produce a composition which is visually satisfying. Even after the Stranger has vanished, and the narrator, by now conventionally grief-stricken, is staggering back to his hut, even then he reflects,

...det kan ikke nægtes, der var *effekt*
i den dobbelte natbelysning!

it can't be denied, it *was* effective,
that double glow, illuming the night!

From this knowledge there can be no retreat. To be able to transform human suffering into aesthetic experience involves acquiring perspective, a sense of absolute detachment. The narrator has lost his mother and his home; in the poem's final section he is to see (again from above) his sweetheart marry someone else. But by now he has lost the power to react; -

> *...jeg tror jeg mærker i bringens hvælv*
> *alleslags tegn til forstening.*
>
> [H, XIV, 400]

> I believe I notice within my breast
> all the signs of petrifaction.

The man has become - or at any rate has made what he believes to be the necessary sacrifice to become - an artist. He no longer feels the mountain cold, or any urge to participate in life. For experience he has substituted an aesthetic understanding denied to those *som nede i sværmen sidder*, 'who stay down there, amongst the herd'.

'Paa Vidderne' seems, on the face of it, an uncompromising statement of the price to be paid for becoming an artist. But the inner contradictions and bad faith of the narrator, his weakness of will and readiness to consent to the sacrifice of others should warn us against equating his thoughts with Ibsen's. Ibsen himself referred to the *frigørelsestrang*, the 'need' or 'urge' for liberation (the word is ambiguous) which runs through this poem and which was to find full expression in *Love's Comedy*, written a couple of years later. But both in that play and in the poem *'Byggeplaner'* [H, XIV, 208], 'Building Plans' (the first version of which was written before 1858) Ibsen is concerned to question what seem in *'Paa Vidderne'* to be immutable truths. 'Building Plans' records, retrospectively, his own creative plans at the beginning of his career. In that first version of the poem, he likens his ambitions to a dream-castle with two *Formaal*[9] or 'purposes';-

> *Det Store var at blive en udødelig Mand,*
> *Det Lille var at eie en deilig Liljevand.*
>
> [H, XIV, 208]

The greater was to achieve undying fame,
The lesser was to own a beautiful lily-pond.

In a later version, these wishes are clarified - there the two wings of the castle would house an immortal *skald* and a *pigebarn*, a 'girl-child' or 'young girl' (the word is, perhaps significantly, ambiguous). But the most significant aspect of these plans is what experience has made of them. And in the earlier version,[10] a total revaluation has taken place:-

Alt som jeg blev fornuftig, blev det Hele splittergalt:
Det Store blev saa lidet, det Lille blev mig Alt.

As soon as I got wisdom, the whole scheme seemed to fall;
The greater purpose dwindled, the lesser one grew to be all.

The implication here is surely that, even by 1858, emotional happiness seemed to him much more important than success or reputation.

'On the Heights' and 'Building Plans' represent the two contradictory terms of the central tension in Ibsen's work at this period, a tension which underlies, in various forms, all his later work as well. What makes the poems and plays of 1858-64 so exciting in themselves and so crucial to an understanding of all that came later, is that they express so trenchantly, so recklessly, the thesis and antithesis between which the later work seeks to mediate. It was all very well for Kierkegaard to posit two separate modes of existence, the Aesthetic and the Ethical - and a final transcendent Beyond to which only the man of faith might attain. But the creative artist, unlike the saint (and Ibsen again and again insists upon the unlikeness) *cannot* simply transcend the separate limitations of aesthetic and ethical truth. If he (unlike the speaker in '*Paa Vidderne*') is to remain both artist and human being, he must, somehow, reconcile the two.

This is the problem, never finally to be resolved, which was to haunt the rest of Ibsen's career. Is it necessary for the writer to sacrifice in order to create? Is he ethically justified in so doing? Is this readiness to sanctify one's own egotism not a pathway to megalomania, the mark of the false saint, eternally ready (like so many of Ibsen's later heroes, from Brand to Rubek) to sacrifice others to his own vanity? When he wrote that

> *At* digte, - *det er at holde*
> *dommedag over sig selv.*
>
> [H, XIV, 461]

> To *write* is to hold
> judgement-day over oneself.

Ibsen was not indulging in hyperbole, but expressing what was, for him, a sober and exact truth. However manifold and various the charges which his characters must face in the intensely imagined and individuated worlds of their separate dramas, a sense of *self*-accusation lies somewhere behind them all - the dreadful possibility that, in one or in several senses, the sacrifice has been in vain. Hence that succession of characters, each of whom believes that he or she has been offered some special exemption from the moral laws which govern the rest of the world, 'fumbling about below'. And not only the moral laws. For what these 'disinherited children' (the term is at least as applicable to them as it is, in a different sense, to those they sacrifice) seek to deny is their own mortal nature, their existence in time. They are, characteristically, prisoners of a childhood which they cannot or will not outgrow, transfixed in a Romantic dream which demands the sacrifice of other real or imagined children so that their own inner worlds may remain intact.

(iii)

Nowhere in Ibsen's work is the antinomy between poetry and life more explicit than in the plays and poems of the early 1860s. *Love's Comedy*, in particular, can be read as an almost Shavian comedy of debate concerning the relative claims made on a young poet by life and art. But whereas Shaw tends to depress us by his conviction that problems can be solved and the world saved by argument alone, the context in which the characters of *Love's Comedy* conduct their debate suggests how humanly inadequate the terms of that debate really are. Pastor Straamand's conviction that he must sacrifice whatever creative ambitions he has had for the sake of his multifarious brood of children, and Falk's insistence (only stilled by the briefest imaginable engagement to Svanhild) that the poet should have no human ties or responsibilities whatever - both are, considered in any wider context, unacceptable alternatives. And Falk's position, at least, with its glorification of the life of aesthetic irresponsibility, is undercut throughout the play by the imagery in which it is expressed. Ibsen may have re-entitled the song with which Falk begins the play *'Digterens vise'*, 'The Poet's Song', but it seems very unlikely that he intended this as an endorsement of Falk's beliefs. For the glorification of blossom over fruit, aesthetically attractive potential over fertile achievement,

Hvad vil Du om Frugten spørge
Midt i Træets Blomstertid?

[H, IV, 143]

Would you start to weigh your apples
when the blossom's on the bough?

[O, II, 99]

is only too apt. This song - indeed, much of the play - may be interpreted as a gloss on the scene in J. L. Heiberg's *A Soul after Death*[11] in which the central character, the very soul of mediocrity, after sampling the Christian Heaven and Pagan Elysium, finds his true home in Hell. Heiberg's Hell, like Falk's Paradise, is a place where blossom never sets and spring can never lead to harvest; it is *Begyndelsens evige Land*, 'the land of eternal beginnings', a world which is eternal precisely by token of its incapacity to develop. And whereas Heiberg shows us his true poet, Aristophanes, as rumbustiously questioning and sharp-witted as ever, in a pagan Paradise to which the bourgeois Soul is denied entrance, the Poet whom we see in Hell is a human inadequate who has sought to use art as a compensation for an ill-spent (or un-spent) life:-

Om ei mig selv jeg havde lukt
Fra Godhed og fra Fromhed ud,
Da toned ei mit Qvad af Længsel...

If I had not locked out myself
From Goodness and from Pious Deeds
My song could not resound with longing...

But even the poet's alibi for the inadequacies of his human existence:-

Hvis jeg var god, jeg digted slet,
Men jeg er slet, og digter godt.

If my life were good, my verse would be bad
But I have lived badly, and my poems are good.

is specifically undercut by the comment of Mephistopheles:-

At han selv er slet, er det Visse i Sagen,
Men om Digtet er godt, kommer an paa Smagen.

> That *he* is bad, that is true at least;
> That the poem is good, is a matter of taste.

The Poet remains in Hell, and though he has been taken as the mouthpiece for Heiberg's belief in a necessary separation between a writer's life and his art, in this play, at least, no-one is left to quarrel with Mephistopheles's dismissal of his beliefs as *mærkelig Inconsequens*, 'a notable non-sequitur'.

And the same, surely, is true of Ibsen's Falk. I can see no substantial evidence in the play for Francis Bull's view that Falk learns, and in learning transcends Heiberg's aestheticism. For, like Peer Gynt with Solvejg, all Falk wants of *his* beloved, Svanhild, is the memory of her, a matter for poetry divorced from time and development. He may compare his poetic soul to a *langelek*, a fiddle with sympathetic strings which supply a note of longing beneath the cheerful melody of life. But there is not much more evidence of the power to transform talent into achievement in his case than there is in Peer Gynt's. Falk's departure at the end of the play, renouncing Svanhild and responsibility as he heads for the mountain wastes, does not solve the problems of the play, but gracefully bypasses them. For all his talk of turning the blossoms' nectar into honey (not fruit), the play is haunted to the end by a sense of decorative sterility. To Ibsen, even at this stage, a retreat into anacreontic irresponsibility was neither attractive nor even possible. Some other resolution of the conflict had to be found.

(iv)

Not until the plays of his final period was Ibsen again to be so explicit in his discussion of the conflicting claims of art and life. But there are a couple of instances in the works he produced immediately after *Love's Comedy* which shed light on the more positive way his thoughts were developing in the crucial years before the writing of *Brand*. In each passage a poet reflects on the nature of inspiration. Each provides a sort of commentary on Falk's unrepentant aestheticism and each does so through the imagery of childhood and sacrifice.

The first instance is perhaps as unexpected in its context as Ørnulf's lament in *The Warriors at Helgeland*. In the fourth act of *The Pretenders* (*Kongs-emnerne*, 1864), King Skule asks the Icelandic poet, Jatgejr, *Sidder du inde med mange udigtede kvad*, 'Have you any other unspoken ballads in your head?' [H, V, 106/ O, II, 298]. Jatgejr replies:-

Nej, men med mange ufødte; de undfanges
et efter et, får liv og så fødes de.

No, but many unborn; they are conceived one
after the other; they are given life and are born.

In itself, and in another context, the metaphor might seem unremarkable enough.[12] But in the context of this conversation, Jatgejr's conceit has a special resonance. What fascinates Skule, the statesman-warrior gnawed by envy and unfulfilled ambition, is whether Jatgejr's 'children' can be subjected to the same pressures as ordinary human children. Do poets envy each other their poems? Would they, if they could, kill each other to get those poems? Jatgejr refuses these speculations - he has his own children, and no need to find others to love. But Skule persists. He must have someone near him who will believe in him absolutely, whom he can trust. (*Køb eder en hund*, 'Buy yourself a dog', the poet suggests [H, V, 108/ O, II, 300].) Will Jatgejr become his son and heir? There is, of course, a condition. In order to achieve the (to Skule) inconceivably higher destiny of becoming a lord over men, Jatgejr must renounce poetry:-

SKULE ... digt aldrig mere, så vil jeg tro dig!

> SKULE ... Write no more poems, then I will trust you!
>
> [O*]

For Jatgejr, the price is too high. No matter that it is *kun dine udigtede kvad du skal ofre* 'only your unborn songs that you sacrifice'; it is just these which are the most beautiful. The only person whom Skule needs to trust in him is (says Jatgejr), precisely, Skule himself;- *da er I frelst*, 'then you will be saved'.

Such self-sufficiency is beyond Skule. Like Hedda Gabler's,[13] his frustration and envy are the outcome of an incapacity for self-estimation or self-trust. Like Hedda's his instinct is to destroy. Soon after learning that she herself is expecting a child, Hedda first burns the manuscript which has been like a child to Løvborg and Thea, then destroys her own child and herself. Later in *The Pretenders* Skule's reaction, on learning that he himself has a son, is to attempt to kill the son of his rival to the throne.

Thus the conversation between Skule and Jatgejr, though it seems in its immediate context to be a mere interlude, soon swept aside by the action of the play, does provide a parallel and commentary to that action. In his obstinate insistence on the value of his craft, Jatgejr provides an important counter-truth to the ideal of aesthetic irresponsibility cultivated by Falk. Jatgejr's vocation as poet also springs from the failure of love. But the crucial difference is that his has been no light-hearted, irresponsible renunciation. He has loved and been betrayed; it is out of sorrow that poems are made. *The Pretenders* does not really explore further the relationship between art and life; but it does affirm that the life of the artist (and life *to* the artist) can be something more than the self-indulgent affair which too simple a reading of *Love's Comedy* might suggest.

For a revealing (and, in Ibsen's work, unique) glimpse into how poems are born, we must turn to a fascinating and rather neglected lyric which he wrote sometime in 1864, *'Fra mit*

Husliv', (literally) 'From my domestic life'. The scene is the poet's home. It is evening; house and street are quiet. Out of the silence, out of the veil of cigar-smoke, the children of his fantasy come tripping forth;-

... mine vingede børn, på rad,
viltre gutter og piger...

[H, XIV, 383]

my children, winged row upon row,
boisterous lads and girls...

But just as their games reach their height (symbolizing the play of the poet's fantasy) *gennem alle de dejlige riger*, 'through all the realms of delight', there is a sudden interruption. For the poet happens to glance at the mirror:-

Derinde stod en adstadig gæst
med blygrå øjne, med lukket vest.

Within stood a sombre, sober guest
with lead-grey eyes, waistcoat-buttons tight.

What has brought the play of fantasy up short is, of course, awareness of himself, a self-image staring back into the room, the waistcoat of his personality buttoned tight. What his strait-laced guest represents could be some sort of moral censor, I suppose; but it is more likely to be simply awareness of the world outside the imagination. Although the sudden apparition causes the children of fantasy to quail and fall silent, the moment is surely a necessary one in the creation of any poem. It is the beginning of that inner judgment-day which Ibsen was to define as the true nature of poetry. It is certainly the absence of such self-awareness which will doom Brand to the Ice-Palace, Peer Gynt to his perpetual quest of self-evasion.

Yet, even so, the playing children are as necessary to the

poet as the self-image staring reproachfully from the mirror on the wall. It is the interplay between these two forces from which poetry is made. *Løgn er den Poesi, der ikke kommer af Livet*, 'That poetry which does not spring from life is a lie', wrote the Danish philosopher-novelist Poul Møller; it is an aphorism which might serve as an epigraph to the whole of Ibsen's work. Yet poetry without fantasy is not poetry at all. Imagination and responsibility, those aesthetic and ethical spheres which Kierkegaard so carefully distinguished, must somehow combine if an art is to be produced which can express the fullness of human development, the awareness of youth and age. The struggle to find a dramatic form to express this awareness was to preoccupy Ibsen for the rest of his creative life.

CHAPTER ONE

Brand

More insistently, perhaps more convincingly than any other Ibsen character, Brand seems to confront us with 'the claims of the Ideal'. Mankind must choose, he says, either a life of spiritual fulfilment, or the living death of a merely material existence. Those who believe in the possibility of evading such a choice (as Ejnar seeks to do) delude themselves. The choice is unavoidable and absolute; and those who choose self-fulfilment must understand that the price of spiritual life is *Offervill-igheden* - the willingness to sacrifice.

Ibsen himself seemed to side with those who would take Brand's doctrines as - with whatever reservations - the message of the play. In a letter to the Danish critic Peter Hansen, denouncing Norway's failure to aid Denmark in the war of 1864, he invoked a readiness to sacrifice individual life in a higher cause, which he specifically linked with his own feelings in writing *Brand*:-

> Those were the days when *Brand* began to grow within me like an embryo. When I arrived in Italy, unification was complete as a result of a boundless spirit of self-sacrifice [*Offervillighed*] whilst at home in Norway...! That Brand is a priest is really immaterial [*uvæsentligt*]; the demand of All or Nothing is valid for all aspects of life... Brand is myself in my best moments.[14]
>
> Letter to P. Hansen, 28 Oct 1870
> [H, XVI, 317-8/ O, III, 442-3]

This seems, on the face of it, as clear an assertion of authorial intention as we are likely to find in Ibsen's work. Yet a closer examination of Brand's 'willingness to sacrifice' and its roots in his character suggests how great may be the distance between the author's conscious beliefs and the way in which they are embodied in the work of art - may even suggest how suspicious were Ibsen's feelings about those who believe they have received such a call to sacrifice. That he identified a character's beliefs with his own is certainly no unconditional endorsement of either beliefs or character. On the contrary, it is an indication that both will be subject to close and unforgiving scrutiny. Self-identification implied for him that *dommedag over sig selv*, 'judgement-day over oneself' which he was to define as the true purpose of writing.

One of Ibsen's most powerful means of exploring the relationship between his characters' conscious beliefs and their unconscious motives is by adding an extra dimension to character through the implication of an imagined past, beyond the immediate scope of the action on stage, yet influencing, even controlling that action, as inheritance and early environment define adult personality. Brand's beliefs are not only the outcome of some elective decision; it is clearly implied that it is in his childhood that the roots of these beliefs, and with them the shape of the play's dramatic action, must be sought. As so often in Ibsen's plays, it is only by examining closely what we are told of the past that we can understand what happens in the dramatic present.

It is vital to any understanding of the play to recognize that Act I represents for Brand a return to his childhood home. After his meeting with Ejnar and Agnes, as he begins the precipitous descent towards the sea, he begins to recognize his surroundings. Looking down on the valley, he describes the landscape below, with its huts and boathouses under rocky screes, the shabby church and, lastly, the cottage where

... imellem Strandens Stene,
blev min Barnesjæl alene.

[H, V, 198]

... among the stones along the shore
My child-soul dwelt alone.

[O, III, 95]

The feelings which the once-familiar landscape wake in him are powerful, negative and contradictory; coming home he feels a stranger; -

vaagner bunden, klippet, tæmmet,
Samson lig i Skjøgens Skjød.

I wake bound and tame and shorn
like Samson in the harlot's lap.

[O*]

What associations the landscape holds for him, that it can evoke such a sense of impotence and claustrophobia, only becomes clear later. Yet all that happens later can be traced back to this moment of awakening and self-recognition. Somehow, in spite of or even because of these feelings, comes that decision to remain in the village as its priest which precipitates all that follows.

The way in which Brand makes that first decision demonstrates how inexorably past determines present in the play. After his bravery on the fjord, the villagers beg him to stay as their priest. Yet their entreaties seem in vain; and even Agnes's vision of his mission fails to convince him that this is his appointed place. Brand's true mission, he says, is *indad*, within:-

der *skal Viljegribben dødes,*
der *den nye Adam fødes.*

[H, V, 218]

> *There* shall the vulture of the will be slain,
> And *there* shall the new Adam be born...
>
> [O*, III, 115]

But where in the physical world can he find a fit starting point for this journey of spiritual self-discovery, which will allow him (in an alarming anticipation of Peer Gynt) to be 'entirely oneself'? And how can that self be purified of its earthly antecedents, *Vægten/ af ens Arv og Gjæld fra Slægten*, 'The weight of one's inheritance of guilt'? At this moment he spies the personification of that burden, his own mother, clambering up the hill. Suddenly afraid, he asks:-

> *Hvilket iskoldt Barneminde,*
> *hvilket Gufs fra Hjem og Fjord*
> *drysser Rim om denne Kvinde, -*
> *drysser værre Rim herinde --?*
> *Naadens Gud! Det er min Moer!*
>
> [H, V, 219]
>
> O, what ice-cold childhood memory,
> what chill blast from home and fjord
> casts its bitter frost about this woman...
> and casts an even sharper frost within?
> God have mercy! It is my mother...
>
> [O, III, 115]

Brand's horror at her appearance reflects not just the bitterness of childhood memories, but the recognition that the inheritance of materialism and guilt she represents is indeed part of himself. The more he has tried to nullify that *Arv og Gjæld fra Slægten* (the phrase is ambiguous - literally it means 'inheritance and debt from the family' *or* 'from Mankind' - thus it could refer to original sin, or to heredity, or to the affairs of a single family) by turning his back on his childhood home, the more firmly that inheritance has imprinted its limitations on his view of the world. Earlier Brand has brooded on the fate of the surviving children of the child-murderer whose last moments he has eased,

> de, *hvis Livsens-Elv skal rinde*
> *ud fra dette stygge Minde,* -

> those, whose stream of life must flow
> out of that foul memory, -

and has asked, anguished:-

> *Naar begynder Ansvarsvægten*
> *af ens Arvelod fra Slægten?*
>
> [H, V, 211-12]

> When does the weight of blame
> for our inheritance begin?
>
> [O*, III, 109-10]

Now Brand's mother comes to lay upon him the burden of responsibility of a literal, material inheritance, the store of gold she has put aside through a lifetime of brutal meanness and hard work. All that matters to her is that he should 'sustain the family-line from son to son' (*Hold Ætten oppe, Søn for Søn*) that he should not squander either his life or the inheritance in which she has invested her own life and soul. Brand is disturbed by much more than the idolatry which this implies. He knows, too accurately, the cost of this inheritance. One of those 'ice-cold childhood memories' rises to the surface of his mind - the image of his mother ransacking the mattress of his father's death-bed for the family fortune.[15]

This sense of coldness, encirclement, repressed horror, brutality, which explains Brand's hatred and fear of his family inheritance, also goes far to explain his own attitude to anyone not possessing his own will to escape, to transcend the merely *jordvendt*, the 'turned to earthward'. When Brand faces his mother we see two utterly opposing views - the purely material, the uncompromisingly spiritual - yet their equal ruthlessness in the struggle which follows suggests how deep an influence family inheritance has exercised on Brand.[16] And when he speaks of his mother sullying the image of God in herself, as *din Gjaeld*, her 'debt of sin', and says that he will redeem that indebtedness to the Almighty and purify His image by will alone:-

> *Gudsbilledet, som du har plettet,*
> *i mig skal rejses viljetvættet!*
>
> [H, V, 225]

> The image of God which you defiled shall be restored,
> Cleansed by the fire of my will.
>
> [O, III, 121]

- we recognize the same brutal obstinacy in the saint as in the sinner.

No wonder that when his mother first sees him, she cannot 'distinguish priest from peasant' (*en kan ej skille Prest fra Bonde*) and that, earlier, he has declared war on the evils of the world in a phrase[17] which translates the land-longing of the peasantry into a theological battle-cry, -

> *Till Kamp for Himlens Odelsmænd!*
>
> [H, V, 202]

His mother's sin in marrying an unloved man for his money not merely precipitates, at many removes, the final catastrophe of the play; it prefigures Brand's own fear of and contempt for the love which he has never known as a child, and is thus ready to banish from his life and his world-view as an adult. In the end, the limitations of his childhood form the limits of his religious vision. Where his mother demands perpetual retention, the refusal to let material wealth out of *Slægtens Vold*, 'the grasp of the family' [H, V, 221/ O*, III, 118], Brand demands its mirror-image, total sacrifice. And the ideal to which such sacrifice must be made can only, in the end, be a self-image; for how can Brand, who has never learnt to love others, love or worship anything other than himself? What Evangelical Christianity has given to this damaged self-willed child is what Ibsen's later, more decadent self-worshippers (Gregers Werle, Solness, Allmers, Rubek) can never quite achieve - the certainty that the self is identifiable with God.

It is only after his confrontation with his mother that Brand decides to remain in the village as its priest. And it is the nature of the Being which 'calls' him to remain which is at issue when we come to consider the next, and crucial turning-point of the play - Brand's decision at the end of the next act not to leave the village, even though staying means the sacrifice of his son to his calling as priest.

At this point, Brand is at the height of his power and self-confidence. He has restored the fortunes and self-respect of the parish; he has begun what promises to be a happy married life with Agnes; they have a small son whom he loves dearly. Only the running feud with his mother clouds his happiness. Grandly, inflexibly, he refuses to compromise his beliefs. His mother has idolized wealth; therefore, to be saved, she must give up not less than everything -

> *Jeg har ej Rett*
> *at dyrke Guder i min Ætt.*
>
> [H, V, 232]

> I have no right
> to set my family up as gods.
>
> [O, III, 127]

Here, as throughout the play, Brand is obsessed with images and idols,[18] constantly reproaching other people with the sin of idolatry, whether literally, of gold, or metaphorically, of some false idea, such as that of 'Love'. No word has been more debased by those idolators, he says;

det lægger de med Satans List
som Slør udover Viljens Brist.

they spread it with Satan's cunning
to mask the defects of the Will.

Yet only a moment or two later, Agnes watches him, head bowed in love, almost as though weeping, cradling his young son:-

O, hvilken Sum af Kjærlighed
i denne stærke Mandesjæl!
Alf tør han elske...

[H, V, 238-39]

O what a wealth of love
in that strong manly soul!
Alf he can love...

[O*, III, 133-4]

At this stage, Brand seems able to divide himself in two, one moment fulminating against the inadequacies of merely human love, the next melting with tenderness. For the time being, the contradictions remain in equilibrium, undeclared. But he is already aware that they *are* contradictions. When Agnes says happily that there is one sacrifice which even God cannot demand, Brand immediately asks himself whether this is true:-

Men hvis han turde? Herren tør,
hvad 'Isaachs Ræddsel' turde før.

[H, V, 243]

But if he dared? The God who struck
Terror in Isaac may do so again.

[O*, III, 138]

The speculation seems ominous. Even before there is any reason to imagine that anyone need be sacrificed, Brand's mind is running on Biblical (and, one might say, Kierkegaardian) precedents. For the moment he seeks to comfort himself with the idea that he has already made his sacrifice by giving up his vocation to be an itinerant preacher - yet has to admit that this is no real sacrifice. Then he distracts himself by wondering when his dying mother will show some *Offervillighed* ('willingness to sacrifice')[19] and by wrangling with the Mayor about the gulf between life and faith, between deeds and ideas.

But the discussion has a more immediate relevance than even Brand expects. No sooner has he delivered (in reply to the Doctor's admonition *vær human*, 'be humane') a stirring speech about the inadequacies of human love (*Var Gud human mod Jesus Krist?* - 'Was God humane to Jesus Christ?' [H, V, 254/ O, III, 147]) than his own son is found to be dangerously sick. The family must leave the valley at once, says the Doctor - otherwise the child will die.

It is the decisive moment of the play. In Acts I and II, as Bjørn Hemmer has pointed out, all choice has been easy. Now it becomes 'endlessly difficult'.[20] From Brand's decision to sacrifice his son to his mission as a priest springs, directly or indirectly, the action of the rest of the play. Any interpretation of the play as a whole must be founded on an assessment of the nature of this sacrifice, and of the God in whose name it is made.

Traditional criticism of *Brand* - even that prepared to accept the importance of Kierkegaardian ideas within the play[21] - has been inclined to accept Brand's conception of his God as being, at worst, inadequate, lacking in *caritas*, over-identified with the strivings of a purely human will and thus, in Kierkegaardian terms, too much bound within the ethical sphere. The question facing Brand is indeed that discussed with such intensity by Kierkegaard in *Fear and Trembling* - whether Abraham is right to be prepared to sacrifice his son, whether there *can* be such a thing as 'a Teleological suspension of the Ethical', a cancelling of all merely human (and humane) morality as the price - the necessary sacrifice - for moving from the ethical to the religious sphere of existence.

Kierkegaard is prepared to take Abraham's faith in God as an unquestioned absolute. Only thus is he able to interpret the leap into the Absurd (the preparedness to sacrifice Isaac) as being the action of a true believer rather than a murderer. Brand, of course, is similarly inclined to take his own faith on absolute trust. But Kierkegaard explicitly argues that such a sacrifice cannot remain within the ethical sphere. If Abraham is not a saint, inspired by the true God, he must be a criminal:-

> [Abraham] acts by virtue of the absurd, for it is precisely absurd that he as the particular is higher than the universal. This paradox cannot be mediated; for as soon as he begins to do this he has to admit that he was in temptation, and if such was the case, he never gets to the point of sacrificing Isaac, or, if he has sacrificed Isaac, he must turn back repentantly to the universal. By virtue of the absurd he gets Isaac again. Abraham is therefore at no instant a tragic hero but something quite different, either a murderer or a believer. The middle term which saves the tragic hero, Abraham has not.[22]

Whether or not Ibsen had read *Fear and Trembling*, or was merely familiar with its ideas at second hand, the dilemma described in this passage is unmistakably relevant to *Brand*. If we accept Kierkegaard's argument, Brand cannot be seen as the tragic hero which so many critics have imagined him to be. Nor, after Act III, can he be seen as remaining within the ethical sphere. He can only be *en Troende* - a true believer - or a deluded murderer. The teleological, supra-ethical 'justification' of his actions, therefore, must depend even on its own terms upon the nature, the quality, the authenticity of his belief.

Brand is very sure - unnervingly so - of the nature, even the appearance of his God. There are moments in the play at which he seems to be thinking in graven images. When in Act I he denounces Ejnar's vision of God as a balding silver-bearded old man, a bespectacled, carpet-slippered *paterfamilias*, strict but kindly - exactly the kind of God Kierkegaard had denounced the late Bishop Mynster for believing in - it is so that Brand can substitute a divine image of his own:-

Min er en Storm, hvor din er Vind,
ubøjelig hvor din er døv,
alkjærlig der, hvor din er sløv;
og han er ung, som Herkules, -
ej nogen Gudfaer paa de treds!

[H, V, 191]

My God is storm where yours is wind,
unbending at moments where yours is deaf,
all-loving just when yours is listless,
and he is young, like Hercules -
not some Godfather in his sixties!

[O*, III, 91-2]

Brand the iconoclast does have icons of his own, it seems; his God, if not humane, is unmistakably human in outline[23] - and, indeed, difficult to distinguish from His ideal creation, the primal, resurrected Man:-

... frem af disse Sjælestumper...
... et helt *skal gaa, saa Herren kjender*
sin Mand *igjen, sit største Værk,*
sin Ættling, Adam, ung og stærk!

[H, V, 195]

> Out of these broken shards of soul...
> ... New wholeness will be born, so that the Lord
> will know once more his Man, his masterwork,
> his offspring Adam, young and strong!
>
> [O*, III, 93]

It would be possible, of course, to take this for the conventional language of a revivalist, muscular Christianity - the ideal of the self, cleansed of sin and weakness, reborn. Much of what Brand says could be interpreted in those terms. But the difficulty of telling creator from creation - Christ/Hercules from his Michelangelesque Adam - and of distinguishing both from their apostle/mediator/creator Brand himself is disturbing. His idea of God is so man-, indeed so self-centred that his use of these terms reveals much more than a mastery of evangelical rhetoric. *Aesthetically*, much of the imagery of these passages may well have derived from Ibsen's first encounter in Rome with Italian Renaissance painting and sculpture - especially with the paintings of Michelangelo.[24] *Dramatically*, however, what it suggests is unmistakably an aesthetically-conceived self-image. Earlier, Brand has told Ejnar,

> *knappt ved jeg, om jeg er en Kristen;*
> *men visst jeg ved, jeg er en Mand.*
>
> [H, V, 191]

> I hardly know if I am a Christian;
> But I do know this: I am a man.
>
> [O, III, 89]

and there is something in all this glorification of masculine strength and will, this invocation to human strong-men (Samson, Hercules, even, in his Michelangelesque form, Adam) which recalls the ambivalence of the cancelled epigraph to the play:-

Og han skabte Mennesket in sit Billede.

[H, V, 429]

And He created Man in His image.

[O, III, 433]

All that Brand says about his God suggests that their relationship is precisely the reverse.[25] No less than Ejnar, the hedonist artist, Brand has confused the aesthetic, the moral and the religious, not (as in Ejnar's case) in a spirit of lax self-indulgence, but rather in the militant faith of one who intends to stamp that self-image into the face of the world.

For exactly the charge which Brand lays against Ejnar - that he has failed to choose either the life of a hedonist or a moralist - has refused to live, in Kierkegaardian terms, wholly in the aesthetic or the moral sphere:-

Lad gaa at du er Glædens Træl, -
men vær det da fra Kveld till Kveld...
Det, som du er, vær fuldt og helt,
og ikke stykkevis og delt.

[H, V, 191-2]

What matter if you are a slave to joy
Just as long as you stay that way...
In what you are, be true and whole,
Not half-and-half, dividedly.

[O*, III, 89]

is surely true of Brand himself. No less than the man who was perhaps the most important model for the character of Brand - Pastor G. A. Lammers[26] - Brand carries into his ministry an element of aesthetic self-regard, a lack of humility *vis-à-vis* the otherness of God, a tendency to glorify the all-sufficiency of the human will (*Mandeviljens qvantum satis*) which excludes him from wholeness and grace;

> For he who lives in the aesthetic sphere does not choose; and he who, after ethical truth has been revealed to him, chooses the aesthetic way - he is no longer living in the aesthetic sphere, but in a state of sin.[27]

Perhaps, indeed, one token that this conception of God is dangerously false is that Brand's God, unlike Abraham's, really does demand human sacrifice. Certainly, Brand's behaviour during the crucial scene at the end of Act III is far removed from Abraham's other-worldly faith and confidence. When Brand learns of the danger to his son, his first reaction is that the family should leave 'that day, that very hour'. He only begins to doubt when the Doctor points out the discrepancy between Brand's attitude to his mother, and his reaction when someone he *does* love is threatened:-

> *... fra en selv er Modet veget*
> *i samme Stund som Loddet faldt*
> *og Offerlammet var ens eget.*
>
> [H, V, 256]

> ... in oneself the courage wavers
> at the hour when fate decrees
> the lamb for sacrifice shall be one's own!
>
> [O*, III, 149]

Until this moment in the play, Brand has successfully managed to divorce his own precariously cultivated emotional life from the havoc he has been creating in other people's. Now, after a moment of uneasy incomprehension, he realizes the inconsistency:-

> *Er* nu *jeg blind!* Var *jeg det før!*
>
> [H, V, 257]

Am I blind *now*? Or *was* I blind before?
[O*, III, 150]

For the first time he has been forced to see his own reactions as relative, not *absolutely* valid - though, significantly, the revelation comes through recognition of an inconsistency in himself, not because his reactions have been tested against some external reality. Hitherto, those reactions *have* been his external reality - that self-image which he calls God - and what disturbs him now is the threat to his self-image, not the ethical implications of the possibility that he may have behaved wrongly in the past. The Doctor hastens to assure him that flexibility is not the sign of spiritual weakness, that he is a greater man now than before. But the Doctor cannot resist adding a final homily:-

Farvel! Nu har jeg rakkt Dem Spejlet,
brug det, og sukk saa: Herregud,
slig ser en Himmelstormer ud!

Farewell! And now I've handed you a mirror
Make use of it, then sigh, 'Oh God!
So that's how a Heaven-storming Titan looks!'

The image is fatally apt. When Brand does look into the mirror, what he sees is a reflection of his own paranoia. The sun sets, and out of the gathering darkness, out of Brand's own darkness, a man hurries in. He is never described or identified. His first words are exactly calculated to re-awaken all those darker feelings which domestic life has, for the moment, tamed:-

Hør Prest, du har en Avindsmand!

Listen, Priest, you have an enemy!

The idea of a secret, personal enemy (*Avindsmand*) and the suspicion of a secret disease threatening the hero's seed:-

... Vær paa din Post mod Fogden.
Din Sæd skjød frodigt over Land
till han med Rygtets Brandpest slog den.
[H, V, 257-8]

... Be on your guard with the Mayor.
Your seed was sprouting richly in the land
Till he with rumour's canker killed it.
[O*, III, 150]

- all this is the language not of the reborn soul striving towards God, but of irrational panic in that older, hidden, rejected self. Combined with the Mayor's allegations that Brand would desert his parish as soon as he inherits his mother's fortune - all this appeals to (even springs out of?) the dark side of Brand's nature, his suspicion and vanity. No wonder that he hears the man's words as an echo of his own thoughts:-

Hvert klangfuldt Ord, mod Bergvægg sagt,
mig slaar med tifold Gjenlyds Magt.
[H, V, 259]
Each resonant word, declaimed to the mountainside,
now echoes back to me with tenfold force.
[O*, III, 151]

No wonder, also, that what finally decides him to sacrifice his son is the arrival of the mad girl, Gerd, who now appears (providentially? As an echo of his darker self?) at the garden gate.

Gerd is used in the play economically, and to precisely calculated effect. She appears only three times, at the end of the first, the third and the final acts; and at each point she reveals, through her seeming madness, a side of Brand which has lain partly hidden. At the end of Act I, it is she who reminds him of the Ice Church, that image of mad, limitless, inhuman purity, in whose perspective all human life seems petty and ugly. Now, at the end of the Third Act, at the moment of decision which lies at the centre of the play, she presents Brand with the vision of what will happen to the village if, bereft of *his* will, all the phantasmagoria of superstition and the collective unconscious flood forth:-

Har I hørt det? Bort fløj Presten! -
Ud af Bakken, opp af Houg,
myldrer baade Trold og Draug,
svarte, stygge, store, smaa...
Ned fra Svartetind min Høg
rapp bortover Lien strøg...
... og en Mand paa Ryggen red, -
det var Presten, det var Presten!

[H, V, 259]

Have you heard? The Priest has flown!
Out of the hillsides,up from the barrow-mounds
Are swarming trolls and headless ghosts,
Black ones, foul ones, great and small...
Down from Svartetind swooped my hawk,
Flashed across the mountainside...
... And a man rode on his back -
It was the Priest! It was the Priest!

[O*, III, 152]

This is the frenzied language of madness. To any sane listener, it would preclude taking seriously anything else the speaker had to say. Brand, however, merely asks who has induced this 'broken soul' to entrap him with *Afgudssange*, 'idolatrous songs' - thereby revealing once more his own obsession with images, real and false, and permitting Gerd to make the final, decisive attack:-

Afgud! Hør, du; ser du hende?
Kan du under Klædet kjende
Barnehænder, Barneben?

Afgud! - Mand, der *ser du* en!

[H, V, 260]

Idol? Listen, do you see her?
Can't you make out, under her shawl
The shape of infant hands and feet?

Idol? Man! You see one, *there*!

[O*, III, 152-3]

Brand is now helpless, trapped within the logic of his chosen view of the universe. To the deity of his world, any merely human object of love must in the end challenge the monotheism of God himself - must, logically, be classed as idolatry. Gerd's madness, echoing and amplifying Brand's own, has reminded him of the *rationale* for excluding human love from his view of the world. With much less pain than it cost him to accept the sanity of the Doctor's advice, Brand accepts Gerd's madness as a paradigm of his own truth:-

Agnes, Hustru, - ve, jeg skjønner,
hende har en større sendt!

[H, V, 260]

Agnes, wife, I fear, alas,
she has been sent by a Greater Power!

[O*, III, 153]

The sacrifice must be made; the child must die.

Henceforward, Brand cannot retrace his steps, cannot reconsider or reform his idea of God, because to do so would be to accept himself the guilt for his son's death. There are moments when his faith wavers, when he can almost see God as loving father rather than avenging Lord. But such moments cannot be allowed to last. Agnes may see God in this way if she wishes; Brand cannot, must not, dare not:-

jeg maa se ham stor og stærk,
himmelstor.

[H, V, 266]

I must see Him great and very strong...
As great as Heaven itself.

[O, III, 159]

Pity and love have no more power over him; now he can only think in terms of atonement and sacrifice. When he learns the secret of Gerd's ancestry, learns that she is the product of the same tangle of embittered, loveless, mercenary relationships as himself, Brand is overcome by the thought that Gerd's injunction to sacrifice his son may have been less a message from God than the logical outcome of - indeed a kind of poetic revenge for - his mother's sin in jilting Gerd's father for a richer man:-

Mit lille Barn, skyldløse Lam,
du fældtes for min Moders Gjerning;
en brusten Sjæl bar Bud fra ham,
som troner over Skyens Kam,
og bød mig kaste Valgets Terning; -
og denne brustne Sjæl blev till,
fordi min Moders Sjæl foer vild.

[H, V, 287]

My little child, innocent lamb
you had to die because of my mother's deeds;
a broken soul brought word from Him
who has His throne above the clouds
and bade me cast the die of choice -

and that same broken soul was born
because my mother went astray.

[O*, III, 178]

By this stage, the logic of Brand's thought is contorted almost beyond belief. Now that Alf's death can safely be blamed on the sins of someone else (that is, neither Brand nor his God) the child can be hailed as an innocent Lamb, and both his death and Gerd's existence can be interpreted as atonement for the misdeeds of the same hated human agency. Yet at the same time Gerd must still be seen as God's messenger - though the purpose of the message, it now seems, is to avenge his mother's sin, presumably against that 'Love' which Brand so despises? But, even stranger and more chilling, the decision to sacrifice Alf is now described as 'bidding me cast the die of choice'. Whatever the complacent uncompromising cruelty which has been attributed to his God up to now, at least Brand's picture of His Will has had a certain consistency. Now, in his confusion and anguish, Brand seeks to justify a God who, in his concern for *Ligevægt*, 'equity', seems only concerned to exert vengeance on guilty and innocent alike. Brand seeks to pray, calls for light. But he is so deeply trapped in complicity with his vision of a God who serves more and more to justify his own *Offervillighed* (i.e. his willingness to sacrifice others) that neither self-questioning nor prayer can deliver him.

Even in the final moments of the play, Brand is trapped by the same heroic (or criminal) refusal to face the implications of what he has done. The Chorus of Spirits (the voice of his own discouragement?) seeks in vain to persuade him that he cannot become one with the image of God:-

Aldrig, aldrig blir du lig ham, -
thi i Kjødet er du skabt.

[H, V, 354]

Never, never will you be like Him...
For of flesh are you created.

[O, III, 241]

The dream-spectre of the dead Agnes offers the vision of a world in which, if only he will renounce the path of Will, all can be forgiven and made new. But Brand cannot, will not recant. Even now, he would be prepared again to sacrifice his child to his vision.

This may seem like the obstinacy in error of the true tragic hero. But, again to use Kierkegaardian terms, the hero of whom one is reminded is not Abraham, nor even Euripides's Agamemnon, sacrificing his daughter yet remaining within the ethical sphere. Rather it is the Don Juan described in *Either/Or*, a being whose sins are confirmed by no universal law, who resists, to the last, the injunction to recognize any reality save his own. - Or, in Brand's case, *almost* to the last. For where the voices of love and reason have failed to persuade him, Gerd, the reflection of his own madness, succeeds. When she hails him as the Redeemer -

I din Haand er Naglehullet; -
du er udvalgt; du er størst.

[H, V, 360]

In your hands are the holes of the nails...
You are the Chosen One... the Greatest.

[O, III, 248]

Brand begins to understand the extent of his blasphemy - not against God but against his own human nature. At this moment the mists clear; and he realizes where they are. He has at last reached the Ice-Church, the shining, barren symbol of his own purity of will.

Now, and only now, he can weep. Until this point his life has been like a blank snowfield - an image of his own frozen childhood; now

> *fra idag mit Livsensdigt*
> *skal sig bøje varmt og rigt.*
> *Skorpen brister. Jeg kan græde,*
> *jeg kan knæle, - jeg kan bede!*
>
> [H, V, 361-2]

> - from today, the poem of my life
> shall yield its fertile riches.
> The snow-crust's breaking. I can weep;
> I can kneel; I can pray!
>
> [O*, III, 249]

But it is Gerd, the reflection of his own *hubris*, who has made this self-recognition possible; and it is Gerd's obsession with the imaginary Hawk, and all those feared possibilities which it represents, who brings about the final catastrophe. As Brand becomes able to see love, self-surrender, maturity as the way forward from the *impasse* of his frozen self-love, Gerd finally sees the hawk as within her sights.

The family tradition which has sacrificed Brand's wife and child to a distorted vision of God, which has destroyed Gerd's father and driven Gerd into madness, now claims its last victims. As Brand recognizes the logic of a self-destruction as complete as those which will destroy the houses of Rosmer and Allmers:-

> *Ja, hver Slægtens Søn tilldøde*
> *dømmes maa for Slægtens Brøde!*
>
> [H, V, 362]

> Yes, each son of man must die[28]
> condemned for the sins of the race!
>
> [O*, III, 250]

- the mountain snows, white now as a Dove, but deadly as the imagined Hawk, pour down in thunder. And as Brand makes his final appeal to the God of Thunder whom he has called his own:-

> *gjælder ej et Frelsens Fnug*
> *Mandeviljens qvantum satis - ?!*
>
> [H, V, 362]

> weighs not an ounce in Redemption's scales
> the whole sufficiency of human will?
>
> [O*, III, 250]

his question contains, in Kierkegaardian terms, its own answer. For, 'a man can become a tragic hero by his own powers - but not a knight of faith'.[29] Brand's attempt to substitute will for faith as effectively debars him from the Religious sphere as the sacrifice of his son has expelled him from the Ethical. When a voice within the avalanche utters the final disavowal:-

> *Han er deus caritatis!*

> He is the God of Love!

it is not the voice of God's judgment over Brand but Brand's own recognition, beyond the icy walls of the self, of that reality which pride and idolatry have conspired to hide. Brand has excluded himself from grace. That grace is the love of *this* world was to be the theme of all Ibsen's later drama.

CHAPTER TWO

Peer Gynt

In the last act of *Peer Gynt*, as Peer traverses a burnt-out forest at night, voices come to him out of the ash-laden, mist-laden wind and darkness. He stops to listen:-

> *Hvad for Graad af Barnerøster?*
> *Graad, men halvt paa Vej till Sang.* -
>
> [H, VI, 213]

> What is that sound of children's voices weeping,
> Weeping, but half-way to song?
>
> [O*, III, 398]

It is, in itself, a moving and suggestive image. But to sense its full resonance, to grasp its significance for Peer's character and the play's structure, we must return to the beginning, to what we learn of his own childhood.

In doing so, we shall already be re-enacting the characteristic motion of the play, in which every attempt to 'go round' merely takes us back to where we started. For *Peer Gynt* is concerned with, in a literal and entirely un-Nietzschean sense, 'Eternal Recurrence', a reaching back to and re-living of the past, of which Aase's last sleigh-ride in the plundered cottage is one example amongst many.

The play's opening sets the tone for all that is to follow:-

> *Peer, du lyver!*

Nej, jeg gjør ej!

[H, VI, 59]

Peer, you're lying!

No, I'm not!

[O*, III, 255]

As Aase's first words are an accusation, so Peer's are a lie - that is, both refutation and confirmation. The ambivalence of the exchange reflects the peculiar kind of tautology which infuses their relationship. Neither of them has any clear sense of where lies start, of what divides truth from fantasy. More firmly than in any marriage between equals, mother and son act out rituals in which the duality of truth/falsehood has been replaced by the private monistic world of children's games and fantasies. Despite the parody of a *Bildungsreise* in Act IV, Peer has no wish to learn, to attain knowledge through experience of the adult world. Far from maturing him, all the events of the first four acts, at least, seem to confirm his belief that, as the chosen one of fortune, he will be able to evade the consequences of his actions by re-making the world in the image of his own imagination. As far as he is concerned, time *is* reversible, and deeds can be unmade with the same blithe facility that words can be unsaid and lies, when occasion demands, turned inside out.

On one level, of course, both Peer and Aase know that, as far as the rest of the world is concerned, Peer's stories are usually fantastic embroideries of his own or other people's experiences.

O, din Fandens Rægglesmed!

[H, VI, 62]

Oh, you bloody story-teller!

[O*, III, 258]

Aase bursts out when at last she cottons on to the source of the tall story about the buck on the Gjendin-Egge. But her use of the word *Rægglesmed* is, significantly, both accurate and indulgent. For, in an oral culture, a 'story-teller' (here, at least, the ambiguity of the English matches that of the Norwegian) *does* like Peer purvey old stories *i en nygjort Ham*, 'dressed up in new clothes' [H, VI, 63/ O*, III, 258]. But even in such a tradition, distinction is likely to be made between *saga* and *eventyr*, between history and imagination, the real and the fantastic. The point about Peer's stories is that they have been invented to confuse the two, to ward off an unbearable reality and blur the distinction between what is and what might have been.

Aase is partly aware of this. As they both pursue the absconding Peer, she tries to explain matters to Solvejg. Her only resource in holding the household together as the drunken spendthrift father racketed round the neighbourhood had been to retreat into a fantasy-world:-

> *... imens sad jeg og Vesle-Peer hjemme.*
> *Vi vidste ikke bedre Raad, end at glemme...*
> En *bruger Brændevin, en anden bruger Løgne;*
> *aa, ja! saa brugte vi Eventyr*
> *om Prinser og Trolde og alleslags Dyr.*
> *Om Bruderov med.*
>
> [H, VI, 89-90]

> ... whilst Little Peer and I sat at home
> The best we could do was to try and forget...
> One person uses brandy, another one lies!
> So, yes, we used fairy tales
> about princes and trolls and all manner of beasts.
> About bride-stealing, too.
>
> [O*, III, 286]

What she has used as a means of protecting little Peer from

the reality of his father's decline has been only too effective. Fantasies, like *Brændevin*, have become a method of sealing off the outside world, of establishing a secret compact against time and decay, and against any human relationship between separate equal selves which might threaten that compact. Aase's disingenuous surprise at the consequences -

Men hvem kunde tænkt,
de Fandens Ræggler skulde i ham hængt?

But who could have thought
Those blasted tales would have stuck in his mind?

is as much a kind of indulgent complicity as are her prophecies of Peer's impending doom. When she describes Peer a few lines later as *Mit fortabte Lam*, 'My poor doomed lamb', Solvejg's father, with a pious complacency worthy of the redeemed Ejnar, agrees, *Ja, rigtig. Fortabt*, 'Yes, truly. Doomed'. Aase is outraged. For she, too, has fallen into the habit of using words in a way quite divorced from reality. To hear her own words used by someone who does mean them is also an invasion of the imaginary world she has invented with Peer.

Peer's relationship with his mother is almost a negative image of Brand's. Whereas Brand's family have achieved wealth and success through the ruthless exclusion of 'what men call Love', Peer - another only child[30] - has built up with Aase a compact so strong that it can withstand almost any shock which external reality can administer. Within that relationship, love and mutual esteem (and in Peer's case, self-esteem) are given quantities, absolutes, unconditional on time or conduct or consequence. Aase's passivity and acceptance create expectations in Peer which no adult relationship could satisfy. He abducts Ingrid only to prove that he can do so, not to restore the family fortunes by marrying her. Ingrid has shown independence by rejecting Mads Moen and running off with Peer - and a headstrong wife with a large farm to be worked is the last thing he wants. Only the endlessly patient Solvejg can be admitted to his imaginative world - and that only because she is prepared to assume the role of undemanding indulgence which has been Aase's. When Peer hails Solvejg at the end of the play as

> *Min Moder; min Hustru; uskyldig Kvinde!*
> [H, VI, 241]
>
> My mother, my wife, innocent woman!
> [O*, III, 421]

he is defining the only kind of relationship he can have, either with another human being or, indeed, with the world. His return to Solvejg/Aase's lap is as much a return to, and a logical projection of, his own childhood as Brand's death in the Ice-Church.

Ibsen's contemporaries were very much aware of these elements in the play, and were inclined to stress - rightly - affinities with classic Danish literature of the early and mid century. Certainly, *Peer Gynt* has features in common with Oehlenschläger's fairy tale drama *Aladdin* (the ironic orientalism of Act IV; the idea of the hero as god-graced child of fortune), with J. L. Heiberg's *A Soul after Death* (the studied, pungent, ironic poise of the verse; the judgment on Peer's lukewarm, mediocre record of sin), with Paludan-Müller's Byronic, anti-Byronic epic *Adam Homo*, with Kierkegaard's Seducer in *Either/Or*, with the characters in H. E. Schack's novel, *The Fantasts*. There is no doubt that Peer's failure or refusal to grow up can be seen as both part of and a commentary on a whole tradition in the literature of the Danish 'Golden Age'.[31] Yet a close reading of *Peer Gynt* will show how far Ibsen diverged from that tradition - even the part of it (Heiberg, Paludan-Müller, Schack) which spelt out the danger of fantasizing for real life. Ibsen's criticism was much more radical, his irony correspondingly deeper. Georg Brandes denounced

Oehlenschläger's *Aladdin* (which he loved) as 'Poetry about poetry... poetry which gazes at itself in the mirror and wonderingly admires its own beauty'. Ibsen shows us in *Peer Gynt* the logical outcome of such a view of poetry and life.

Or, to be more precise, of such a divorce between poetry and life. When Peer, returning to his native valley at (or after) the end of his life, asks who *was* this legendary Peer Gynt, the Sheriff's Officer answers,

> *Aa, der siges, han var en vederstyggelig Digter...*
> *... alt, som var stærkt og stort,*
> *det digted han ihob, at* han *havde gjort.*
> [H, VI, 208]

> It's said he was some confounded romancer
> ... everything strong and great
> He changed into stories, as if *he* had done it himself.
> [O*, III, 394]

Ibsen, of course, is playing here upon an ambiguity which is present in Norwegian, untranslatable into English. *At digte* can mean either to create imaginative literature, or merely to fantasize.[32] It is precisely the tension behind this ambiguity which is at the root of Peer's character, and at the root, too, of much critical misunderstanding about the play. Poets, genuine poets, are also in one sense liars - like Peer, they *digter ihob*; that is, they re-order reality, alter historical truth, impose in some sense their own personality upon the world they transform into art.[33]

But this does not mean (though some have argued[34]) that *Peer* is a poet. On the contrary, his refusal to accept any discipline or commitment, even to his own lies, and his inability to see any connection between words and deeds, exclude him irrevocably from the role of the poet as artist. He shows no sign of what Foldal in *John Gabriel Borkman* calls *digterkald*, 'poetic vocation'. For Peer, poetry and lies *are* co-terminous, and both are to be used to impress others or himself, or to extricate himself from the consequences of his actions. *Digt og forbandet Løgn!* [H, VI, 94], 'Poetry and damned lies' [O*, III, 290] is how he dismisses his exploits, real and imaginary, up to the Rondane-scene, and (just to rub the equation home) adds, a few lines later, *Løgn og forbandet Digt!* Thus W. H. Auden's suggestion that 'Ibsen is trying to show us what kind of person is likely to become a poet', is inadequate, and the added proviso, 'assuming, of course, that he has the necessary talent' is downright misleading.[35] What Ibsen is surely demonstrating is that a talent for fantasy is not enough to turn a fantast into a poet, and that the kind of relationship which Peer enjoys with Aase - 'the kind of love that is unaffected by time and remains unchanged by any act of the partners' - is exactly calculated to destroy both poetry and human nature.

The weeping children's voices, 'half-way to song', which Peer hears in the darkened forest, represent just this half-way region, suspended uneasily between inspiration and experience, yet partaking fully of neither. By Kierkegaard's definition of a poet, at the beginning of *Either/Or*:-

> An unhappy man who hides deep pain in his heart, but whose lips are so formed that when sighs and screams pass through them, it sounds like beautiful music.[36]

a poet is just what Peer can never become. The inner voice which constantly advises him to *Gaa udenom*, 'go round' - to evade difficulty, suffering, responsibility - cannot destroy Peer, even by stealth; but it can and does deflect him into his long self-admiring pilgrimage away from and back to the kind of truth which should be a starting-point, not a destination. The moral stalemate which results, reflected again in his confrontations with the Button-Moulder, means that, like Heiberg's Soul after Death, his life remains in a state of moral and imaginative Limbo,[37] in some ways as terrible as Brand's icy Hell. Peer cannot even say, with another of Heiberg's characters, the Poet:-

> If my life were good, my verse would be bad;
> But I have lived badly, and my poems are good.

The voices which Peer hears on the wind are only 'half-way to song'; and the songs of the threadballs, the withered leaves, the wind, the dew, the broken straws, are the cries of children unborn, poems unlived or unwritten, potentialities destroyed by evasion, by the refusal or inability to escape from the magic circle of childhood:-

Vi er Tanker;
du skulde tænkt os...
Vi er et Løsen;
du skulde stillet os...
Vi er Sange;
du skulde sunget os...
Vi er Taarer,
der ej blev fældte...
Vi er Værker;
du skulde øvet os!

[H, VI, 213-4]

We are thoughts:
You should have thought us...
We are the password
You should have given...
We are songs;
You should have sung us...
We are the tears
You never let fall...
We are the deeds
That you left undone...

[O, III, 398-9]

This is not Shelleyan rhetoric, though one may be reminded of the invocations to poetic inspiration in the first act of *Prometheus Unbound*. But it is just that lack of power or will to distinguish between self and world (defined by Herbert Read as the characteristic quality of Shelley's poetry) which Ibsen diagnoses in Peer. It is the essential circularity of Peer's relationships (with Aase, and in a double sense with Solvejg) which unfits him both for the limited integrity of the ordinary life (as, for example, of the man whose funeral Peer attends a few scenes earlier) and the more dubious but equally dedicated life of the artist. Peer has neither warred with trolls nor, even for a moment, held judgment-day over himself.[38] For the concept of self-judgment implies the capacity to stand outside oneself, to overcome the self-imprisonment of the Troll watchword,

> *Trold, vær dig selv - nok!*
>
> [H, VI, 100]

> Troll, to yourself be - enough!
>
> [O*, III, 295]

That Peer is incapable of such self-distancing is shown by his response to the accusing voices on the wind. To the unborn thoughts, he can only reply,

> *Livet har jeg skjænkt till* en;-
> *det blev Fusk og skjæve Ben!*
>
> [H, VI, 213]

> Life I only gave to *one* -
> A bungled job with crooked limbs!
>
> [O*, III, 398]

referring, presumably, not to a thought but to his child by the

Dovre-King's daughter.[39] That child, like Eyolf Allmers, is lame - and there is no doubt that in each case the lameness is symbolic, the physical manifestation of spiritual and emotional bad faith. Symbolic, too, is Peer's reaction to the threadballs' reproach - in a stage direction he is made, as so often, to 'go around'.

As the voices which call out to him grow more urgent and bitter, Peer's responses[40] become more aggressive and confused:-

I din Hjertegrube
har vi ligget og ventet;-
vi blev aldrig hentet.
Gift i din Strube!
PEER *Gift i dig*, *dit dumme Stev!*
Fik jeg Tid till Vers og Væv?
[H, VI, 214]

In the vaults of your heart
we have lain and waited;
we never were sent for.
Poison, lodged in your throat!
PEER Poison to *you*, you foolish rhyme!
When had I time for verses and prattle?
[O*, III, 399]

Yet this poet *manqué*, who claims to have been too busy living - and lying, his own special contribution to imaginative truth - to bother with mere poetry, cannot pretend even to have lived with the full-hearted intensity which would justify, in a sense, his existence as a sinner. His life has been as devoid of feeling as of artistic seriousness:-

Isbrodd, som saarer,
kunde vi smelte.
Nu sidder Brodden

i Bringen lodden...

[H, VI, 214]

Ice-spears which wound
We could have melted;
Now the spear's point lies
Lodged deep in your breast...

[O*, III, 399]

It is surely no coincidence that the imagery here recalls both *Brand* and H. C. Andersen's *The Snow Queen.*[41] No less than Brand's, Peer's life has been marked by coldness of heart. He may have *Kvinder bag ham*, 'Women behind him' [H, VI, 110/ O, III, 305] - but they are precisely that, figures from his childhood, mother or mother-substitute, not people he has *grown* to love. No wonder that Peer's answer to the unshed tears is confused, silly and irrelevant. His response to all these accusations recalls his notebook-entry on Memnon's Statue:-

Støtten sang. Jeg hørte tydeligt Klangen,
men forstod ikke rigtig Texten till Sangen.
Det hele var naturligvis Sansebedrag.

[H, VI, 172]

The statue sang. I distinctly heard the sound
But didn't exactly take in the words of the song.
The whole thing clearly a trick of the senses.

[O*, III 362]

He cannot or will not understand what the unsung songs, the unshed tears tell him, because to do so would destroy in a moment his own special ice-palace where, alone, he is *selvets Kejser* - 'emperor of self' [H, VI, 186/ O*, III, 374].

The phrase, of course, is not Peer's but Begriffenfeldt's. Yet the director of the Cairo Lunatic Asylum, in which

Den absolute Fornuft
afgik ved Døden iaftes Kl. 11.

[H, VI, 176]

Absolute Reason
departed this life at 11 o'clock last night.

[O*, III, 366]

and in which, accordingly, the inmates have changed places with their keepers, is only articulating, with absolute logic, the consequences of Peer's unreflecting, totally self-reflective solipsism, his monstrous self-sufficiency. In Peer's world there *can* be no Absolute Reason, for the very concept implies the capacity to stand outside individual subjective experience; and Begriffenfeldt's New World Order is to be founded on that *selvets Fundament*, 'foundation of self' [H, VI, 175/ O*, III, 365] which excludes all Kantian notions of external Reason, all possibility of agreed systems of ethics.

Yet the point about the Gyntian Self[42] is that it *has* no foundations. Peer, when asked to describe it, does so in terms which imply that it is as multifarious as an army, as boundless and ungovernable as the sea:-

Det gyntske selv, - *det er den Hær*
af Ønsker, Lyster og Begjær, -
det gyntske selv, det er det Hav,
af Indfald, Fordringer og Krav...

[H, VI, 141]

The gyntian *self* - it is the host
of wishes, appetites and desires; -
the gyntian self - it's the sea
of notions, claims and demands...

[O*, III, 334]

Yet all this heaving ocean of hungers and lusts, precursor of the monarchy of absolute self-gratification established by Alfred Jarry's Ubu[43], is no more than

Den Verden bag mit Pandehvælv.

[H, VI, 140]

The world behind the curve of my brow.

[O, III, 333]

It has no more objective existence than the subjective consciousness which gave it birth.

Which is to say that it has no distinctive existence, any more than Peer has a developed sense of true selfhood. In one sense, indeed, Peer *has* no self - only an endless sequence of disguises, the skins of the onion (again, an appropriately circular image) surrounding an identity which has failed to develop. World Empire and the absconding self, Gyntiana and the onion-skins, the impossibly grandiose, the unbearably small - all are reflections of a self which, unable to contract relationships with others, creates fantasy-empires as defence against its fears of emptiness and extinction. When Peer meets the Button-Moulder, and, horrified at the idea of being melted down 'together with Peter and Paul', declares

dette Støbeske-Væsen, dette gyntske Opphør, -
det sætter min inderste Sjæl i Opprør!

[H, VI, 220]

this life in the melting-pot, this Gyntian ceasing-to-be,
it sets my innermost soul in revolt!

[O*, III, 404]

the Button-Moulder affects surprised incomprehension:-

Dig selv har du aldrig været før; -
hvad skiller det saa, om tillgavns du dør?

You have never been yourself before: -
what difference if you are wiped out now?

And all those whom Peer calls on to attest his selfhood can only agree with the Button-Moulder. To the Troll-King of the Dovre, now old, down at heel and evilly pathetic, Peer is the 'Lord Prince' whose desertion of the Green One has been an act of shrewd common sense, and whose renunciation of Trolldom has only been *pro forma*:-

Som Trold har du levet, men stødt holdt det hemmeligt.
[H, VI, 225]

You have lived as a Troll, but always kept it a secret.
[O*, III, 408]

For Trolls are never sufficiently conscious of other people's existence to be truly sinners; and Peer's own record of sin, despite the first tiny pangs of conscience which he coyly confesses to the Button-Moulder:-

... *nylig, da jeg vandred her saa ensom paa Moen,*
følte jeg et Trykk af Samvittigheds-Skoen;
[H, VI, 229]

... just now, wandering alone on the moor,
I felt the shoes of my conscience pinching;
[O, III, 411]

is entirely unimpressive. To the Thin Man, priest and devil, a connoisseur of sins, Peer's misdeeds are bagatelles, peccadilloes, *en Halvvejs-Snakk*, 'half-way talk' [H, VI, 234/ O*, III, 415] or mealy-mouthed prattle, entered into without commitment or conviction.[44] Only negatively can Peer claim to have been himself; only by the process of inverse development, of purgatory (*Jeg damper, jeg dypper, jeg brænder, jeg renser* - 'I steam [the soul], I dunk it, I burn it, I cleanse it' says the Thin Man describing this new process of spiritual photography) can Peer be turned into his positive image, his true self - a genuine sinner, presumably like Brand. Yet faced with this one chance of salvation through damnation, Peer hastily evades his fate. There must, he feels, be less painful ways of attesting one's damnation.

And it is in this context, wriggling to evade the Button-Moulder's ladle, the Thin One's baths of sulphur, that Peer makes up his mind to cease going round, to return to his starting-point, the arms of Solvejg:-

> *Ja, der, - der finder*
> *jeg Synderegistret -*
>
> [H, VI, 238]

> Yes, there - there I shall find
> the true register of my sins.
>
> [O*, III, 419]

Yet Solvejg is no more willing to admit this than the Troll-King or the Thin One. The irony is perfect; Peer has chosen for his Penelope the one person who will refuse to admit, in any circumstances, that he has done wrong, the one witness who regards *everything* he has done as forgivable:-

> *Intet har du syndet, min eneste Gut!*
>
> [H, VI, 239]

> You've done no wrong, my only boy!
>
> [O, III, 420]

She is, literally and figuratively, blind to his faults, and therefore, as a witness, useless.

Yet the unwanted alibi she gives him is the true one. Peer has never sinned because, essentially, he has never left her side, never grown up. Peer himself is *Gutten derinde*, 'the boy inside there', the child-man who has never left home and seeks only to return to the womb of Aase-Solvejg: -

Min Moder; min Hustru; uskyldig Kvinde!
[H, VI, 241]

My mother, my wife, innocent woman!
[O*, III, 421]

These words do not impress the Button-Moulder, and they should not impress us. This all-accepting love is proof against time only because it exists in an infantile world for which time, context, consequence, selfhood have no meaning. To return to the womb of undemanding infancy may well be the only redemption to which Peer can aspire. But that in itself would surely be proof that the Button-Moulder is right.

It seems only just and appropriate that Peer's dissolution should be threatened by the echo of one of his childhood games (for Peer, too, has had a casting-ladle and has played Button-Moulder; begging his father for pewter he has been given silver - by such moments of unthinking extravagance and indulgence are human souls corrupted [H, VI, 115/ O, III, 310]). All wheels have now come full circle. It is to this infantile fiction of self that Peer has sacrificed his adult self, his marriage (in any meaningful sense) to Solvejg, and all those thoughts, deeds, songs, poems of which he might once have been capable. This is the true record of sins; and its only just conclusion would seem to be the casting-ladle.

CHAPTER THREE

A Doll's House

> *Der er øvet megen uret imod mig, Torvald. Først af pappa og siden af dig. . . Han kaldte mig sit dukkebarn, og han legte med mig, som jeg legte med mine dukker. Så kom jeg i huset til dig -*
>
> [H, VIII, 357]
>
> I've been greatly wronged, Torvald. First by my father, and then by you. . . He used to call me his baby doll, and he played with me as I used to play with my dolls. Then I came to live in your house. . .
>
> [O, V, 280]

There is no doubt that Nora's self-diagnosis is one with which, in some sense, we are bound to agree. *A Doll's House* is a play which resounds with the images of childhood. Even the title is redolent of the nursery; and Nora herself is a character trapped within multiple and contradictory roles of child-woman, child-mother, child-wife.[45] But the effects of this are far more complex and interesting than Nora is able or willing to realize; and to understand what happens in the play, we must begin by examining what can be deduced about the two homes in which she has lived out her protracted childhood.

It is worth noting here that the problem of the critic parallels that which faced the dramatist. Examination of the drafts for *A Doll's House* reveals a curiously retrospective method of composition. That is to say, the part of the final act in which Nora denounces her father and husband had assumed something like its final shape in the first extant full draft,[46] well before many of the aspects of her character had been developed. Thus Ibsen seems to have begun with an idea which had interested him for a decade or more, [47] with the situation which forms the conclusion of the play, and revised the play to give psychological plausibility and dramatic force to that conclusion. The question as to what sort of character, with what sort of antecedents, would behave as Nora does in the final act, seems to have prompted Ibsen to make of her something so complex and self-contradictory, that the original abstract victim became someone much more subtle and ambivalent whose very ambivalence gives the play's ending an entirely different tonality. The Nora of the play's final version is so steeped in childishness, so much the prisoner of her upbringing, that the apparent transformation of her character comes to seem disturbingly ambiguous.[48]

The alterations which Ibsen made in the earlier scenes are often seemingly trivial. At the beginning of the first act, for example, she arrives loaded with presents for the children - trumpets, swords and toy horses for the little boys, a doll and a doll's bed for her daughter. In the final version, she also carries, concealed about her person, a bag of macaroons. They are forbidden fruit, so to speak - and this is exactly their attraction. Nora fibs about them not only to Torvald (which is perhaps understandable) but to Doktor Rank as well;

> *RANK: Se, se; makroner. Jeg trode det var forbudne varer her.*
> *NORA: Ja, men disse er nogen, som Kristine gav mig.*
> *FR. LINDE: Hvad? Jeg - ?*
> *NORA: Nå, nå, nå; bliv ikke forskrækket. Du kunde jo ikke vide, at Torvald havde forbudt det.*
> [H, VIII, 293]
> RANK: Look at this, eh? Macaroons. I thought they

> were forbidden here.
> NORA: Yes, but these are some Kristine gave me.
> MRS. LINDE: What? I. . .?
> NORA: Now, now, you needn't be alarmed. You weren't to know that Torvald had forbidden them.
> [O, V, 219]

Nora fibs almost without thinking, when she has nothing to gain by it, for the sheer pleasure of deception. The forbidden macaroons, munched in pleasurable, guilty secret, suggest not only self-indulgence but a vivid enjoyment of deception and masquerade for their own sake. It forms comic relief to Nora's other, much grander act of fraud, the forged signature which has assured the trip to Italy and (she says) saved Torvald's life; but it must also vitally affect our view of Nora's behaviour elsewhere in the play. It confirms what we might anyway have suspected from her school-girlish boasts to Fru Linde - that the excitement of illicit role-playing has meant nearly as much to her as saving her husband's life. Nora as lark and squirrel, Nora as schoolgirl heroine of the hour, Nora as noble-minded suicide or apostle of personal freedom - all these are roles to be assumed and played with style and gusto. That hidden bag of macaroons suggests more than one kind of appetite.

It suggests, too, how much of a piece Nora's character has become in the play's final version, not just in terms of her behaviour within the stage-time of performance but also in the coherence of imagined past with dramatic present. The new and disturbing elements which Ibsen introduced when revising the play do indeed derive from the implications of her accusations against her father, but they do so in a way which the original draft does not seem to have envisaged. Her role-playing and extravagance - the elements which Ibsen most emphasised in re-writing the play - become in this final version precisely congruent with the ethos of that childhood home, the original doll's house, of which we are made aware throughout the play. It is clearly understood between Nora and Torvald that she is very much her father's daughter. Torvald tells her early in the first act, that she is *en besynderlig liden en. Ganske som din fader var* [H, VIII, 276], 'a funny little one. . .Just like your father'[49] [O, V, 205] and what he has in mind is her extravagance and greed for money. Like her father, she is a spendthrift (*ødeland*) and this, Torvald thinks, is an inherited quality:

> *Det ligger i blodet. Jo, jo, jo, sligt er arveligt, Nora.*
>
> It's in the blood. Oh yes, it is, Nora. That sort of thing is hereditary.

Nora is unrepentant, sorry only that she has not inherited more of papa's qualities. What disturbs Torvald, on the other hand, is the suspicion that she *has* inherited many of these qualities. When, in the final act, he is confronted with the knowledge that she has forged her dying father's signature, almost his first reaction is to blame heredity for her lack of legal scruple:-

> *Alle din faders letsindige grundsætninger har du taget i arv. Ingen religion, ingen moral, ingen pligtfølelse.*
>
> [H, VIII, 352]
>
> All your father's irresponsible ways are coming out in you. No religion, no morals, no sense of duty.[50]
>
> [O, V, 276]

Obviously, Nora's background has represented something deeply antipathetic to Torvald's own temperament and (presumably) upbringing. To some extent, this must reflect a difference of ethos and *class*, between the freethinking (in an old fashioned Francophile sense[51]) cultivated, carefree, commercially irresponsible world of Nora's father, and the rectitude-as-an-end-in-itself of the civil servant.

But Torvald's alarm at this recrudescence of inherited

qualities in Nora has a much more immediate and personal cause then mere generalized disapproval:-

> *Å, hvor jeg er bleven straffet for, at jeg så igennem fingre med ham. For din skyld gjorde jeg det; og således lønner du mig.*
>
> Oh, this is my punishment for turning a blind eye to him. It was for your sake I did it, and this is what I get for it.

In the first draft, these sentences are present, but without any supporting evidence earlier in the play. In the final version they become the core of a *forhistorie*, carefully worked into the fabric of the earlier acts, which goes far to explain both Torvald's hysterical fright and some of the odder features of Nora's behaviour.

What the final version of the play makes clear is that this is not the first time Torvald has come close to professional ruin on account of Nora's family. Her airy remark to Fru Linde near the beginning of the play:-

> *Du ved vel, at Torvald gik ud af departementet da vi blev gift?*
>
> [H, VIII, 281]
>
> I suppose you know that Torvald left the Ministry when we got married?
>
> [O, V, 209]

takes on an entirely altered significance when we realize that her thin-sounding and rather contradictory explanations - that there were no prospects of promotion with the Ministry, and that *therefore* he had to leave a secure post and work all hours as a struggling lawyer in private practice - are a polite way of concealing the true reasons for his resignation. No wonder

Nora's account is evasive. What we must presume to have happened is that Torvald, as a civil servant with legal training, has been called in to head some kind of Board of Trade enquiry to investigate irregularities in the books of her father's firm. Even Nora recognizes the seriousness of the matter (and by implication her father's guilt?):-

> *Jeg tror, de havde fået ham afsat, hvis ikke departementet havde sendt dig derhen for at se efter, og hvis ikke du havde været så velvillig og så hjælpsom imod ham.*
>
> [H, VIII, 316]

> I honestly think they would have had him dismissed if the Ministry hadn't sent you down to investigate, and you hadn't been so kind and helpful.
>
> [O, V, 242]

What Torvald has done, it seems, is to enter some kind of exculpatory report ('turned a blind eye') then resigned his post and married the offender's daughter.[52] Such recklessness appears entirely out of character in the Torvald we see on the stage - indeed such is his habitual caution that surely only the risk of dismissal or even prosecution could have persuaded him to give up a secure post for the uncertainties of beginning a private practice.

Yet - 'such things are hereditary' - Nora seems to have learned nothing from the experience. Within moments of the play's beginning, she is trying to persuade Torvald to raise a loan on his future salary to pay for the Christmas shopping. What would happen, asks the prudent Torvald, if he were to be killed on New Year's Eve by a falling roof-tile? If that were to happen, says Nora, things would be so terrible that it wouldn't matter if she were in debt or not. As for the unlucky creditors:-

> *De? Hvem bryr sig om dem! Det er jo fremmede.*

[H, VIII, 274]

> Them? Who cares about them! They are only strangers!
>
> [O, V, 202]

This is all of a piece with her conception of 'natural' law as something according to which personal motivation and, above all, personal loyalty to those one knows and loves should take precedence over any Kantian ideal of universal equity. For her, as for Peer Gynt, Absolute Reason is dead, or applies only to others. It is sufficient justification for her actions that *Jeg gjorde det jo af kærlighed*, 'I did it for love. . .' [H, VIII, 304 / O, V, 229], sufficient guarantee against unpleasant consequences that *Jeg har jo tre små børn*, 'Why, I have three small children' [H, VIII, 309 / O, V, 235].

It should not be too readily assumed that Ibsen intends us to sympathize unreservedly with Nora's conception of what the law should be - even if it does accord with what is argued in his earliest known drafts for the play.[53] His dramas are full of characters who imagine they have acquired some overriding moral dispensation permitting them to defy the moral and legal codes which bind other people. Yet it is difficult to think of a single character - from Brand and Peer Gynt to Solness, Borkman and Rubek - whose conduct justifies such a 'suspension of the ethical'. Even in cases where there is ground for believing that Ibsen actually sympathized with ideas which the characters express (with Brand's stand against compromise, for example, or Gregers Werle's pursuit of absolute honesty, or Rebekka West's declaration of the rights of passion) the translation of ideals into dramatic and human truth always involves the recognition of mixed and impure motives, self-love, bad faith.

So too it is with the final version of *A Doll's House*. Nora does not actually commit any crime worse than the fairly technical one of forging her father's signature as guarantor. But her behaviour in other contexts constantly warns us that the motives for her actions are not at all what she would like to believe. Even her apparently disinterested actions are tainted by self-indulgence and the appetite for manipulating others. It might seem a pure kindness, for example, that she should arrange for her old friend Fru Linde to gain a post in Torvald's new bank, even if it is at Krogstad's expense. But there is more than one sort of pleasure to be had from using one's position to do favours to one's friends:-

> *Ja det er rigtignok umådelig fornøjeligt at tænke på at vi - at Torvald har fået så megen indflydelse på mange mennesker. [tager posen op af lommen.] Doktor Rank, skal det være en liden makron?*
>
> [H, VIII, 293]

> Yes, it really is terribly amusing[54] to think that we. . . that Torvald now has power over so many people. [She takes the bag out of her pocket.] Dr. Rank, what about a little macaroon?
>
> [O, V, 219]

This revealing little exchange, with Nora's verbal slip, and the hint (macaroons again) that her view of this new-found power is dangerously self-indulgent, is not in the play's first draft [H, VIII, 386-91 / O, V, 299-302]. Together with her preceding sneer against the nature of the society which sustains her (*Hvad bryr jeg mig om det kedelige samfund?* 'What do I care about your silly old society?' [H, VIII, 292 / O, V, 219]) and her bare-faced, unnecessary lie about where the macaroons have come from, the whole passage suggests, quietly but eloquently, what a world ruled by Nora's moral principles might be like.

Torvald's earlier, apparently more indulgent explanation for this moral phenomenon - *Nora, Nora, du est en kvinde!* - 'Nora, Nora! Just like a woman!' [H, VIII, 274 / O, V, 203] - is characteristically beside the point. Everything we discover about 'papa's qualities' suggests that, far from being the result of mere womanliness, Nora's attitude to public and private morality is a pretty accurate reflection of her father's. It would seem to follow that her claim in the first draft to be the victim of *tyrannens mishandling af det værgeløse offer*, 'the tyrant's maltreatment of the defenceless victim' [H, VIII, 447 / O*, V, 341] is, in any general sense, highly misleading. Defenceless she certainly is not. Indeed, one suspects that the multiplicity of roles she plays in the marriage, far from being imposed by Torvald's bullying, are all part of a curious kind of marital conspiracy - the first of many examined by Ibsen in his dramas of contemporary life - in which certain patterns of behaviour and certain fictions about reality are tacitly accepted by both partners so as to ignore unpleasant or dangerous realities. The baby-talk about squirrels and larks forms a kind of Biedermeier shorthand for a deeper and more damaging fantasy which reduces not just Nora but the marriage as a whole to the level of the nursery. It is, as much as anything, a way of shutting out the implications of adult sexuality; and it is part of a game which Nora plays with far more apparent enthusiasm than Torvald.

Nor is her interpretation of the rules entirely straightforward. For, unknown to the other player, she has added a sort of extension to the game in which she plays a series of secret roles; - the breadwinner; the heroine of the hour; the *mère coupable* who will sacrifice herself for the sake of her children. When, in the last act of the play, she is found to be cheating, she demands that the rules be changed, then (when the other player offers to change them) storms out. It would be unwise as well as unfair to regard this as mere gamesmanship. For Nora, the price of victory which she demands of Torvald - the maturing of their marriage into an adult relationship - is precisely what she cannot bring herself to pay.

It is revealing to examine in this connection the changes which Ibsen introduced into later drafts concerning Nora's relationship with Doktor Rank. In the first draft he is merely a family friend, as well-intentioned and disinterested (and as dramatically unsatisfactory) as the character of Relling in *The Wild Duck*. In the final version, Rank's character and dramatic function are entirely altered. He is now a more sinister figure with whom Nora has developed a curious, uneasy relationship just this side of flirtation. Nora preens, teases, shows off her new stockings:-

> *Kødfarvede. Er ikke d e deilige! Ja, nu er her så mørkt; men imorgen -. Nej, nej, nej; De får bare se fodbladet. Å jo, De kan såmæn gerne få se oventil også.*
>
> [H, VIII, 322]

> Flesh-coloured! Aren't they lovely! Of course, it's dark here now, but tomorrow. . . No, no, no, you can only look at the feet. Oh, well, you might as well see a bit higher up too.
>
> [O, V, 247]

When he responds just a little, with a sort of tentative arch formality, she taps him lightly on the cheek with the stocking. The dialogue and action are heavy with innuendo.[55] One even begins to wonder at this point what their relationship can have been in the past - and even what might have lain behind Rank's advice to Nora to take Torvald to the south.

Yet within moments of this suggestive passage of dialogue, when Rank does openly confess his attraction to her, Nora reacts with shocked distaste:-

> *Ak, kære doktor Rank, dette her var virkelig stygt af Dem.*
>
> [H, VIII, 324]

> Ah, dear doctor Rank, that was really unpleasant[56]

of you.

[O*, V, 249]

What is unforgivable in his behaviour is not that he loves, or at least desires her (which even she must have realized, at least subconsciously) but that he has been open enough to say so. The moral which Nora draws from this exchange is presumably that since all men are beasts, it is unreasonable to expect disinterested behaviour from any of them. But the context in which the Doctor's pass at Nora is made and the inconsistencies of her own behaviour suggest a very different conclusion - not about Rank, who reacts in a straightforward obvious way to what looks like a fairly obvious piece of flirtatiousness, but about Nora herself.

Her confusion at the incident suggests a much deeper confusion about different kinds of human relationships; and it is significant that when a puzzled Rank asks her to explain her behaviour - for, he says, she has seemed as happy to be with him as with Torvald - her answer takes us back to the nursery. There are the people one loves most, she explains, and the people whom one would almost rather be with:-

> *Da jeg var hjemme, holdt jeg naturligvis mest af pappa. Men jeg syntes altid det var så umådelig morsomt, når jeg kunde stjæle mig ned i pigekammeret; for de vejleded mig ikke en smule; og så talte de altid så meget fornøjeligt sig imellem.*
>
> [H, VIII, 325]
>
> When I was at home, I loved Daddy best, of course. But I also thought it great fun if I could slip into the maids' room. For one thing, they never preached at me. And they always talked so entertainingly amongst themselves.
>
> [O*, V, 250]

Her childhood, oscillating between strong-willed father and

gossiping maids, has left her, she seems to be saying, with an instinctive tendency to divide herself between emotional and social life, between feeling and pleasure. It is a curious sort of explanation to give in this context - certainly Rank finds it so - but it does indicate how pervasive and how crippling is the influence of *hjemme* - her childhood home. Her conception of all human relationships is essentially manipulatory. The image she uses to Torvald about her relationship with her own children:-

> *. . . de har igen været mine dukker. Jeg syntes det var fornøjeligt, når du tog og legte med mig, ligesom de syntes det var fornøjeligt, når jeg tog og legte med dem.*
>
> [H, VIII, 358]

> [they] in turn have been my dolls. I thought it was fun when you came and played with me, just as they thought it was fun when I went and played with them.
>
> [O, V, 280-1]

is precisely applicable to all her dealings with other people - hence her delight in the thought of being able to exercise, through Torvald, power over the employees of the Bank. Human dolls are not compliant, passive objects content to lie prone on the nursery floor. They too manipulate - especially when they have the advantage of being brought up as only children in troubled or inadequate households, hardened early in the techniques of emotional survival.[57]

For the effect of growing up in the doll's house is that, eventually, its limitations become the perimeters of one's own emotional world. In time, denial of freedom creates fear of freedom. As long as Nora can convince herself that in some sense she is still in the nursery, as long as she can maintain the fictions which allow her to remain child-woman, child-wife, child-mother, her marriage to Torvald poses no threats. Essentially, nothing has changed; the tensions between childishness and physical maturity, between emotional fiction and biological reality, are subsumed in a sequence of assumed roles, carefully controlled games, the purpose of which is to preserve that timeless, a-sexual inner world intact. Rank is no threat to this compact; for it is in the rules of the game that such provocation as he has been offered can be denied the instant that either party begins to take the matter seriously. This is the essence, and the great advantage of flirtation. Nevertheless, the incident is of considerable significance when we come to assess Nora's confrontation with Torvald in the final act.

Taken at face value, Act III of *A Doll's House* presents the critic with an insoluble problem - or rather, with a problem which is only soluble if we assume that Ibsen miscalculated. On the one hand, we are clearly expected to agree with much of Nora's denunciation of Torvald and her father - she has languished in childish subservience; upbringing and marriage have hindered her development as a human being. On the other hand, the dramatic context into which her transformation is placed in the play's final version throws anything she may say into doubt. This tension is perhaps present by definition in any reading of the play. After all, the more convincingly Nora establishes her credentials as one whose personality has been limited and distorted by marriage, the less likely the audience will be to believe in her instantaneous conversion from terror-stricken squirrel to emotionally liberated woman. But the changes which Ibsen introduced in the final version make it (deliberately, I believe) *more* difficult to believe in this transformation.[58] They suggest, instead, a much more complex form of dramatic irony in which we are intended to believe simultaneously that Nora means what she says; that what she says is in some sense (indeed, in several senses, not all of them intended) true; and yet that everything she does and says indicates that she is still firmly locked within her nursery-self.

What *has* changed by the final act is that her immaturity has now entered a much more dangerous phase, in which play-acting is replaced by melodramatic fantasies of self-immolation and sacrifice. Elements of this are already present in the first draft - the sudden lunge towards the river and suicide when Torvald discovers the letter, her longing for him to take all the blame on himself. But in the play's final version, what Nora now calls *det vidunderlige*, 'the miraculous', is firmly established, from the end of Act II, as the scenario which Nora has devised for herself and Torvald, the pattern and indeed the motive for all her actions.

Nora's 'miracle' is the stuff of which melodramas are made. According to the sequence of events which she has devised, Torvald, far from explaining what has happened or giving in to Krogstad and hushing the matter up (the two possible sensible courses of action open to him), will stand up and declare himself the guilty one. And in order to prevent this ruinous self-sacrifice, Nora will pre-empt his confession by throwing herself in the river. As a scenario, the plan is melodramatic and silly; as a solution to their difficulties it is absurd. But it is also revealing about the nature of her response to the adult world. For in this context her innocent-sounding words to Torvald at the end of Act II, *Du må ofre dig ganske for mig iaften*, 'You must devote yourself exclusively to me this evening' [H, VIII, 333 / O, V, 257] take on a second and much more sinister meaning. *Ofre* does indeed mean, it its original, carefree context, 'devote' or 'give yourself up'. But it can also carry the much more serious sense, 'to sacrifice'. And confronted with a threat to her enclosed *borgelig* idyll, Nora's immediate instinct *is* to look for a sacrifice. Torvald's career, her own life and (when neither of these seems likely to be offered up) her links with her own children - all these are nominated in turn as sacrificial victims. In the last case, the sacrifice is made. Nora leaves home.

Whether Ibsen himself saw - or could permit himself to acknowledge - the full implications of Nora's action is unclear. In a letter to Erik af Edholm, he speaks of her as

> a great grown-up child (*et stort voksent barn*) who

> must venture out into life to discover herself and thereby perhaps at some later stage become suited (*skikket*) to bring up children - or maybe not; no-one can be sure. But this much is certain - that with the view of her marriage which Nora has acquired in the course of that night, it would be immoral of her to continue living with Helmer. That she cannot do, and so she leaves.[59]

One detects here an element of belated special pleading on behalf of that original conception of Nora as heroine and martyr from which the final version of the play so markedly diverges. The instability of her character in the final version, her greater capacity for self-deception and emotional dishonesty, means that her new-found view of her marriage at this moment of crisis is unlikely to be rationally arrived at or valid for very much longer than the moment of high passion in which it is articulated. The character on the stage may well be describing the weaknesses of a certain kind of relationship in a way that the playwright agrees with, and from which, in general terms, it would be difficult to dissent. But in revising his play, the playwright has also made it much more difficult to believe that this particular 'grown-up child' can or will understand the significance of the night's revelations.

For if we regard her actions only in the light of the Nora we see on stage rather than in that of Ibsen's initial (and half-abiding) intentions, doesn't her final dramatic gesture seem like one more evasion of the issue? Isn't this sacrifice, like the others, designed not to help her grow up, but to preserve her infantile self intact? If growing up implies learning to live in an equal relationship with others, then Nora's behaviour in the last act is surely preposterous - a parody of that process of maturation, and at the same time its complete denial. Her decision to leave a fuddled, bewildered Torvald some ten minutes after he has been shown what she now says is the error of his ways, less than half an hour after she has been about to throw herself in an ice-cold river for his sake, before he has had the slightest chance to accept any change in their relationship - that decision is itself at best a piece of petulant childish impatience, even in the terms in which Nora justifies it. Nor can it be justified, as Ibsen seems to be half-hinting that it might in his letter to Edholm, by reference to the interests of her children. For it is entirely characteristic of Nora, and crucial to the patterning of the play, that she is abandoning them to a childhood, oscillating between father and nursemaid, which will be an exact copy of her own.

Yet if we look beyond the terms of Nora's discourse, to the dramatic context in which they are placed, then her behaviour does become entirely consistent. Her sudden exit can only really be construed as an attempt to evade precisely that mature relationship - at least with Torvald - which she claims she wants. If Nora, as is suggested throughout the play, has designated Torvald as father-substitute, then the dual nature of their relationship hitherto - lurching from parent/child didacticism, *vejledning*, to collusive infantilism - has skirted the implications of this essentially incestuous relationship for as long as possible. When the falseness of the situation is made plain to them both, it is Nora who must act to end the marriage at whatever sacrifice to herself or to the lives or happiness of others.[60] But nothing in the play suggests that the resounding boom of Nora's final exit can be taken as a signal of liberation. It rather denotes a final defensive retreat, a refusal to grow up, the self-incarceration of the heroine within her own childhood.

CHAPTER FOUR

Ghosts

...*Jeg tror næsten, vi er gengangere allesammen*, 'I'm inclined to think that we are all ghosts...every one of us', Mrs Alving tells Pastor Manders. And she is not speaking only of genetic inheritance, she says, but of all the *gamle afdøde meninger og alskens gammel afdød tro*, 'old defunct theories, all sorts of old defunct beliefs' by which society is ruled [H, IX, 92/ O, V, 384]. There is a sense, willingly seized upon by the Shavian tradition in Ibsen-criticism, in which this is indeed the subject-matter of *Ghosts*; for, on one level at least, the play does present an argument for just that sexual honesty and *livsglæde*, 'joy in life' which the young Helene Alving had denied her husband and which Osvald (the victim in a figurative and literal sense of that repression) now defends to Pastor Manders. Much - perhaps rather too much - of the play functions on the level of a debate about the social issues of the day - the sort of debate which is to be found throughout the Scandinavian literatures of the early 1880s, above all in the works of Bjørnson and Alexander Kielland.

But *Ghosts* is very much more than a play about social problems, about the effects of mercenary marriage and inherited disease. The characters do 'set problems under debate'. But the way in which the past dominates and determines the present, as the failed marriages of the parents destroy their children, means that the terms of the debate become, at least as far as the fates of those children are concerned, largely irrelevant. It is the nature of the relationships between the characters (alive and dead - for at Rosenvold as at Rosmersholm, the dead are as real as the living) which gives the play its tautness, its power, its formal intensity. Of the characters on the stage, three are directly related, Engstrand is Regine's putative father, and Pastor Manders is (somewhat implausibly) someone with whom Fru Alving has been in love and for whom she should have left her husband. It is thus, in a very literal sense, a 'family drama'; and in the family, the most passionate feelings and drives, untamed by society, are free to ravage its members behind closed doors.

This is surely the significance of the play's title: *Gengangere* in Norwegian means something more specific than 'Ghosts'. Its literal meaning is 'those who walk again'; and the power of the past to live again through the present (a power of which inherited disease is only one very literal metaphor) forms the true subject matter of the play. Each of Captain Alving's children has grown up in innocence of this inherited past - Osvald because he has been sent away from home as soon as he became old enough to understand what was happening in the household, Regine because she has been kept unaware of her true parentage. But Osvald's physical revolt from this *tilsølede hjem*, this 'polluted house' [H, IX, 83/ O, V, 376] and Regine's ignorance of her origins, have not sufficed to save them. In a more literal and terrifying sense, we are taken back to Torvald Helmer's *sligt er arveligt*, 'That sort of thing is hereditary' [H, VIII, 276/ O, V, 205]. In *Ghosts*, the patterns of heredity assume the force of an implacable law which no idealism, no attempt at meliorism, can withstand. What gives the play its special claustrophobic power is the way in which the symbolism of the play and its assumptions about the determined nature of human existence combine to render Osvald a helpless passive victim.

Yet this power is also the source of a certain rigidity in the play's development which is, in its way, a sort of weakness. It is perhaps no coincidence that in the months before he produced the first draft of *Ghosts*, Ibsen had become fascinated by what was to become one of the classics of Scandinavian Naturalist fiction, J. P. Jacobsen's *Niels Lyhne*.[61]

Jacobsen's novel also deals with the decline of a sensitive individual blighted by inherited weakness and by incompatibilities in his parents' marriage; and his hero, too, is characterized by helpless passivity.[62] But whereas Jacobsen had been able to cast his novel in a sinister dream-like prose which enacts the uneasy bewilderments of its hero (and which so enraptured many German writers of the 1890's, Rilke and Thomas Mann amongst them) the problem of expressing such passive decay in *dramatic* form was almost insoluble. Osvald Alving is helpless to avoid his fate; all he can do is to become aware of it - and it is this process of gradual revelation which constitutes the dramatic movement of the play. The first act ends with the symbolic embrace between Osvald and Regine which recalls, like a ghost of the past, the coupling of Osvald's father and Regine's mother which became so traumatic a moment in the Alvings' marriage; the second act ends with the equally theatrical burning down of the Children's Home with which Fru Alving has sought to allay rumour about her marriage and to expiate her bad conscience about it. Yet these climaxes, though dramatically effective in themselves and symbolically related to the themes of the play, are only punctuation marks, as it were, in the process of revelation. Before the end of Act I, Fru Alving has told Pastor Manders of the unrepentant, unreformed licentiousness of her late husband; two thirds of the way through the second act we become aware of the nature of Osvald's illness. The only relevant person *not* to realize it by then is Osvald himself, for he still believes his father to have been the blameless public figure Fru Alving has described in her letters. From that point onwards, the only remaining source of dramatic tension is in the dramatic irony of Osvald not realizing the falseness of this picture. When, eventually, Fru Alving does tell him [H, IX, 122/ O, V, 413] the remainder of the play takes on the character of the final stage in the progress to a martyrdom.

Criticism (it is one of its more natural attributes) abhors a vacuum. Faced with the strangely bare and vacant structure of *Ghosts*, some modern commentators have hastened to supplement it with readings-in of their own. Perhaps the most influential of these has been an article by Derek Russell Davis (1963) in which he argues that Osvald's condition has been mis-diagnosed - that what he is suffering from is not inherited syphilis at all, but some form of family-induced schizophrenia.[63] It is not clear whether Davis believes that Ibsen himself consciously intended us to understand that he was talking about psychological disorder rather than a physical malady; and one must say that it seems improbable, given the scandal and the damage to Ibsen's reputation caused by the play, that he should have given no indication to anyone if he had been misunderstood on so crucial a point. Moreover, since Ibsen had introduced the subject of venereal disease in *A Doll's House*, at least by implication, it is scarcely probable that he would appear to make the condition central to the dramatic issue of his next play, if he were really talking about a different illness entirely.[64]

If, on the other hand, Professor Davis's case is that Ibsen himself misunderstood the matter (in common with established medical opinion of his time) and mistook a psychological malady for a physical illness, even then serious difficulties still attach when one tries to apply this interpretation to *Ghosts*. It is all very well to claim that Osvald's symptoms, case-history and prognosis would be more appropriate to a mental condition than to inherited syphilis; but it really does seem rather far-fetched to treat as a case of 'family mad-making' a young man who has experienced so very little of *any* form of family life. Osvald has been sent away from home at the age of six or seven. His conscious memories of infancy are disconnected and vestigial; the remaining fragments, whilst not all idyllic, are scarcely the stuff of which psychoses are made. If there are other, darker memories, the text of the play gives no hint of them. As for his memories of later childhood and adolescence, none of them, apart from rosy letters from his mother, can concern his home, for he has been absent from Rosenvold until the age of sixteen or seventeen, when his father dies. Although Davis claims that Osvald has then come home and stayed 'for a while' with his mother, and that 'his incestuous desires for her are likely to have been revived in this situation', there is no evidence in the text to support this. Indeed, all the evidence of their conversations together points to the *distance* between mother and son, a distance not of estrangement or suppressed desire, but rather (not surprisingly in the situation) of the wariness of two people who feel they should have some form of relationship but who don't yet know each other very well. As for Osvald's feelings for Regine, he is surely attracted to her precisely because she is vital, life-asserting, all that life at Rosenvold otherwise is not. There may be a terrible and appropriate irony in her being his half-sister, but it is not one of which he can possibly be aware. In sum, the idea of life at Rosenvold - at least before the extreme situation of the final act, which none of the characters knows enough to foresee - as being a seething cauldron of over-intense emotions cannot be justified in terms of the play's *forhistorie*, of what the characters say to each other, or of the play's dramatic structure.

And if interpretation of the play is restricted to what Ibsen actually wrote, rather than what critics feel he should have written, the deficiencies of that dramatic structure remain. *Ghosts* is a curiously static play. It depends for its dramatic momentum on the articulation of a sequence of revelations; yet the fearful intricacies of inquisition and self-revelation which Ibsen was to explore in *Rosmersholm* and *Little Eyolf* were still beyond his grasp in this earlier play. Nevertheless, *Ghosts* does possess a dramatic power in excess of its somewhat broken-backed and tenuous plot, and the abiding, though somewhat melodramatic horror of its ostensible subject-matter; and much of this power derives from the intricate *thematic* unity throughout the play, from the title-page to the final tableau. Spectres of childhood damaged or destroyed haunt the imagery of the play. Osvald, exiled from his childhood home to protect him from knowledge of his debauched father's true nature; Regine, foisted with her mother on Engstrand so as to preserve the purity of the Alvings' family name; the children's home with which Fru Alving seeks to sanctify her husband's reputation and to still her own conscience by ridding herself of his money - all of these reflect a world in which adults manipulate and destroy their children so as to preserve an untrue image of themselves. When Engstrand seeks to wheedle Regine into becoming the hostess of his projected seamen's hostel/bordel, his hypocrisy is so blatant that the effect is comic as well as nasty. But the comedy is only a distorted surface-reflection of the way in which the gentry, too, prostitute their children and dependents. It is the power of the Alvings' money which has made Regine into Engstrand's putative daughter in the first place; and it is entirely appropriate on more than one level that the money which should have gone to support the children's home may instead be diverted into Engstrand's enterprise: - *...får jeg styre det huset efter* mine *funderinger, så tør jeg love, at det skal bli' salig kammerherren værdigt*, 'if I can run it *my* way, I think I can promise it'll be a place worthy of the Captain's memory' [H, IX, 119/ O, V, 410]. The irony cuts several ways - for what is to Engstrand a piece of pure manipulative hypocrisy is also no less than the truth, not just about Captain Alving but about the respectable world as a whole. Indeed the price of that very respectability has to be paid by those children whom it is supposed to preserve. The children's home, which *skal ... helliges til en højere livsopgave*, 'is to be consecrated to a higher purpose' [H, IX, 67/ O*, VI, 361] becomes instead a symbol of the way in which children are sacrificed to preserve lies or assuage guilt, in the name of that 'higher purpose' with which so many Ibsen characters, from Brand to Rubek, justify their actions.

Yet childhood exacts its own revenge. It is central to the play's symbolic structure that at the moment at which the sacrifice is made manifest and Osvald's disease assumes absolute power over its victim he regresses to helpless, permanent infancy. He has felt himself deprived of a childhood, thrust out too early [H, IX, 73/ O, V, 368] from a family he can scarcely remember. His return to Rosenvold is thus a sort of quest for something which has never really existed there - that same ideal of family life which he has sought in the bohemian households he has visited in his youth. But the fact that it has never existed, and the *reasons* for this (his father's debauchery, his mother's repression) combined with the fact of his illness, mean that Osvald's return takes on the character of a regression. Indeed the whole play forms a sort of retrogression from the articulate young artist whom we see in Act I to the crippled child of the final scene. It is as though, impossibly restricted in the development of a character who can do nothing to alter his fate, Ibsen resorts to a kind of anti-development, unbuilding Osvald's personality before our gaze.

To add richness and complexity to this negative motion, moreover, Ibsen surrounds his central character with others who become symbols of his regression, and others still who parallel it in their failure to grow up. Osvald's longing for the apparent health and vitality of a girl who turns out to be his half-sister;[65] Fru Alving's weird half-anguished, half-victorious crooning over a child she has never really known -

> *Å, jeg kunde næsten velsigne din sygdom, som drev dig hjem til mig. For jeg ser det nok; jeg* har *dig ikke; du må vindes.*
>
> [H, IX, 125]

> Oh, I could almost bless this illness that drove you home to me. I can see I haven't made you completely mine yet - I must still win you.
>
> [O, V, 416]

- both are symptomatic of the contracting, imploding nursery world which the house of Alving comes to represent for him. His degeneration into idiocy is a medical condition, but it is also the logical conclusion of forces at work within his own character, which are an essential part of the play's symbolic framework and which parallel features of his parents' marriage.

For the Alvings' marriage has been blighted not only by its mercenary nature, but by a kind of obstinate childishness which has made both parties incapable of inner growth. Fru Alving says of her husband that in the earliest days of their marriage he was

> *sligt et livsglædens barn, - for han* var *som et barn, dengang....*
>
> [H, IX, 122]
>
> a child so full of the joy of life - for he *was* like a child in those days....
>
> [O*, V, 412]

a child-man whom the life of a public official in a remote town and her own devotion to *pligter* ('duties') had prevented from growing up.[66] But it is surely significant that this is one of the only passages in the play in which she speaks of him with any affection. Equally revealing, the only point at which we can gain any sense of what has attracted her to Manders is when she sees him completely taken in by Engstrand:-

> *FRU ALVING. Jeg siger, De er og blir et stort barn, Manders.*
> *MANDERS. Jeg?*
> *FRU ALVING [lægger begge hænder på hans skuldre]. Og jeg siger, jeg kunde ha' lyst til at slå begge armene om halsen på Dem.*
>
> [H, IX, 101]
>
> MRS ALVING. I say you are a great child, and always will be, Manders.
> MANDERS. I?
> MRS ALVING [places both hands on his shoulders]. And I say I could almost feel like flinging my arms round your neck.
>
> [O*, V, 392]

Her fascination with the childish qualities in men seems, on its own terms, innocent enough. But considered in relation to her attitude to Osvald - her hunger for his company, her evident pleasure (after 20 years) at having him home so that she can relive her own youth - a side of her character emerges rather different from the noble liberated woman she has so often been taken to be. For Ibsen is surely suggesting here that she *needs* to be surrounded by child-men - derives, even, a certain satisfaction from their weakness and immaturity (a satisfaction very evident in her almost welcoming the illness which has returned Osvald to her) which colours her relationships with all men.

It is one of the most sinister ironies in the play that the son she has regained in perpetuity enacts helplessly, literally this fantasy-relationship between child and mother. And more sinister still, seen in the context of Ibsen's plays as a whole, is the lineage, as it were, of this fantasy. For Osvald's return to his mother has more than a passing kinship with Peer Gynt's return to Solvejg/Aase - indeed the final moments of *Ghosts* are an exact and terrible parody of the closing scene of *Peer Gynt*, as the tableau of mother and errant son is gradually bathed in the light of sunrise. Fru Alving soothes Osvald, as Solvejg soothes Peer, with the assurance that everything is *en forfærdelig indbildning*, 'a horrible delusion' but that now he is safe with his own mother:

> *Alt, hvad du peger på, skal du få, som dengang du var et lidet barn.... - Og ser du, Osvald, hvilken dejlig dag vi får? Skinnende solvejr. Nu kan du rigtig få se hjemmet.*
>
> [H, IX, 130]

> Everything you point to, you shall have, just like when you were a little child....And look, Osvald, what a lovely day we're going to have. Shining sunny

> weather. Now you'll be able to see your home properly.
>
> [O*, V, 421]

In the sunrise of *Ghosts*, however, there is nothing of that promise of transfiguration which, in spite of all evidence to the contrary, may be sensed at the end of *Peer Gynt*. This cold dawn gives light, not warmth - we do see, though Osvald cannot, what his home is really like; and the sun he craves, with its promise of richness and growth in a wider world,[67] is cut off for ever, outwardly by the snowy peaks and glaciers which stand like a shining barrier around the house, inwardly by the disease which is both product and symbol of a marriage as icy and loveless as that which produced Brand. For Osvald's slumped, hopeless form, a moribund death-in-life image of that marriage, life is frozen into the timeless moment of still-birth, infancy is a terminal condition. *Alting vil brænde. Der blir ingenting tilbage, som minder om far*, 'Everything will burn. There'll be nothing left to remind people of Father' [H, IX, 120/ O, V, 411]. In these images - the burned children's home, the child degenerating into the helpless second infancy which he himself has foretold moments before (*som et lidet spædebarn, uhjælpelig, fortabt, håbløs* - 'like a tiny infant, helpless, doomed, hopeless' [H, IX, 129/ O*, V, 420]) the unsatisfied fires of the young father's nature and the cold devotion to duty of the young mother are combined. From such a marriage, nothing can grow.

Yet the conclusive force of this ending, enormously powerful though it is in the theatre, must also have suggested to Ibsen how sterile, how terminal the logic of such a determinist view of life might be for the dramatist. He might defend, in *An Enemy of the People*, his right and duty to diagnose social and human ills. But it is significant that he did so in a dramatic form which was swiftly put together, is open-textured, defiantly optimistic and full of energy, movement and life. When he came to write his next major tragedy, *The Wild Duck*, he would take great care to ensure that the issues would be more complex than in *Ghosts*, the action less predictable, the symbolism richer and less explicable. Above all, he would shift the centre of dramatic attention away from the victim of the sacrifice, and towards those who demand that sacrifice be made.

CHAPTER FIVE

The Wild Duck

Amongst Ibsen's major dramas, *The Wild Duck* is one of those which deal most directly with the sacrifice of a child. Yet to regard it as principally Hedvig's play, or as a family-tragedy about the Ekdals, would be to distort and diminish the play's design. *The Wild Duck* is built first of all on the interaction between two families, and in particular between two ruined only children, Hjalmar and Gregers, who together precipitate the tragedy. It is their relationship which constitutes the dynamic, indeed the daemonic element in the play; and only by a close examination of that relationship can we understand what happens to Hedvig.

The first act of the play concentrates on the Werles, father and son.[68] At the opening of the play, Gregers has just returned from the family *Værk* up in those forests which are to play so significant a part in the play's imagery. He has been living there, it seems, for the whole of the period - some 17 years - since the scandal which shook the Werle-Ekdal business and ruined Hjalmar's father. Outwardly, the situation is preposterous; Gregers and Hjalmar have been school-friends, yet after the crash Gregers seems to have made no attempt to contact Hjalmar. Instead, he has first tamely accepted, and later insisted upon, exile up in the forests. Now, nearly two decades later, his first action on being summoned back to the town is to insist that Hjalmar be invited to his welcome-home party.

It comes as no surprise to learn that the motives behind the invitation are anything but sociable. Gregers's attempts to conceal this are disingenuous and entirely unconvincing:-

> *Hvad! Det heder jo at selskabet skal være for* mig. *Og så skulde jeg ikke be' min eneste og bedste ven -*
>
> [H, X, 48]

> What! They say the party's for *me*. Am I not allowed to invite my best and only friend....
>
> [O, VI, 134]

If Gregers has sought a reunion with his 'best and only friend' (the phrase does convey the ring of a sort of truth, if not the one Gregers means or Hjalmar understands) the reasons will have to be sought elsewhere than in warm-hearted nostalgia. Nor are they hard to find. Gregers is indeed interested in the past, but only in so far as it can be of use to him. Little by little, with systematic cunning, he extracts from Hjalmar the details of old Werle's conduct towards the Ekdals since the trial. The scene is a masterly example of Ibsen's power to use a conventional theatrical device - the creation of an historical perspective to the play's action by means of a question-and-answer dialogue - for psychological and dramatic effect. By the time the other guests return, and Hjalmar is eased uneasily out through the door, his purpose for the moment served, the essentials of Gregers's case against his father are all in place.

Initially, at least, Ibsen seems to have thought of the ensuing scene, with its conflict between father and son, as the central event of the first act, the motive force of the play as a whole. Step by step, Gregers establishes innocent-seeming, even creditable facts about his father's treatment of the Ekdals, only to use them, moments later, to cast doubt on the motives behind all this helpfulness. Hasn't it all been a mixture of guilty conscience and opportunism - all a cover for palming off onto the young Hjalmar old Werle's mistress, the housemaid Gina? And isn't even the party at which this conversation is taking place inspired by similarly Machiavellian motives? -

> *I anledning af fru Sørby skal der arrangeres familjeliv her i huset. Tablå mellem far og søn!*
>
> [H, X, 64]

> A bit of family life had to be organized in the house all for Mrs. Sørby's sake. A little tableau: father and son!
>
> [O, VI, 149]

Here Gregers and reality part company. Up to this point, all his allegations against his father seem to be backed up by the evidence, and borne out by what happens later in the play. But his allegations about his father's *present* motives should give us pause for thought - indeed, should make us examine much more closely Gregers's own motives both in consenting to attend the party and in choosing this moment to expose his father's villainy.

For, on this issue at least, his interpretation of his father's behaviour is not really plausible. Gregers claims that he has been summoned home in order to still the rumours about his father's treatment of his mother:-

> *Hvad blir der så igen af alle rygterne om, hvad den stakkers afdøde måtte lide og døje? Ikke et fnug. Hendes søn slår dem jo til jorden.*

> What will be left then of all the stories about the things the poor dead wife had to put up with? Not a whisper! Her own son kills them all stone dead.

But do these 'stories' really exist in the form that Gregers imagines? There are rumours, as we have seen in the first lines of the play, that the old man *har nok vær't en svær buk i sine dage*, 'has been a bit of a lad in his day' [H, X, 45/ O, VI, 131] and that there is 'something between' himself and Mrs Sørby. But the rumours which Gregers imagines refer to a period long before, vividly present only to him. If, as is implied, Gina has been the last of old Werle's conquests, if he and Mrs Sørby have been so discreet that no one is sure of their relationship, then the idea of the old merchant as heartless philanderer is no longer very plausible. What *is* clear from Gregers's melodramatic language, his obsessive bitterness, the inconsistencies in his *overspændt*[69] behaviour, is that the first act of *The Wild Duck*, which seems on one level to be an unmasking of the sins of the father, functions on a deeper and more significant level to expose the neurosis and bad faith of the son. It is in this light that the rest of the play must be judged.

If Act I reveals more about Gregers's character than about anyone else's, Act II performs the same function for Hjalmar. There is a telling contrast - which must be brought out in performance - between the straightness, decency and human niceness of Hedvig and Gina in the first minutes of this act, and the spoilt vanity of the *Paterfamilias* to whom they both defer. For Hjalmar's treatment of his family implies a far more effective and damaging criticism of traditional marriage than anything seen or said in *A Doll's House.* As he describes the Werles' dinner-party to his admiring family in such a way that every humiliating aspect - his naive and panic-stricken attempts at conversation, his confusion and inadequacy, his hurried early departure - becomes transformed into an occasion for gloating self-satisfaction, the pathos of his appearance in the first act is swiftly qualified by the realization that we are observing an untrustworthy self-deceiver. And as, oblivious to poor Hedvig's mounting impatience to see what titbits he may have brought home from the dinner-party, he uses wife and daughter as a chorus to his own vanity:-

> *...en sådan løs og ledig husdragt passer også bedre til min hele skikkelse. Synes ikke du det, Hedvig?*
>
> [H, X, 73]

> ...an informal, loose-fitting jacket like this suits me better, on the whole. Don't you think so, Hedvig?
> [O*, VI, 158]

then, when he is at last reminded of his promise, presents the child with a menu-card instead and, when she is disappointed, blusters and sulks - it is clear that the man who appears to the world in general as an inadequate outcast and to Gregers as a wronged hero is, in fact, a spoilt, vain, lazy, childish domestic tyrant. We scarcely need Relling's later information[70] that Hjalmar has been brought up by *to forskruede, hysteriske tante-frøkenerne*, 'two crazy, hysterical maiden aunts' [H, X, 142/ O, VI, 224], to recognise him as a really rather unpleasant variant on the type of the emotionally retarded spoilt child who spends his life manipulating other people.

Separately, Gregers and Hjalmar, though unattractive enough in their respective ways, are relatively harmless. Together, they are deadly. As the play progresses, their relationship reminds us more and more of the accusations which Gregers has levelled against his father -

> *Når jeg ser tilbage på al din færd, da er det, som om jeg så ud over en slagmark med knuste menneskeskæbner langs alle vejene.*
> [H, X, 64-5]

> When I look back on everything you've done, it's as if I looked out over a battlefield strewn with shattered lives.
> [O, VI, 150]

It is entirely characteristic of Ibsen's major drama that the final outcome of this fatal partnership between Werles and Ekdals - immature resentment playing on immature vanity - should be the sacrifice of a child.

Gregers gets to work swiftly. Within minutes of leaving his

father's house, he turns up at the Ekdals, continues his interrogation of Hjalmar, and ingratiates himself sufficiently to be shown the family's cherished secrets:- the loft in which they play out their memories of a happier, freer, richer past; and the crippled, tamed wild duck.[71] For the Ekdals the duck is merely a pet. If it stands for anything in their lives, it is perhaps the survival of their instinctive selves, even within the cage of misfortune and (relative) poverty.

But for Gregers, once he has discovered its origins, the wild duck becomes a symbol; and all its natural qualities - the wildness, the shyness, the habit when wounded of diving down into the depths rather than be captured - become metaphors for the murkier secrets, common to both families, which must be brought up to the light, and extirpated. More, he is at least half-aware of the origins of this drive within his own boundless self-hatred. He speaks to Hjalmar of the 'cross' of bearing the name 'Gregers Werle'; and when Hjalmar (who cannot imagine such a feeling - for how can absolute vanity conceive of absolute self-hatred?) asks him what he would like to have been instead, Gregers replies:-

> *...en rigtig urimelig flink hund; en slig en, som går til bunds efter vildænder når de dukker under og bider sig fast i tang og tarre nede i mudderet.*
>
> [H, X, 86]

> ...a really absurdly clever dog; the sort that goes in after wild ducks when they dive down and bite on to the weeds and tangle in the mud.
>
> [O, VI, 171]

Imaginatively, Gregers, like Iago, is parasitic. None of the images which he uses is of his own creation. He needs the Ekdals with their 'great trusting childlike natures' (*store troskyldige barnesind* [H, X, 64/ O*, VI, 150]) to supply those straightforward pictures of reality which, out of his own self-hatred and self-contempt, he can forge into the metaphors which are his instruments of destruction. And the person whom he finally does destroy, his half-sister Hedvig, is 'chosen' not just because she is vulnerable, but because she is in so many different ways a self-image - the natural child of the father with whom he cannot exchange love and the woman who has supplanted his own mother; the sibling with whom he is in unconscious rivalry; the putative child of the friend whom he loves and hates and despises and envies.

The action of the last four acts of *The Wild Duck* is Gregers's (as that of *Othello* is Iago's). But whereas Iago's tactics are planned and only his motives remain buried in darkness, Gregers lives all the time an existence in which conscious and unconscious motives are in flat opposition to each other. After his first appearance at the Ekdals', Hedvig says of him that *det var ligesom han mente noget andet, end det han sa' - hele tiden,* 'all the time it was just as though he meant something different from what he was saying' [H, X, 87/ O, VI, 172]. This is normally taken to mean simply that he makes (on Ibsen's behalf) symbols out of reality. But it is true also at another level - for what he says, and the consequences of what he does, are so consistently at variance that it becomes difficult to think of him as 'merely' accident-prone. That unconscious willing of disaster with which Solness will reproach himself in *The Master Builder* is already a part of Gregers's existence as he sleepwalks, uttering high moral sentiments, towards Hedvig's destruction.

As Gregers rightly intuits, it is the mysterious loft which is at the centre of Hedvig's existence, and of all the things in the loft, it is the wild duck which is *vel den aller fornemste der inde*, 'the most distinguished[72] of all the creatures in there' [H, X, 98/ O*, VI, 182]. For, as Hedvig says, *det er jo en* rigtig, *vild fugl. Og så er det så synd i hende; hun har ingen at holde sig til, hun, stakker...* 'she's a *real* wild bird. It's such a shame, poor thing, she hasn't anybody to keep her company'. No family, like the rabbits? (i.e. the Ekdals?) prompts Gregers, as he leads

Hedvig on towards the equation between the loft and that *havsens bund*, 'nethermost depths of the sea', from which he intends to drag up the 'truth', though (or because) intuitively, half-consciously, he realizes that it is a truth which will kill.[73]

Once again it is the Ekdals who, this time almost literally, place the loaded weapon - that is, the image to be transformed - into Gregers's hand. Hjalmar confides in his friend, first the plans for the invention which will shake the world, and then the real purpose behind his work as an inventor. His *livsopgave*, 'task in life', [H, X, 103/ O*, VI, 187] is to rescue the silver-haired old fantastic who is contentedly drinking himself silly in the next room, to *opvække hans selvfølelse fra de døde, i det jeg hæver det ekdalske navn til ære og værdighed igen*, 'restore his own self-respect by raising once more the Ekdalian name to a place of honour and dignity'. Appropriately, the final symbol which Hjalmar presents to Gregers is that of the pistol, which the two retarded men of the family now spend their copious spare time playing with. For the pistol, too, has played its part in *den ekdalske slægts tragedie*, 'the Ekdalian family tragedy'. When the Lieutenant had been found guilty of fraud, his first reaction had been that he would shoot himself. But, says Hjalmar, he dared not do it. *Han var fejg....Å, kan du begribe det?*, 'He was a coward... Oh, can you imagine it?'. Gregers can. After all, Hjalmar and his father are only Ekdals. (Hjalmar, it seems, has also been tempted to end it all. But in his case, naturally, cowardice, or common sense, is made to sound like bravery - *der hører mod til at vælge* livet *under* de *vilkår*, 'it takes some courage to choose *life* under *those* circumstances' [H, X, 104/ O*, VI, 188].) But Hedvig is not an Ekdal. And it is on Hedvig that Gregers, armed now with the further idea of a sacrifice to the family honour, sets to work.

He is nothing if not radical in his methods. First he disrupts the communal breakfast (prepared at short notice by the long-suffering Gina, the unnoticed victim in the tragedy) by declaring that *Jeg, for min del, trives ikke i sumpluft*, 'Personally, I don't thrive in a poisoned atmosphere' [H, X, 110/ O, VI, 193]. Then, his determination only strengthened by a visit from his father, he takes Hjalmar off for a long walk so that the secret of his marriage may be revealed. Until the links of family loyalty are broken, the wild duck will be safe among the rabbits, and nothing can be achieved. But Hjalmar is an easier target than even Gregers can have suspected. He has only to supplant Hjalmar's self-image of the fond father and happily married man with an equally touching one of Hjalmar the put-upon, the cuckolded and deceived, and Hjalmar's love for his family dissolves without trace. As he says, *En mands hele moralske grundlag kan svigte under hans fødder;* det *er det forfærdelige*, 'The whole moral basis of a man's life can crumble beneath his feet - *that* is the terrible thing' [H, X, 125/ O, VI, 207]. And he is quite right. For the 'moral basis' of his existence is vanity; and it is on his vanity that Gregers has successfully played. Hjalmar's first reaction, before he has had time to realize the (probable) truth about Hedvig's parentage, is to see himself as her saviour, her final hope;- *Så længe barnet har* mig *- ! Så længe* mit *hode er oven mulde - !*, 'As long as the child has *me*...! As long as I can keep body and soul together...!' [H, X, 126/ O, VI, 208]. But no sooner does he put two and two together, - as Gregers must have realized he would - than he rejects her completely:- *Gregers, jeg har ikke noget barn!*, 'Gregers, I have no child!' [H, X, 136/ O, VI, 218]. Hedvig is ready for the sacrifice.

For, unlike Gina, who takes them literally,[74] and Hjalmar, who sees them as merely decorative, Hedvig understands symbols and takes them seriously. When she talks to Gregers of her favourite book from the store in the loft, *Harryson's History of London*, it is the 'pictures' or 'images' (she uses the word *billeder*, which can mean either) which she mentions first, and first of all the frontispiece:- *Foran står afbildet døden med et timeglass, og en jomfru. Det synes jeg er fælt.* 'In the front there's a picture of Death with an hourglass, and a maiden.[75] I think that's horrible' [H, X, 97/ O*, VI, 181]. The image has far more relevance to her own situation (and to the symbolic structure of the play) than Hedvig can realize. The action of the play takes place on the two days before her fourteenth birthday; she is, as Relling says, *i en vanskelig alder*, 'at a difficult age' (- and when Gregers still cannot or will not understand, Relling puts it in terms which even *he* will grasp:- *Hun er i stemmeskiftningen, far*, 'Her voice is breaking, man' [H, X, 126/ O*, VI, 208]). Thus like most bright children at the onset of puberty she is both highly emotional and enormously suggestible. Hjalmar, in a moment of self-dramatizing fury, has talked of wringing the wild duck's neck. Gregers now seizes on Hedvig's passing mention of the bird and, closing in, puts the suggestion,[76]

> *...om nu* De *frivillig offred vildanden for* hans *skyld?....Om De nu for ham offervillig gav hen det bedste, De ejer og véd i verden?*
>
> [H, X, 138-9]

> ...Supposing *you* offered to sacrifice the wild duck for *his* sake?....Suppose you were ready to sacrifice for him the most precious thing you had in the world?
>
> [O, VI, 221]

It could plausibly be argued, of course, that Gregers here means exactly what he says, and no more; that the traditional view of his character as being dangerously deluded, fatally wrong about human nature, but not actually willing harm to Hedvig, is entirely correct; and that when he says to the Ekdals, just before Hjalmar's departure,

> *Sammen må I tre være, hvis du* [Hjalmar] *skal vinde frem til den store tilgivelsens offerstemning.*
>
> [H, X, 136]

> The three of you must remain together if you, Hjalmar, are to win through to the sacrificial spirit of forgiveness.
>
> [O*, VI, 218]

the 'sacrificial spirit'[77] of which he speaks is something entirely vague and general. But Gregers's generalities usually have a sharp point; and there is an absolute congruence (though not the one he says he expects) between the ideas of sacrifice he invokes and the actual outcome of the play. This congruence could, again plausibly, be ascribed to the playwright's predilection for patterning, for creating a structure of action to match the structure of the play's imagery. And certainly no other character in the play shows any awareness of the abyss in Gregers's personality which a more causative reading of the relationship between his words and deeds would suggest. Even Relling, when he accuses Gregers of *retskaffenhedsfeberen* ('inflamed scruples') and of blind *tilbedelses-delirium* ('delirious fits of hero-worship') [H, X, 143/ O*, VI, 225] in his idealization of Hjalmar, doesn't seem to be hinting at anything more sinister than an adolescent troublemaker with ignorant and silly ideas about human relationships. And since this is a play, and we only know about the characters from what they say and what other characters say about them, it would be safer to assume that Relling is right.

But a safe, sound reading is not always the best or most satisfying. And one can also argue that, because this *is* an entirely realistic play on one level, and a carefully worked-out symbolic drama on another, we should examine very carefully indeed the relationship between these different planes of meaning, in particular for what it can tell us about the inner lives of the characters. For here one might find grounds for believing that forces are at work in Gregers which Relling does not understand at all. In any case, what Relling does *not* know - though after Hedvig's death he comes to suspect it[78] - is how far Gregers has used the wild duck as a symbol to appeal to just that passionate, unformed side of Hedvig's nature which the Doctor's bluff good-sense cannot fathom. Yet if the way in which Gregers thinks and Hedvig acts is (as we can see from the rest of the play) entirely alien to Relling's nature, that does not mean to say that it does not exist - or that, in a special way, Gregers does not understand - precisely *because* he is 'neurotic', 'over-romantic', 'half-crazed', 'a queer fish' and the rest of it - the way in which Hedvig's mind works. And if we read the play in this light, then Hedvig's death, rather than being merely the pathetic outcome of a silly man's well-meaning self-deceptions, becomes tragic at a much deeper level. For our perception of the action of the play on a 'realistic' level would then be in accordance with just that symbolic pattern of sacrifice which so obsesses Gregers; and Hedvig's action, far from being 'accidental', would be the logical outcome of that imaginative order which the damaged lonely child in Gregers seeks to impose on the world.[79]

Certainly, his behaviour immediately after the shooting accords with this view of his character. He is besotted as ever with the idea of sacrifice. Hedvig, he assumes, has persuaded her grandfather to shoot the poor duck. It is, he proclaims, *vidnesbyrdet... en barnlig offerhandling*, 'the proof... the child's sacrifice' [H, X, 156/ O, VI, 237]. Not for nothing did Ibsen make Gregers say in a draft version of Act IV, *De må ikke tvile på offervillighedens magt; den er just det ideale i familjelivet*, 'You must not doubt the power of self-sacrifice, it is the real ideal in family life' [H, X, 255/ O, VI, 278]. It is only through sacrifice that Gregers's ideal, like Brand's God, can be appeased. His exultant *gennem barnet vilde oprettelsen ske*, 'redemption would come through the child' [H, X, 157/ O, VI, 238] suggests how fused the images of child and wild duck have become - to the point where reality can no longer challenge or disturb the symbolic pattern.

When symbol and reality *are* seen to be one - when it is realized that Hedvig has shot herself and not the duck - Gregers, though for the moment confounded, does not lose sight for a moment of his 'ideal' reality. His first words, *på havsens bund* - 'in the nethermost depths of the sea', are a direct reference to the symbolic games he has played with Hedvig. They reflect, perhaps, a kind of awe at what has happened. But they do not indicate any sense of personal responsibility, any self-examination, any self-immolating declaration of guilt such as Rebekka makes in the last act of *Rosmersholm*. When Relling indirectly accuses him of complicity, Gregers (who has stood silent for several minutes) just replies *Ingen kan sige, hvorledes det forfærdelige gik til*, 'Nobody can say how this dreadful thing happened' [H, X, 160/ O, VI, 241]. For his part, he will not, cannot see the distinction between the ideal and the human reality it destroys. Is Hedvig dead? Very well then, her death must be accounted, by the logic of his own view of human relationships, a blessing. *Hedvig er ikke død forgæves*, 'Hedvig has not died in vain', - because her death has made Hjalmar behave as, in Gregers's ideal picture of reality, he *should* behave. When Relling tells Gregers that this transformation of reality will not last, that within nine months Hedvig will be no more for Hjalmar than *et vakkert deklamationstema*, 'a subject for fine speeches' [H, X, 160/ O*, VI, 241], Gregers's response is to declare that, if this is so, life is not worth living. The implication of his final proclamation of his life's mission - 'to be the thirteenth at table' - is surely that if life cannot be recreated in terms of his own ideal, then it is life which must be sacrificed. Gregers cannot, dare not learn from what has happened, any more than Hjalmar can. It is the prospect of this invincible, unassuageable ignorance which is the most disturbing aspect of the play. For Ibsen, himself a moralist and idealist in a world which he recognized to be neither moral nor ideal, there could be no more pessimistic conclusion.

CHAPTER SIX

Rosmersholm

Rosmersholm is a very different play from its predecessor. In *The Wild Duck*, the tragic tone is constantly modified by moral passion, irony, and the desire to show 'the whole truth'. *Rosmersholm*, by contrast, is Ibsen's closest approach to the form and spirit of classical tragedy. The central characters are treated with a seriousness untainted by any suggestion of satire; even the play's one apparently farcical character, Brendel, becomes in the final version an integral part of the tragedy. In *Rosmersholm*, everything is subordinate to, and perfectly integrated into the play's overall design. It is Ibsen's most perfect formal achievement.

It was not easily gained. No Ibsen play for which the drafts have been preserved shows a more profound and dramatic development in the writing than this one. Indeed, there is an almost uncanny analogy between the motive power of the final version - the gradual rediscovery of a past which will overwhelm and destroy the present - and the process of discovery which we can observe in the drafts, as Ibsen labours to explore his characters' thoughts and motives. The effect of this exploration and revision is not to 'point-up' (as in *The Wild Duck*) but to work the inner lives and secret motivations of the characters so deeply into the fabric of the play that only the most subtle and sensitive reading will have a chance of revealing what lies beneath. There is no Relling or Håkon Werle to tell us of the forces and experiences which have created character. We discover, as Rosmer and Rebecca do, from within;

and the process of discovery is itself fate.

Rosmersholm contains no child;[80] and what we learn of the childhood of the central characters has to be gleaned from their own words. Yet the play conveys, perhaps more subtly and profoundly than any other, how strict and inescapable are the limits which childhood experience imposes on the development of character. This is most obviously true of Johannes Rosmer, and any study of the play must begin with his birthplace, Rosmersholm itself. Yet here we are immediately confronted with the dual nature of the house's symbolism, reflecting in turn the very different levels on which the play works. To Kroll and Mortensgård, Rosmersholm is the potent symbol of a threatened social and political order; and Kroll's description of what the house stands for in the district:-

> *Rosmerne til Rosmersholm, - prester og officerer. Højt betroede embedsmænd. Korrekte hædersmænd alle sammen, - en æt, som nu snart i et par hundrede år har siddet her som den første i distriktet.* [H, X, 358]

> The Rosmers of Rosmersholm... clergymen and officers... high officials... punctilious gentlemen, all of them... a family which has been established here for nearly two hundred years as the foremost in the district. [O*, VI, 305]

is certainly correct within its own terms. This is what the house has represented to others;- the incarnation of a social order - almost a hereditary official caste, part aristocracy, part bureaucracy, guardians of temporal and spiritual truths ('clergymen and officers') - which had ruled provincial Norway since the seventeenth century. Kroll's fury at Rosmer's apostasy, Mortensgård's anxiety to capture his allegiance *without* breaking his links with the Church - both reflect the political manoeuverings necessary in *den borgertvist, - borgerkrig kunde jeg gerne sige,* 'this civil dispute - civil war, I'd almost call it' [H, X, 348/ O*, VI, 296] which raged in Norway in the early and middle 1880s, and which Ibsen himself had witnessed at first hand in Molde and elsewhere during the summer of 1885.

Yet Kroll's and Mortensgård's preoccupations are not those of Johannes Rosmer, nor of Ibsen's play.[81] For Rosmersholm is not inhabited by the ideals represented in the family portraits on the wall, but by real people who have been emotionally crippled by these ideals. Rosmer describes his father 'rather bitterly' as *major her hjemme i sit hus også*, 'very much the major, even at home' [H, X, 359/ O, VI, 306]. And when Rebekka suggests to Mrs Helseth that it may be a good thing that Beate had no children, because Rosmer would find it difficult to put up with crying infants, the housekeeper replies,

> *Små barn skriger ikke på Rosmersholm, frøken... Men det ligger til slægten... Når de blir større, så lér de aldrig. Lér aldrig så længe de lever.* [H, X, 402-3]
>
> Children never cry at Rosmersholm, miss... But it runs in the family... When they grow up, they never laugh. Never laugh, as long as they live. [O, VI, 347]

The ethos of Rosmersholm is one in which the heirs to the tradition do achieve a kind of nobility, but only through the repression (whether through inherited inclination or education) of what makes people human at all. A tradition in which children neither laugh nor cry has, in effect, achieved nobility by impairing human nature. In a special sense, *all* the heirs of Rosmersholm are, and remain, unborn.

It is thus peculiarly appropriate, both on the plane of narrative and of symbolic form, that unborn children play a vital part in the structure of the drama. It is Beate's obsession with her inability to bear children which has triggered her final illness; and it is that obsession, fuelled by the belief that Rebekka is bearing Rosmer's child (*For nu* må *Johannes* straks *gifte sig med Rebekka*, 'For now Johannes *must* marry Rebekka *at once*' [H, X, 380/ O*, VI, 327]) which drives Beate into the mill-race. All this, of course, has happened in the play's dramatic past. But in this play, to a degree unusual even in Ibsen's work, past can come to seem as real as present - comes to dominate, indeed, the characters' present actions. *Det er de døde, som hænger så længe ved Rosmersholm*, '... it's the dead that cling to Rosmersholm' [H, X, 346/ O, VI, 294]; and, in a much more subtle and patterned way than in *Ghosts*, the past here does remake itself in the present. Hence the circular nature of the play's plot and imagery; - the first act begins with Rebekka and Mrs Helseth watching through the window as Rosmer takes the long path round, rather than pass too near to the scene of the tragedy which he wants to, yet never can forget; and the play ends with Mrs Helseth watching alone as Rebekka and Rosmer relive in fact the moment of Beate's self-immolation, the true nature and cause of which it has taken the whole play to discover. In the end of the play, dramatic time (the action of the play) and imagined time (the past lives of the characters) become one. They cancel each other out. And in the perfect symmetry of this conclusion, Beate's posthumous revenge (if that is what it is) also enacts her worst fear. The line of Rosmer has died out.

But this is a symmetry of which we only become aware at the end of the play; it is not (as it can sometimes seem in *Ghosts*) a form imposed from outside into which the actions and motives of the characters must somehow fit. If Rosmer and Rebekka's plunge into the mill-race fulfils an inherited pattern, aligns them (rather than Kroll) with the austere, self-denying, ultimately self-destructive ethos of Rosmersholm, everything which drives them to that moment of self-destruction is the natural, logical outcome of their respective past selves, repossessing the present. It is the coming-together of these two *fortider*, Rosmer's and Rebekka's, which defines the course of the tragedy.

It must be stressed that neither character has a straightforward relationship to the past - and that, in each case, something of the past's ambivalence has become an established part of present character. In Rosmer's case, the tensions engendered by his upbringing and especially by his education are unmistakably reflected in his personality and in his relationships with others. Unlike his forbears, he has not been reared exclusively in the Rosmersholm tradition. In the play's final version Rosmer has had Ulrik Brendel as his tutor[82] - and to Brendel's influence, it is hinted, can be ascribed something of Rosmer's capacity for freedom of thought and his longing for happiness and liberty from the past. Brendel's *oprørske meninger*, 'revolutionary ideas' [H, X, 359/ O, VI, 306] may have been countered by his expulsion from Rosmersholm. Rosmer may have turned to Kroll, the ideological image of old Major Rosmer, as his counsellor and confidant from student days onwards [H, X, 352/ O, VI, 300]. But something of Brendel's teaching has taken root in the young Rosmer - that openness to experience and outside influence which Kroll[83] so resents [H, X, 365/ O, VI, 312].

If, by inheritance, Rosmer is firmly tied to the values of Rosmersholm, by upbringing he has wavered for long between the extremes of liberty and convention. The consequent uncertainty and fear of conflict seems to be reflected as much in his emotional life as in his political views. It is manifest in his fear of giving offence to former friends; and is visible, too, in what we learn of his past relationships with both Rebekka and Beate. When Kroll cross-questions him as to the real reasons for Beate's suicide, the first proof Rosmer offers of her madness is *hendes ustyrlige, vilde lidenskabelighed*, 'her wild fits of sensuous passion' [H, X, 377/ O, VI, 324] to which she has expected him to respond.[84] (Whether or not these advances have been the result of Rebekka's schooling is unclear.) Rosmer's reaction is entirely characteristic. It is *rædsel*, 'horror' (as Rebekka, at least, would have expected it to be). One suspects that the chaste purity of the relationship between Rosmer and Rebekka has not been entirely of her choosing. It has also been dictated by Rosmer's own temperament - his tendency, caught between opposing sides of his nature, to withdraw or evade.

No wonder he speaks with wistful admiration of Brendel's having had the courage to live life in his own way [H, X, 365/ O, VI, 312]. The paradox is that, for all Rosmer's rather desperate talk of spreading joy (*glæde*) in the neighbourhood, he completely lacks the will to find happiness in his own life. And what has destroyed his will-to-happiness is not, one suspects, the repressiveness of his background (it is a little difficult to imagine the older Rosmers putting up with this gnawing unhappiness and lack of personal fulfilment) but rather his own divided nature, caught between different aspirations, different cultures. In this, he betrays kinship with those other 'superfluous men' caught between uninhabitable past and unattainable future who fill the pages of Turgenev, J. P. Jacobsen and (a little later) Thomas Hardy. Yet, though the causes of Rosmer's crippled emotional life lie in his uneasy relationship with the Rosmer traditions, the effects are precisely congruent with the outward teachings of that tradition. To one unable to express emotion, the most fundamental of human passions can come to seem terrifying or disgusting.

And here we come to the crux of the tragedy. Rosmer's timorous diffidence is not in itself the stuff of which drama is made - he is, in that sense, the least probable of heroes. What gives *Rosmersholm* its extraordinary force and resonance is the inherent conflict between his nature, his upbringing, his relationship to the past, and Rebekka's. Rebekka West represents something almost entirely new in Ibsen's drama. In most of the plays before *Rosmersholm*, women's sexuality is scarcely perceptible, let alone central to the dramatic issue.[85] In no play afterwards is it ever far from the centre of the drama. And it is significant that, from *Rosmersholm* onwards, the attitude of women to childhood, their own and other people's, and (in various literal and metaphorical senses) to childlessness, is also vital to the drama. Rosmersholm may be the scene of the action, and the traditions of the place may supply the stage for the drama. But it is Beate's madness and Rebekka's determination and strength of character which drive on the action; and it is Rebekka's childhood which will lead to the final catharsis.

For Rebekka comes from a different culture, almost a different world. She has grown up in the far north of Norway, in Finnmark - an area which held a special significance for Norwegian writers and artists of the period. To many of them, the far north offered something of the same fascination which the writers of Britain and Germany felt for the south - it was seen as representing sensuality, unregulated emotion, violence and magic.[86] Ibsen, who (until his cruise to the North Cape in 1891) had never travelled north of Trondheim, nevertheless made use of this association of ideas in the two plays specifically set in Northern Norway - *The Warriors at Helgeland* (1858) and *The Lady from the Sea* (1888).[87] Critics have long considered the heroine of *The Warriors* to be a direct forerunner for the characters of both Rebekka West and (less convincingly) Hedda Gabler. What has not been sufficiently appreciated, however, is the extent to which the themes and imagery of the earlier play anticipate *Rosmersholm*. For Hjørdis is not just a study in Viking strength of character. More important, she is a woman in whom sexuality, frustrated, has turned to intrigue and violence. All this is concomitant with the Nordland landscape:-

> *Her nordpå er hver nat en vinter lang... du skal se bølgerne flyve mod land som vilde, hvidmankede heste... Ha, hvilken lyst at sidde som heksekvinde på hvalens ryg, at ride foran snekken, vække uvejr og lokke mændene i dybet ved fagre galdrekvad!*
>
> [H, IV, 54-5]

> Here in the north every night is as long as a winter... You'll see the waves racing for the shore like wild, white-maned horses... What fun it would be to sit like a witch on a whale's back, and ride round the ships, and call up the storms, and lure men down

to the depths of the sea, singing sweet enchantments! [O, II, 53]

Here we can see already motives which Ibsen was to use 28 years later in *Rosmersholm*:- the white-maned wave-horses, the woman as witch luring men to a watery death (compare Rebekka's image of herself as *havtrold*, 'sea-troll' [H, X, 437/ O, VI, 379] and Kroll's accusation that she has *forhekset*, 'bewitched' both himself and Beate [H, X, 409/ O, VI, 354]), and the related image, a few lines later, of *draugen, der græder i bådhuset*, 'the banshee[88] who wails in the boathouse' [H, IV, 55/ O*, II, 54]. It is also notable that, at the end of the play, Hjørdis's spirit is borne away on a black cloud-horse; and even more so that the child she believes to have been murdered is central to much of the play's action.

Rebekka is not a heroic figure in the sense that Hjørdis is.[89] The heroine of *The Warriors at Helgeland* is a noble's daughter, kidnapped by one hero acting in the guise of a gentler, weaker friend (as Brynhild is in the *Volsung saga*). Her tragedy is that she has only once known a kind of sexual fulfilment, on the night of her abduction, with (unbeknown to her) the man who is not her husband. The traumatic events of Rebekka's past are more deeply buried, more shadowy and uncertain. For the first half of the play, all that we know is that she has been adopted as a child by her foster-father, Doktor West, that after her mother's death she has looked after him, and that together they have come south to Rosmersholm. What we are not told is that, up in Finnmark, she has had an affair with her foster-father. And what even she does not realize - or at least not consciously - is that Doktor West is also her own real father.

Yet it is only very slowly that we become aware of the significance of Rebekka's origins. They are, like so much in the play, hidden - and even Kroll who seeks, with an almost disinterested malice, to reveal the secret of her illegitimacy, has no idea of what his revelations imply. His patient, short-sighted industry (or has it been his wife's?) has discovered only the murky secret of the relationship between Rebekka's mother and Doktor West, a relationship of which she is presumably the offspring. As far as Kroll is concerned, the mere fact of her illegitimacy is enough to explain both her lack of moral scruple and her (unconscious) filial devotion to the old doctor. But, as Freud[90] pointed out, and as a comparison of the draft with the final version confirms,[91] Rebekka's anguish and terror at Kroll's words must come not from realization of illegitimacy, but from the fact that up in Finnmark she has been her father's mistress. Yet Freud is surely also right in his acknowledgement that Rebekka has other and more conscious motives for rejecting (as she has done before Kroll's revelations, too) Rosmer's offers of marriage, that this is 'a case of multiple motivation in which a deeper motive comes into view behind the more superficial one'.

Yet the significance of Rebekka's unwitting crime goes deeper than the slightly mechanical interpretation which Freud places upon it. Rebekka's change of attitude is important within the drama, not so much because Rebekka finds herself on the verge of an act which she associates too closely with the Oedipal fantasy she has already acted out in a traumatic adolescent affair, but much more because her redoubled sense of guilt has induced in her a state of mind tragically similar to the Rosmer family's view of life. Her childhood, as the natural child and adopted daughter of Doktor West, places her as the last in a line of characters that also includes Regine in *Ghosts* and Hedvig in *The Wild Duck*. But, unlike them, Rebekka *has* been brought up as a member of the gentry.[92] Knowledge of her true parentage brings several sorts of shame; but also the realization that her actions, her beliefs, even her very existence, have been conditioned by forces which will be for ever beyond her control. If, as she says in the last act, *Aldrig har jeg stået længere fra målet end nu*, 'I have never been further from my goal than I am now' [H, X, 427/ O, VI, 370], it is not only because Rosmersholm has robbed her of the power to will or act, but because she has discovered in her previous life and actions a pattern which makes a mockery of individual choice and free will. More than the one, more obvious kind of irony is implied in retrospect by Kroll's praise of her at the beginning of the play, *således at la' hele sin ungdom gå hen under opofrelser for andre*, 'giving up the best years of her young life, sacrificing them for the sake of others' [H, X, 349/ O, VI, 297]. Rebekka, after all, *has* been sacrificed by the libertine doctor (for he at least must have realized the implications of what he was doing) just as she has sacrificed Beate in their *kamp på bådkølen*, 'fight to the death'.[93] Yet both the power which enabled her to act to remove Beate (*Det var over mig... som et af de vejr, vi kan ha' ved vintertid der nordpå*, 'It swept over me... like one of those storms we sometimes get in the winter up North' [H, X, 426/ O, VI, 369]) and the stillness of spirit in which she has learned to love Rosmer (*... en stilhed, som på et fugleberg under midnatssolen oppe hos os*, 'a stillness like that which comes over a colony of sea-birds on the Northern coast under the midnight sun' [H, X, 428/ O, VI, 371]) are forces entirely beyond the control of her free will. It is significant that the imagery she uses to describe these conflicting forces evokes the landscapes of her childhood. For, in the end, what has 'infected her will' (*smittet min vilje*) is not Rosmersholm, nor even her incestuous affair, but in a much wider sense, the whole of that *fortid*, or past, which has made of her what she is.

And this, much more than the secrets of her origins, is what constitutes the dramatic momentum of *Rosmersholm*. Rebekka's confession cuts off Rosmer's own path of escape from the *mørke og tyngsel*, 'gloom and oppression' [H, X, 382/ O, VI, 329] of his family past to the outer world where he, too, can begin to live.[94] As in *Ghosts*, the forces of circumstance are infinitely stronger than the power of the individual to choose life and happiness. But the tragic force of *Rosmersholm* goes far beyond that of the earlier play. Left to himself, Rosmer might well subside into the pathos of an Osvald Alving, living, in one sense or another, a posthumous existence in his family mansion. But the pent-up energies of Rebekka make such a conclusion unthinkable. If it is in Rosmer's nature to ponder and self-question - here as always he is, in Kroll's terms, *den stille forsker*, 'the quiet scholar' [H, X, 382/ O*, VI, 329] - Rebekka must act, must create certainty through decision.

Hence the extraordinary nature of the play's final act. Rebekka's confession at the end of Act III should be, by all conventional standards, the play's dramatic climax. The slow and agonizing journey towards knowledge is complete; there is little more to know, or to be said. Yet it is only here that the characters' true self-examination can begin. And the revelations which follow can only be made beyond the point at which we - and they - realize with certainty that there can be no escape from the force of circumstance, the fetters of childhood. Rebekka speaks of travelling *nordover*, 'North', back to the land of her childhood. But we know instinctively that the past is no more a refuge than the present. That road, too, is closed. For what her childhood has brought her to is, precisely, here - to Rosmersholm and all it represents. And what *she* has brought to Rosmersholm is something which can only be expressed in terms of the imagery of that childhood, something as uncontrollable as one of the winter storms of the north which *tar en, - og bær' en med sig*, 'takes hold of you... and carries you away with it' [H, X, 426/ O, VI, 369].

For the moment Rosmer tries not to understand - *Nu er jeg jo fri, - både i sind og i forhold*, 'Now I *am* free... both in mind and in situation' [H, X, 427/ O*, VI, 370]. But free is what neither of them has been, or could ever be. As Rebekka sees, the only freedom consists in recognizing that one is not, one never can be free - *Aldrig har jeg stått længere fra målet end nu*, 'I have never been further from my goal than I am now'. As Rosmer's scholarly temperament leads him into *denne dræbende tvil*, 'this killing doubt' [H, X, 430/ O, VI, 373], so her energy and will have been transformed into a paralysing guilt for which no action save one can provide any sort of correlative.

It is one of the most astonishing strokes in all Ibsen that this one correlative should be suggested by Ulrik Brendel. At first sight, his entry in the last act seems no more than a daring confrontation between tragedy and farce.[95] Yet in the final version of *Rosmersholm*, Brendel's despair provides a vital commentary on, as well as a counterpoise to, Rosmer's and Rebekka's. In Act I he has left for the town, determined to 'sacrifice' (*offre*) his ideals by making them available to everyone [H, X, 363/ O, VI, 310]. Now he returns from the *store offerfest*, 'great sacrificial feast',[96] only to announce the circus animals' desertion:- *Nu er jeg læns, min kære gut. Blank og bar*, 'I'm cleaned out, my dear boy... absolutely flat' [H, X, 432/ O, VI, 374]. There is not an idea or an ideal left in his head. It is not the Rosmers, he declares, but Mortensgård who will make the future,[97] who will live beyond the bounds of the tragedy:-

> *Han kan gøre alt, hvad han vil... For Peder Mortensgård vil aldrig mere, end han kan.*
>
> [H, X, 433]
>
> He can do whatever he wants... Because Peder Mortensgård never wants to do more than he *can*.
>
> [O, VI, 375]

For Rosmer, on the other hand, such an existence is unthinkable. Yet the price of his 'victory', says Brendel, must be *Rebekka's* sacrifice:- that the woman who loves Rosmer should be ready to cut off her dainty, pink and white little finger, her incomparably formed left ear. For only *then* can a Rosmer's faith be confidently founded on rock rather than on shifting sands.

It is an exact and telling parody of Rosmerholm's outlook on life, a vision of existence which demands that love and faith justify themselves by their readiness to destroy all that has inspired them, by sacrificing not less than everything, as Beate has already done. The only way in which Rosmer's doubts and Rebekka's will to act can be stilled is by re-enacting the past. Their suicide, like Beate's, is a declaration and a proof of love in the only style which Rosmersholm can admit - the sacrifice of self to the patterns of the past.

CHAPTER SEVEN

The Lady from the Sea

A happy marriage! That's easy enough. On the other hand, if ethics were to deliver the address at the wedding service, it would be quite another thing, I imagine. Aesthetics throws the cloak of love over the merman, and so everything is forgotten.... If only it could see what happens afterwards - but for that it has no time, it is at once in full swing with the business of clapping together a new pair of lovers.

Kierkegaard, *Fear and Trembling* (discussing one of the probable sources of *The Lady from the Sea*, the ballad, 'Agnete and the Merman').

In many important ways, *The Lady from the Sea* is a very different work from both predecessors and successors in the Ibsen-cycle. Formally it is as great a contrast to *Rosmersholm* as could be - it is open-textured, loosely constructed, apparently discursive. This reflects a more fundamental difference in *The Lady from the Sea*'s approach to a problem which haunts so many Ibsen dramas. Tragedy in the other major plays often derives from the characters' inability or unwillingness to grow up, to accept the changes that time brings and the responsibilities it imposes. The course of *Rosmersholm*, for example, as of *Brand* and *Peer Gynt*, is the realization, too late, of the incurable distortions, the intolerable limitations which a childish self, not properly outgrown, imposes on adult human beings. *The Lady from the Sea* does not project such a failure - rather, it shows a personality coming to terms with time. That this, too, involves a kind of sacrifice is one of the play's central ironies.

Ellida Wangel, as we see her at the beginning of the play, is stifling in a marriage which seems to demand too little of her, yet prevents her from developing. Her feeling of suffocation takes on a physical form long before we are made aware of its cause. At her first entrance, she greets her husband with effusive and exaggerated relief (after all, he has only been out visiting patients in fine summer weather) then complains bitterly about the waters of the inner fjord:-

> *... Å gud, her er vandet aldrig friskt. Så lunkent og så slapt. Uh! Vandet er sygt her inde i fjordene... Og jeg tror det gør én syg også.*
>
> [H, XI, 64]

> Good Lord, the water here is never fresh. So lukewarm and enervating. Ugh! The water's sick in here in the fjords... And I think it makes oneself sick too.
>
> [O*, VIII, 39]

In one sense, of course, there need be nothing unnatural about this - Ellida could be merely expressing a (very characteristically Norwegian) yearning for freshness in natural surroundings, all the more understandable in one who has been brought up by the open sea. But looking at this exchange and the conversations with her husband and Arnholm which follow, one becomes aware that this apparently naturalistic scene is also an essential part of a wider symbolic pattern. Ellida's *særligt forhold både til havet og til alt, hvad havets er*, 'special affinity with the sea and all that belongs to it', is much more than just a matter of temperament or taste. It is central to the play's structure.

Yet it is not easy to state precisely what the sea does represent for Ellida. It is certainly a part of her past, the element of which she has been most aware, to which she has been most bound since childhood. But it is not, or not principally, her childhood to which the sea draws her back. Nor does that *dragende hjemvé efter havet*[98], 'relentless undertow [of] homesickness for the sea' [H, XI, 85/ O, VII, 59] lead her to want to move physically back to the edge of the open sea. What *det dragende*[99] suggests is something much closer to the inner, irresistible but undirected drives of the unconscious. The personification of these urges is the Stranger, the outlandish seaman for whom Ellida has nursed, through long years of comfortable but sterile marriage, an adolescent passion. It is the nature of this passion, which nearly destroys her marriage to Wangel and has indirectly crippled her relationship with her stepchildren, which offers some clue to her character and to the play's symbolism.

Yet the character of the Stranger caused Ibsen some difficulty and is still a source of critical confusion. The problem derives, surely, from the paradox implicit in the whole design, combining as it does the naturalistic and the symbolic. Ibsen himself went to some pains to define the man's origins and even his naval rank more precisely.[100] Yet he also wrote to Hoffory that 'nobody is to know *who* he is or what he is actually called. Precisely this uncertainty is the main thing in the method I have chosen for this occasion' [14 Feb 1889, H, XVIII, 201/ O, VII, 467]. A few weeks later, he praised the actor in the Weimar performance - 'a long lean figure, hawk-faced, with black piercing eyes and a marvellously deep and hushed voice' [H, XVIII, 204/ O, VII, 468] - in terms which imply a much more mysterious figure.

This may suggest no more than the difficulties a symbolist playwright can experience when he attempts to bring a symbol onstage. But what is crucial to the play is how *Ellida* sees him;

and what she is most obsessively aware of is not the whole figure as he appears to the audience, with his bushy reddish hair[101] and beard, but only his eyes. Indeed, when he first appears on stage, she does not know him [H, XI, 104/ O, VII, 76]; it is only when she sees his eyes that recognition and panic terror set in. It is these eyes which link him to another symbol, buried much more deeply in the fabric of the play, but just as essential to its structure and meaning - Ellida's dead child.

At first sight, the importance of the child to the play's symbolism is far from apparent. It is not mentioned in any of Ibsen's preliminary jottings for the play; Wangel's mention of it to Arnholm in Act I does not appear in the draft, and nor does Ellida's first remark linking the child with her dream-vision of the stranger.[102] Chronologically the first mention of the child in the drafts comes, unprepared and unexplained, at the climax of the second act, when Ellida suddenly asks Wangel *hvorledes skal vi grunde ud - dette her med barnets øjne* - , '... How shall we fathom out... that thing about the child's eyes' [H, XI, 204/ O*, VII, 147].[103] It is almost as though the logic of the symbolism *demanded* that there should be some correlative in Ellida's physical existence - the child which she is bearing when she sees the vision of the Stranger, which becomes, for her, the dream-child of her abortive adolescent love for him - to the pull which the Stranger exercised over her. It is evident that in fact the child is her husband's; and Wangel suggests that though Ellida did indeed have a serious nervous attack at the time that her stranger is believed to have drowned, it had quite other causes, was indeed the outcome of a condition which had lasted for some time, a climax provoked by 'the circumstances' (*de omstændigheder* [H,XI,124/ O,VII,94]) - that is, her pregnancy.

But it is not factual truth that Ellida is concerned with. For her, the child's significance is precisely that it *is* symbolic. And such is the mysterious power of coincidence in *The Lady from the Sea* that her explanation, too, makes a kind of dream-like sense of what has happened. Lyngstrand's narrative of his meeting with the Stranger three years before, at exactly the moment that Johnston/Friman learns of Ellida's marriage to Wangel, just before the shipwreck from which only a handful of men are known to have survived, may seem to make coincidence into a preposterous vehicle for the playwright's artistic convenience. But, on quite a different level, it has a patterned, dream-like logic which exactly suits Ellida's frame of mind. For her, the Stranger's arrival at her bedside, at the moment (she believes, [H, XI, 94/ O, VII, 67]) at which he found out about her marriage, is a living (*lyslevende*) manifestation of both her guilt and her longing. Lyngstrand's fantasy[104] about the drowned seaman coming back to claim his faithless wife [H, XI, 73-4/ O, VII, 48-9] dramatizes exactly her own fears and hopes. No wonder Ellida assumes, against all waking evidence to the contrary, that the child is in some sense the seaman's or the sea's, rather than her husband's.

And no wonder that the child has died in infancy. For what it represents to her is her own, unfulfilled *forhold... til havet og til alt, hvad havets er*, 'affinity... with the sea and all that belongs to it' [H, XI, 64/ O*, VII, 39]. When she tries to describe the child's (and, by implication, the Stranger's) eyes, it is in terms of the sea:-

> *Barnets øjne skifted farve efter sjøen. Lå fjorden i solskinsstille, så var øjnene derefter. I stormvejr også.*
>
> [H, XI, 95]

> The child's eyes changed colour with the sea. When the fjord was calm and sunny, his eyes were the same. The same when it was stormy.
>
> [O, VII, 68]

Wangel's assurance that the child had perfectly normal eyes is beside the point. What Ellida has seen in those eyes is a memory, a longing, a reproach; and the qualities she sees in them are an image of that unformed, immature emotional world which marriage to a man for whom she feels gratitude, not love, has sealed, unused and dangerous, inside her. It is the dead child rather than the spectral lover which points to the true nature of Ellida's predicament.

For the child, like the sea, represents the twofold, apparently paradoxical nature of her longings. Its eyes are constantly shifting, changing, reflecting every mood of sea and sky. Yet, at the same time, the child is essentially static - it cannot change or grow or develop. It is sterile, dead, outside time - as Ellida herself is outside time in her marriage with Wangel, outside time, also, in her longing for the Stranger who has seemed, in his dream-apparition, exactly as he had done seven years before,[105] and whom she has remembered and now recognizes by the changelessly-shifting eyes she also imagines seeing in her child.

In thus linking the eyes - windows of the soul, symbols of love and desire - with the sea, Ibsen comes closer in this play than any other to the greatest and most characteristic celebration of impersonal eroticism in 19th century art - Wagner's *Tristan*. There is, of course, an affinity between the basic dramatic situations from which Wagner's opera and Ibsen's play develop; - the understanding, honourable older husband; the young frustrated wife who falls helplessly, unwillingly in love with the stranger from over the sea. But the two works share a deeper affinity in their use of the sea to evoke the uncontrollable richness and danger of sexuality. In *Tristan*, too, the sea has a complex, multiple symbolic importance - it can signify distance and parting ('Öd und leer das Meer') but also the ecstasy of consummation; in its perpetually shifting, straining harmonies there is a kind of endless modulation which (like the shifting colours of the dead child's and the Stranger's eyes) achieves in the end only suspension and stasis. It is characteristic of the particular variety of love celebrated in *Tristan* that it should be so associated with the restless ever-changing yet changeless sea, with the engulfing of self in an ecstatic vision which can defy change and circumstance because it is outside time, because it identifies consummation with self-annihilation and death.

Yet Ibsen's imaginative world is very different from Wagner's. What Wagner treats as an absolute - the all-absorbing, self-absorbed world which sexual passion makes for itself, annihilating time and context, and with them all other forms of human relationship - Ibsen sees as a stage which human beings must be allowed to live through, if they are to achieve a (very different) kind of self-fulfilment. The climax of *Tristan* is, precisely, orgasmic; past and future are consumed into the eternal, momentary present which is both love and death. Sexual love is thus finally divorced from context, function, consequence - to think of the tragic pair begetting children would be, in the context of Wagner's music, irrelevant, even absurd.

But Ellida's dead child is absolutely germane to Ibsen's intentions. It haunts the play as a perpetual reminder of how limiting, how life-defeating, how incapable of development such Romantic love can be. Ellida's feeling for the Stranger is a sudden, in a way directionless outpouring of feeling; it represents for her the lost, elemental freedom of youth which marriage to Wangel has put an end to - another part of herself which has lain buried, as an insistent memory, an irremovable obstacle to inner growth. Both Ellida and Wangel are forced to realize that whilst the spell of her relationship with the Stranger remains unexorcized, *Det liv, vi* nu *lever, er ikke noget ægteskab*, 'The life we are living *now* is no marriage' [H, XI, 129/ O, VII, 99]. Indeed, she believes that the whole marriage has been based upon a kind of lie, that she has not married him *i frivillighed*, 'of my own free will'; and that therefore the marriage has never been a true one - *Aldrig. Ikke fra først af*, 'Never. Not from the very first'. With her love for the seaman, on the other hand, there *could* have been a true marriage - not just, presumably, because of her *frivilligt løfte*, 'promise freely given' that they will marry; nor merely because the Stranger has a prior claim; but because their relationship has been based on passion and not self-preservation. She has *chosen* to pledge herself to the Stranger, even if her choice was folly. For her, the way in which the child, though it is Wangel's, reminds her of the other unfulfilled relationship, makes it a reminder of what she has sold, of the sterility of her present life.

For the audience, however, though not (consciously) for her, the child has another, rather different significance. Unless Ellida's longing for the stranger is taken at her own evaluation, its (to an outsider) preposterously transient and unreal nature may well suggest - what she has never been able to realize, trapped as she is within the hermetic, timeless world of a marriage in which she cannot mature - that the kind of feelings she cherishes for the spectral, the elemental, the limitless are essentially feelings of dependence, as destructive in their own way as is her marriage to Wangel. Yet at the same time she has been forced to preserve her marriage, too, in a state of dependence which excludes Wangel's other family - her step-daughters Bolette and Hilde.

For Ellida's difficulties are not the sole focus of the play's attention. Indeed, Ibsen specifically refuses, through the structure of the play, to allow Romantic love that independence of context which it demands for itself. Up to a certain point, Ellida has created, even in a literal, physical sense, a separate existence for herself; she tells Arnholm [H, XI, 65/ O, VII, 40-1] that she spends her days in the summer-house, her step-daughters on the verandah - and that her husband has to shuttle between the two. This division has further and darker implications for the family. By ignoring the children, Ellida can isolate herself, and to some extent Wangel too, from his other, more fruitful marriage. It is a measure of the unreason of jealousy that one can envy the unassailable dead their former possession of what, in the present, one does not really even *want* to possess oneself. And it is of the nature of such unhappiness that it craves more and more time to contemplate its own misery - time which would otherwise be given up to relationships with others.

Other people suffer too. Bolette's trapped frustration and

Hilde's anger are in their different ways both the consequence of and an ironic commentary on Ellida's own pain and frustration. Bolette, too, is caught in a situation which stultifies growth. She feels both dependent on her father and guilty about leaving him:-

> *[Ellida] er slet ikke skikket til alt det, som mor havde sådant et godt greb på. Der er så mangt og meget, som denne her ikke* ser. *Eller som hun kanske ikke* vil *se, - eller ikke* bryr sig om.
>
> [H, XI, 100]

> [Ellida's] not very good at doing all the things Mother used to do so well. There are so many things this one doesn't even *see*. Or maybe doesn't want to see... or doesn't care.
>
> [O, VII, 73]

In struggling to fill the emptiness at the heart of this marriage, Bolette is sacrificing herself - is perhaps in the process of becoming a second Ellida, but an Ellida who is much more conscious of the nature of her isolation from experience.

It is Bolette who is clear-sighted enough, towards the end of the play, to give us a clue to the character of her sister, the angry and tormented child who haunts, like a malign spirit,[106] the margins of the play:-

> *Har du aldrig mærket, hvad Hilde dag ud og dag ind har gået og tørstet efter?... Et eneste kærligt ord fra dig.*
>
> [H, XI, 134]

> Have you never noticed what, day after day, Hilde has been yearning for?... One single loving word from you.
>
> [O, VII, 104]

On the purely naturalistic level, Hilde's tense hostility to Ellida,[107] her sneers at Arnholm, her taunting of Lyngstrand, are all accountable for in terms of her double anger at her father's re-marriage and her step-mother's refusal to give praise or affection. This accords exactly with the patterns of frustration and resentment to be found in Ellida and Bolette.

But there is another and much more sinister sense in which Hilde fulfils the pattern of the damaged child taking revenge on her surroundings, though (uniquely in Ibsen's work) this finds full expression only in a later play in the cycle. It has become customary for critics and biographers to assume that the Hilde of *The Lady from the Sea* is an essentially subsidiary character in the play; and that the Hilde Wangel of *The Master Builder* owes much more to traits which he observed in Emilie Bardach and (perhaps) Hildur Andersen, *after* the composition of *The Lady from the Sea*, than to some original, unified conception of an *ur*-Hilde. There can be no doubt that the events at Gossensass in the summer of 1889 made a profound impression on Ibsen. But it may well be that at least part of that impression derived from the recognition in Emilie of traits - *dæmoniske drag*, even - which he had already experienced imaginatively, and had given creative form to in Rebekka, in Ellida and in Hilde herself.[108] In showing two stages of Hilde's development, Ibsen was able to break through the tight conventions of naturalistic drama - was able, indeed, to allow himself something of the freedom of movement to span the whole development of a character (as he had done in *Brand*, *Peer Gynt* and *Emperor and Galilean*) rather than to focus on a single, decisive stage in the process.

To consider the two Hildes side by side is a disturbing experience, not least because it emphasizes the frustrated and morbid element in each. In *The Lady from the Sea*, the trait finds its clearest expression in Hilde's attitude to the young sickly sculptor, Lyngstrand, whom she first of all taunts and insults, then treats with a fascinated, almost prurient intimacy. What so excites her is the knowledge that he is sickly and will not live to be old: - *Det synes jeg er så spændende at tænke på*, 'I think that's such an exciting thought' [H, XI, 81/ O, VII, 55]. As Lyngstrand pursues his own, equally odd dreams of an 'ideal' Bolette - someone he will be able to imagine as thinking of him as he pursues his career abroad, someone whom he cannot think of marrying because she will be too old by the time he returns - Hilde, obsessed by, almost gloating over the vanity of this dream, half-tempts, half-goads him into imagining herself, grown-up, as

> *... en ung, dejlig, sørgende enke.*
> *HILDE. Eller en ung, sørgende brud.*
> [H, XI, 150]

> ... a beautiful young widow in mourning.
> HILDE. Or a young bride in mourning.
> [O, VII, 118]

In the context of *The Lady from the Sea* alone, such ideas could be dismissed as mere adolescent fantasy. But what is true for Ellida in this play - that fantasies not outgrown can have terrible consequences for oneself and others - is shown, in *The Master Builder*, to be true for Hilde as well. Indeed, the two plays taken together suggest that the traumas of the recent past have produced in Hilde scars which go deeper than anything in Ellida or Bolette. Although the ending of *The Lady from the Sea* may make it seem as though all will be well, once Ellida has been able to commit herself to stay, the abiding image one is left with, and one fully confirmed by Hilde's reappearance in *The Master Builder*, is that of the 'demonic' young woman, enclosed in her own imaginative world, and forcing others to play parts in her own inner dramas. When she has persuaded Solness to climb the tower, she is still muttering to herself that it is all *forfærdelig spændende* - '... terribly exciting...' [H, XII, 99/ O, VII, 421]. Perhaps, in the end, it is Hilde, with her dreams of playing the young sorrowing bride - substituting, that's to say, death for sexuality, the momentary image,[109] incapable of development, for maturity and experience - who is the real victim of Ellida's marriage.

But not the only one. For Bolette, too, the play may seem to end happily. But her engagement to Arnholm is surely so reminiscent of Ellida's to Wangel that here also the past is casting long shadows over the present. Here is another young girl longing for both security and the freedom to grow, who allows herself to be bought, as the price of that freedom, by a kindly older man whom she does not love:-

> *Tænk, - at vide sig fri - og få komme ud i det fremmede. Og så ikke behøve at gå og ængste sig for fremtiden.*
>
> [H, XI, 146]

> Imagine! To be free... and to be able to travel. And not to have to worry about the future.
>
> [O, VII, 115]

The tone of the play's ending may tempt us to overlook the implications of what is being said here. Yet if there is one consistent proposition which underlies all of Ibsen's dramas, it is that a marriage based only on security and convenience can destroy all those around it.

The more carefully one considers the implications of the play's final act, the more ambiguous its tonality seems. It is almost as though Ibsen were deliberately combining two sorts of drama - the traditional midsummer night's epithalamion[110] in which warring couples are reconciled, and wander off *parvis*, 'two by two' [H, XI, 151/ O, VII, 118] into the glow of the Northern summer night; and a much sterner tradition in which the illusions and follies of summer are confronted by awareness of approaching winter.[111] In the dreamy, speculative jottings with which he prefaced work on the play, he meditated on the limitation (*begrænsning*) of human existence, which leads to:-

> ... *tungsindet som en dæmpet klagende sang over hele mennesketilværelsen... En lys sommerdag med det store mørke bagefter, - det er det hele.*
>
> [H, XI, 163]

> ... melancholy like a subdued song of mourning over the whole of human existence... One bright summer day with a great darkness thereafter - that is all.
>
> [O, VII, 449]

Some of this melancholy finds its way even into the character of Ellida. Ostensibly, all should be well. In the last act, Wangel finally offers her what (it has been clear for some time) she really wants - the chance to choose her fate rather than leave it to circumstance. She seems to have within her grasp that possibility of willing her own future which Rebekka in *Rosmersholm* longs for and is denied.[112] But, cunningly, Wangel rewords the terms of the choice:-

> *For nu kan du vælge i frihed. Og under eget ansvar, Ellida.*
>
> [H, XI, 154]

> Now you can choose freely. And on your own responsibility, Ellida.
>
> [O, VII, 121]

Or perhaps the cunning, like the re-wording,[113] is really Ibsen's. For the responsibility of which Wangel speaks alters fundamentally both what Ellida is offered and what is asked of her. It is true in more senses than one that, as she says, *Der er - forvandling i dette her*, 'There is - a transformation in all this' [H, XI, 154/ O*, VII, 121] - a transformation of options which imposes on her, not just the freedom of the adult, but the burdens as well. At the end of the previous act, when she is told how much Hilde has needed love from her, she exclaims,

Skulde her *være gerning for mig!* 'Could *this* be where I am needed!' [H, XI, 134/ O, VII, 104]. Already, perhaps, even before her moment of choice, she is learning to realize that what she needs is not just the freedom to love whom she pleases, but the opportunity to live as an adult.

Yet the solemn music of the play's final moments (and no Ibsen play is richer in sounds and images) must not blind us to the fact that Ellida's decision to stay also represents a renunciation, a sacrifice of her former self which in its way, however wise and necessary, is as sad as anything in the play. No wonder that she smiles gravely (*smiler alvorligt*) as she says to Arnholm,

> *Når en nu engang er ble't en fastlandsskabning, - så finder en ikke vejen tilbage igen - ud til havet.*
>
> [H, XI, 156]

> Once a creature has settled on dry land, there's no going back to the sea.
>
> [O, VII, 123]

In showing that she can make such a choice, Ellida is indeed proving that she is *Fruen fra havet*, not *Havfruen* - a human being, not a sea-sprite, not a being like H. C. Andersen's mermaid who *did* find it impossible to acclimatize herself to the human world of change and mortality. But the price of this transformation is the renunciation of youth, the taming of instinct, the submission to what, in a later play, Alfred Allmers will call *forvandlingens lov*, 'the law of change' [H, XII, 240/ O, VIII, 79]. Children grow up, or they die. Yet even growing up constitutes a sort of death, without which there can be no resurrection. Ellida pays the price; but the play leaves us in no doubt that here, too, is sacrifice.

CHAPTER EIGHT

Hedda Gabler

'Mit einem Revolver?... Ja, ja, so ein Rittersmann!... '
Thomas Mann, *Buddenbrooks*

Hedda Gabler is thought nowadays - at least in the English-speaking world - to be the most accessible of all Ibsen's later plays, as it is assuredly the most popular. It is useful to remember that this was not always the case. When the play first appeared in 1890, even sympathetic critics were doubtful, for reasons which perhaps cast a more interesting light on the nature of the play than has some of the uncritical adulation it has received since. When Gerhard Gran argued that the subject matter of the play would be more appropriate to a novel and Edmund Gosse spoke of 'hissing conversational fireworks, fragments of sentences without verbs, clauses that come to nothing, adverbial exclamations and cryptic interrogations', both were pointing to features of the play which are easy to overlook now, but which marked an important stage in the development of Ibsen's drama.[114]

The new dramatic style had implications for the play's content. To a large extent, the nature of *Hedda Gabler*'s narrative method - the short stabbing sentences, the lack of long, introspective speeches - precludes the formal interweaving of past and present to be found in *Ghosts*, *The Wild Duck* and

Rosmersholm. Instead, the audience must struggle to discern even the emotions and motives which underlie the action of the immediate present. In one sense, at least, *Hedda Gabler* has no ghosts.

Yet to accept the dramatic surface, however glittering and impenetrable it may seem, as the whole play, would be to misunderstand the kind of drama which Ibsen sought to create. For all that *Hedda Gabler* is formally, dramatically, a different kind of play from its predecessors, it shares with them a series of motives and concerns which, if properly understood, can transform our view of the play and its characters. It is fascinating to consider in this respect Ibsen's method of composition as revealed by the drafts. Almost as if to compensate for the intended austerity of the chosen dramatic method, he wrote for his own use a quite unusually extensive set of notes, containing not just snatches of dialogue but background details for the characters and comments on the significance of the action. Very few of these details were included in the play's first draft. Yet when he came to write the final version, Ibsen inserted quite a large amount of material from the notebook sketches, and added further detail. It is more than usually illuminating, therefore, to examine the changes which Ibsen made in the final version, since they amount to a careful re-valuation of the apparently impersonal, objective portrait of Hedda herself.

It should come as no surprise that many of the most significant changes from the draft concern Hedda's past, and especially her childhood. The Hedda of the draft is a curiously shadowy figure. We do not even know what she looks like. The final version, however, gives us almost immediately, before we even see her, a glimpse of Hedda's past, as the Tesmans remember it:-

> *General Gablers datter. Slig, som hun var vant til at ha' det mens generalen leved. Kan du mindes når hun red med sin far ud over vejen? I den lange sorte*

> *klædeskjolen? Og med fjær på hatten?*
>
> [H, XI, 296]

> General Gabler's daughter. The way she was used to having things in the General's time. Do you remember her riding along the road with her father? In that long black habit? And with a feather in her hat?
>
> [O, VII, 172]

Hedda remembers it too, for this is how she has grown used to seeing herself, now as then. The vision of what she has once been, of what the world owes her, lies behind much of her later rage and disappointment. It is the disinherited spoilt child's reaction to a world in which things change, fathers die, fortunes or reputations are lost. Nor is this first image of Hedda one which Ibsen allows us to forget. When it becomes clear that the Tesmans may not be as comfortably off as they had expected, it is to the idea of the *Ridehest*, the saddle horse, that Hedda returns. In the last act of the play, she dresses, once more, in black.

But Aunt Julle's description carries other implications (made clearer for the reader by reference to the drafts and sketches) of which neither she nor perhaps Hedda would have been aware. In one of the sketches, it is suggested that, even before his death, the General had been *ikke længere... i nåde*, 'no longer in favour' [H, XI, 513/ O, VII, 477]. In another note, he has even been disgraced and dismissed [H, XI, 505/ O, VII, 485]. Even in themselves these hints are suggestive. Considered in their historical context - the Norway of the late 1880s - they offer an important clue to the interpretation of Hedda's character. The General's fall (and by implication Hedda's) reflects the decline of that class of high officials which had ruled the country for generations. Control of the army had been a vital issue in the political struggles of the '70s and '80s; and there was a direct clash between the army and the victorious government of the left in the middle '80s which led to the resignation of the Army Minister and the reorganization of the high command.[115] Everything we learn about Hedda suggests that her impoverished circumstances reflect this wider social crisis.[116] It is not surprising, therefore, that she equates power with wealth and happiness; for her father has possessed only office and prestige, which cannot be bequeathed, not capital, which can. No wonder that Hedda has longed to live in a house which had belonged to a minister's widow, and that she also nourishes absurd dreams (absurd at least in the new democratic age in which such posts are elective) of making Tesman Prime Minister [H, XI, 302, 337/ O, VII, 177, 212]. Acquiring the house, acquiring a promising husband from the class which seems to be displacing her own - both are means to recreate in life the lost ideal of herself as a girl in a great black cloak, mounted on horseback.[117]

For Hedda's obsessive interest in living with, and in, style - in itself the characteristic defensive reaction of a class which has lost power, prestige and wealth - is sharpened by her own, sometimes panic-stricken immaturity.[118] To her, the grown-up world is a place in which boredom is mingled with terror. The contradictions of her own nature mean that her relationship with that world can never be simple. She has married Tesman not so much in spite of the fact that she does not love him, but rather (one might suspect) *because* she does not - indeed it may be the fact that she has no deeper feelings for him at all which makes him acceptable as a husband. In her eyes - and perhaps in his - Tesman's function is to provide the material security which will make it possible for her to regain the lost world of childhood, with its affluence and style, in which, alone, she can feel safe. Yet whereas the apparent changelessness of Tesman's world, so correct and solid, inspires in her one kind of terror and desperation, the prospect of change in her own life scares her still more. Always she has preferred to play the part of the isolated only child, watching fascinated an adult world in which other people act. It is a role she has clung to even in her relationship with Ejlert Løvborg. Eventually, when at the height of their friendship he has attempted to turn comradeship into physical love, she has been tempted to shoot him, been more tempted still to respond to his advances. But she has done neither. It may be true that, as Løvborg exclaims when, long after, he learns of her true feelings on that night, *Det var* dog *livskravet i dig* –, 'It was, *even so*, your craving for life...' [H, XI, 349/ O*, VII, 224] which underlay her feelings for him. But her 'craving for life' is of a very special nature. For what has given her pleasure in the relationship, apart from its secretive nature, is the chance to hear his confessions of a young man's debauchery, to

> *kikke lidt ind i en verden, som... som en ikke har lov til at vide besked om.*
>
> [H, XI, 348]

> glance in at a world which... which one isn't allowed to know anything about.
>
> [O*, VII, 223]

Similarly, when she interrogates Thea Elvsted on the state of her marriage, dwelling with an almost prurient excitement on Thea's daring in leaving her husband (*at du gik så rent åbenlyst*, 'that you left so openly' [H, XI, 319/ O, VII, 193]) we hear again the note of frightened envy for those who dare to act – a kind of voyeurism, also, which reflects her horrified fascination with what grown up people do.

These are not aristocratic qualities; and it is important to realize that Hedda is, like Rosmer and (legally speaking, at least) Osvald Alving, the last of her line. Here the physical description of Hedda in the stage direction at her entrance implies a warning of what is to come. For whereas the structure, the outline, of Hedda's face is *ædelt og fornemt formet*, 'aristocratic and elegant in its proportions', the texture, the content one might almost say, of this aristocratic frame suggests cultural exhaustion, the decay of the line[119]:-

> *Hudfarven er af en mat bleghed... Håret er smukt mellembrunt, men ikke synderlig fyldigt.*
>
> [H, XI, 304]
>
> Her complexion is of an even pallor... Her hair is an attractive medium brown in colour, but not particularly ample.
>
> [O, VII, 179]

The distinction between formal beauty and inner decay is an integral part of Hedda's behaviour as it is of her appearance.[120] She is consumed with inward rage at the homeliness of the Tesmans, at their lack of outward style. Yet her own behaviour is infinitely shabby - ruthlessness tempered by cowardice, an appetite for dominating others which is only restrained by the fear of what 'people' might say. Above all, her actions are driven by envy, perhaps the most corrosive of emotions, and the most ignoble.

All of these qualities are emphasized by Ibsen's revisions to the play's final draft. Nowhere can this be seen more clearly than in Hedda's first meeting with Thea Elvsted. When Thea's name is announced, Hedda remembers her as *Hun med det irriterende håret, som hun gik omkring og gjorde opsigt med*, 'That woman with the provoking hair that everyone made such a fuss of'[121] [H, XI, 309/ O, VII, 184]. The note of envy is already audible. A moment later she recalls Thea's link with Løvborg. Her manner is transformed; she greets Thea effusively, demanding that they call each other by their first names, as they had done at school. Thea's memories of school are rather different:-

> *Å, hvor gruelig ræd jeg var for Dem dengang!... For når vi mødtes på trapperne så brugte De altid at ruske mig i håret... og en gang sa' De at De vilde svi'e det af mig.* [H, XI, 315]

> Oh, I was dreadfully frightened of you in those days ... When we met on the steps you always used to pull my hair ... and you once said you were going to burn it off.
>
> [O, VII, 190]

What Hedda so hates about Thea's hair is that it is *påfaldende lyst, næsten hvidgult, og usædvanlig rigt og bølgende*, 'strikingly fair, almost whitish-yellow, and unusually rich and wavy' [H, XI, 310/ O, VII, 185] - a symbol, or so it seems to Hedda, of a world of brightness and richness from which she herself has been excluded. To the spoilt child forced to grow up, the irrational bounty of Fate to others can seem unbearable, an affront which no concession can assuage. Even when, at the end of Act II, Løvborg has been lured - or rather stung - into going to Brack's party, and Hedda does at last seem to have achieved that longed-for *magt over en menneskeskæbne*, 'power over a human destiny' [H, XI, 355/ O*, VII, 230] - even then, she is not satisfied. Suddenly, she rounds on Thea, full of a jealous resentment for which even Løvborg's fate cannot compensate:-

> *Å, dersom du kunde forstå, hvor fattig jeg er. Og* du *skal ha' lov til at være så rig! [Slår armene lidenskabeligt om hende.] Jeg tror, jeg svi'er håret af dig alligevel.*
>
> [H, XI, 355]

> Oh, if only you could understand how poor I am. And that *you* are permitted to be so rich! [Flings her arms vehemently round Thea.] I think I'll burn your hair off after all![122]
>
> [O*, VII, 231]

The child is revealed in the adult. For a moment Hedda is once more the bullying schoolgirl cornering her victim. It is not a very heroic sight.

But what is the nature of Hedda's 'poverty'? By this stage in the play, it can no longer be ascribed solely to her marriage to Tesman, nor, exactly, to a frustrated passion for Ejlert Løvborg. Løvborg she could have, it is evident, if only she could bring herself to want him. But she cannot - less, one suspects, because of her fear of scandal (people who take pot-shots at visiting judges cannot be said, in any normal sense, to be over-concerned about propriety or public opinion) than because of what that assumed fear conceals - a fear of herself. It is this, surely, which lies behind what Ibsen describes in a note as Hedda's *grundfordring*, her 'fundamental demand': - *Jeg vil vide alt, men holde mig ren*, 'I must know everything, but keep myself untainted' [H, XI, 512/ O, VII, 489]. In other words, the source of Hedda's frustration is not that she cannot have what she wants, but that her desires are so channelled and circumscribed by inhibition and self-disgust that, even when she *does* get what she wants, its achievement only emphasizes the poverty of what she can bring herself to desire. Implicit in her rounding on Thea is the dim, half-articulated knowledge that the aspiration to live vicariously through Løvborg (and what an aspiration! - the power without responsibility of the manipulating child...) is an admission that she is excluded from living on any richer plane.

It is the combination of (and disproportion between) this knowledge of emotional sterility, and the realization that insultingly, unimaginably, she herself is bearing a child, which drives her on. Confronted with the massive inertia of all that weight of existence which is not herself, she is incapable of desisting from interference. With scared, secretive fascination, Hedda prods events into motion, all the while eaten up with frustrated envy that it is others, and not she, who will act them out. Until, that is, Fate and the guileless Tesman present her with the opportunity - which is also a compulsion - to act herself, in the only way she knows how. She burns, not Thea's hair, but Løvborg's manuscript.

It is a crucial moment for the structure of the play and for the plot, the culmination of a strand of imagery which is of vital importance to the play's imaginative structure and to the understanding of Hedda's character. When Løvborg comes back from the party, having lost the manuscript *en route*, he tells Thea that he has destroyed it. He sees the deed, he tells her, as a sort of self-destruction. But Thea thinks of the book as an act of collaboration between them, and its destruction, therefore, as a kind of infanticide:-

> ... *Alle mine dage vil det stå for mig, som om du havde dræbt et lidet barn.*
> *LØVBORG. Du har ret i det. Det er som et slags barnemord.*
>
> [H, XI, 373]

> ... For the rest of my life it'll be for me as though you'd killed a little child.
> LØVBORG. You're right. It was like killing a child.
>
> [O, VII, 247-8]

Hedda hears this, mutters almost inaudibly[123] to herself *Ah, barnet*, 'Ah, the child'. For what is to Thea, and perhaps to Løvborg, an image of spiritual union, represents to Hedda all of the richness from which she is excluded, and of which the child in her own womb is no more than an insulting, threatening, meaningless parody. Envy, half-masking yet quickened by self-hatred, wells inside her:-

> *Den søde lille tosse har havt sine fingre i en menneskeskæbne.*
>
> [H, XI, 373]

> That sweet little ninny has had a hand in a man's destiny.
>
> [O*, VII, 248]

That it is also Løvborg's book matters little to Hedda - it is, as she says *til syvende og sidst... bare en bog*, 'when all's said and done... only a book' [H, XI, 374/ O, VII, 249]. What makes its destruction imperative is precisely what makes Løvborg stricken with guilt:- *Theas rene sjæl var i den bog*, 'Thea's soul was in that book'.

Thea's existence, as it were, through the book is partially vicarious too, of course; but it is the extent to which the book represents Thea's openness to participation in experience, which is the source of Hedda's vengeful resentment. With the loss of the book, the way is clear for Hedda to supplant Thea's 'meddling' in Løvborg's destiny with her own. Characteristically, however, Hedda substitutes destruction for creation, vicarious action for direct collaboration. Løvborg is sent away with the pistol, and instructions for its use, and Hedda is left alone with the manuscript.

Ibsen describes her next moves carefully, in sequence. She listens a moment, crosses the room to the writing-table, glances at the wrappers round the manuscript, then goes to sit in the armchair by the stove. *Pakken har hun på skødet*, 'She has the packet in her lap' - nursing it, like a child. Then there is a pause, a moment of absolute frozen stillness in the theatre, which must have been prepared for by the slow, half-waking deliberation of her movements up to this point. After a while - a short space of time which must be made to seem endless - she opens the door of the stove, and then the packet. Her next words must be perfectly audible, yet whispered as though to herself:-

> *Nu brænder jeg dit barn, Thea! - Du med krushåret... Dit og Ejlert Løvborgs barn... Nu brænder, - nu brænder jeg barnet.*
>
> [H, XI, 375]

Now I'm burning your child, Thea! You with your curly hair[124]... Your child and Ejlert Løvborg's...

Now I'm burning... burning the child.
[O*, VII, 250]

It is difficult to know on which level the scene is more terrifying. As a matter of straightforward fact, an irreplaceable book is being destroyed. Yet for Hedda, as we have seen, the book is of small importance, except in so far as others value it. Her pleasure, as her words convey, comes not from the act of destruction *as* destruction - which could perhaps have some kind of perverse, barbarous nobility, - but from the infinitely more mean-spirited act of taking from others, of spoiling someone else's creation.

Yet beyond the infantile, spoiler's pleasure in destroying what others have produced, there lies the metaphorical level. Hedda speaks of a morally evil act - burning books - in terms of an act unimaginably more evil still. But how much *is* it a metaphor to Hedda? The process of verbal metaphor can be, in origin as in effect, far more than a decorative play of words. It can also act as a transliteration of a distorted vision of reality. For Hedda, perhaps, the metaphor *is* a reality. *Nu brænder jeg dit barn*, 'Now I'm burning your child', is the culmination of that growing jealousy and rationalized self-disgust which can be traced through the previous three acts. In the image of the burning book, Hedda's jealousy of Thea and her horror of her own pregnancy are fused, as it were, into one. The book is Thea's baby, and thus represents an experience from which Hedda is unbearably shut out. But it is also Hedda's own child - the experience she does not dare to undergo - which she now symbolically extirpates in the flames, as she will in fact destroy it at the end of the play. That these two levels of meaning are brought together thus is more than a formally satisfying literary device. It is central also to the understanding of, and confers a kind of tragic intensity on, a character who is otherwise perpetually reduced by unwitting self-revelation and by the failure of events to validate her vision of the world. Hedda's mistakes, her distorted view of herself and others, her malice and pettiness and envy and psychological cruelty can only achieve tragic force and consistency when seen as part of an aesthetic and psychological pattern, the dominant motive of which is the violation of childhood.

Hedda is not the whole play, of course - indeed what makes this in some ways the most elegantly patterned of all Ibsen's later plays is the extent to which her own obsessions echo and counterpoint so closely those of the other characters.[125] Her own inability to give and receive love, to make contact with the world except through manipulation and destruction, are set throughout the play against the much more amiable deficiencies of the Tesmans. Whereas the Gablers, like the Rosmers, come of a tradition in which essential human reactions are suppressed, Tesmans live by what Ibsen described in sketches for the play as *Tantekærligheden*, 'Aunty-love', a condition characteristic of *De fleste mennesker som fødte af mandlige og kvindelige tanter*, 'Most people as though born of male and female aunts' [H, XI, 510/ O, VII, 488]. Tesman is steeped in *Tantekærligheden*, in the imperative to devote himself to the care and study of other people's lives and work - as Aunt Julle has sacrificed her life to looking after her nephew and bedridden sister. There is a unity and completeness about the Tesman household which Ibsen himself drew attention to, and which is itself a reflection of their limited, limiting, essentially companionable view of life. Whereas Hedda sees her life as a campaign stultified by victories too petty to assuage her self-contempt, the Tesmans live through a perpetual process of submission. Their highest ambition is to sacrifice themselves to someone or something else, as Tesman himself will do with the remains of Løvborg's book; and the highest form of relationship they can aspire to is that 'comradeship' which Tesman will find again with Thea.

For the final irony of the play is that those who live by and for the ideal of self-sacrifice are just those who survive, whereas Hedda, in her compulsion to destroy other people, ends by sacrificing herself. Only thus can the ideal become one with reality. If Hedda's final act is seen in isolation, or as the consequence of mere desperation, the play shrinks to no more than a black comedy. But if we see her suicide as the last, in its definitive way successful attempt to stamp the Gabler view of life on an unsympathetic bourgeois world, as a final answer to Brack's (and Krogstad's[126]) confident *sligt noget* gør *man da ikke*, '... people don't *do* such things' [H, XI, 393/ O, VII, 268] - then beyond her manic, childish dissatisfaction with the particulars of adult life in a world bare of style and enchantment, her act has a kind of tragic integrity. No less than Tesman, Hedda is a damaged child who cannot grow. Unlike Tesman, she has no professional life of self-sacrifice to make the world seem to stand still, nor a fund of *Tantekærlighed* to substitute for the organic growth and intensity of adult relationships. Her fate, no less than his, carries with it the logic of their respective childhood worlds. It is, in the deepest sense, characteristic.

CHAPTER NINE

The Master Builder

> Are you rich and strong enough to pay what it costs?...
> Life for life, that is the price, if life you would create.
>
> Tore Ørjasæter, *Christophoros*

The Master Builder is dense with themes and motives familiar from its predecessors: barrenness and the fear of fertility; hermetic relationships, incapable of growth, which deny growth to others. But these problems are now explored in more personal, even confessional terms. If *Hedda Gabler*, in its detachment from the lives it dissects, is amongst the least personal of Ibsen's works, *The Master Builder* marks a new stage in his development, the opening of that final tetralogy in which the vision of the drama extends to include the figure of the artist himself. In this, the play reflects the interest shown by so many writers of the 1890s for strong and exceptional characters, and is at the same time a return to the themes of Ibsen's own works of thirty years before, *'Paa Vidderne'* and *Love's Comedy*. Yet if *The Master Builder* is a personal play, it is in no specific sense autobiographical.[127] The problems it explores are those of any creative artist who believes that, in Thomas Mann's words, 'wer lebt, nicht arbeitet, und daß man gestorben sein muß, um ganz ein Schaffender zu sein'. Yet Ibsen's analysis goes deeper than Mann's. Solness, like Tonio

Kröger, is a creator with a bad conscience. But the guilt which Solness feels has little in common with Tonio's complacently tormented longing for everyday reality. In Ibsen's play, guilt transforms reality; it maims or destroys the humanity of both the artist and those he loves, and it distorts even his own creative personality.

All of this is foreshadowed in the long, carefully wrought first act of the play, even before the entrance of the instrument of retributive justice, Hilde Wangel. Indeed, any discussion of the play must begin with the Solness household, for it is there, and not in any capricious, troll-like stroke of external Fate, that the motive force of the tragedy is to be found. It is only against the background of those unseen, empty nurseries in which Hilde sleeps *ligesom i en vugge*, 'like a child in a cradle' [H, XII, 73/ O, VII, 396] that her part in the tragedy can be understood.

The Solness household lives in a state of armed truce more damaging, in some ways, than open hostility. Yet it is clear almost from the outset that all this fencing and bickering has other and deeper causes than just the normal resentments and frustrations of middle-age. These marital games of thrust-and-parry form (as so often in Ibsen's plays) a kind of conspiracy against the truth, a means of avoiding discussion of issues which really do matter and which are therefore too painful to be talked about. Aline Solness reproaches herself for not having better fulfilled her *pligter*, 'duties', both to her husband and to her dead children:-

> *Jeg skulde ha' gjort mig hård. Ikke ladt skrækken få slig magt over mig. Ikke heller sorgen fordi hjemmet var brændt for mig.*
>
> [H, XII, 71]

> I should have been hard. Not let the horror of it overwhelm me. Or grief either, because my home was burnt down.

[O, VII, 394]

Yet nothing she says suggests any true understanding of the past - of how it is precisely this rigid, obsessive sense of duty which has led to the family tragedy, the empty nurseries, through her insistence on feeding her babies even though she is suffering from fever. Disaster has only driven her further into a role which denies life in the name of a rigid-childish obsession with the fulfilment of obligation.

Guilty, in the sense of having consciously willed pain or evil, Aline is not. But, Ibsen is suggesting, there is a kind of innocence, that which grows from terror of life, which is every bit as destructive as moral guilt. Her innocence corrodes because it is the outcome of a failure, even perhaps a refusal, to grow and develop. It is not for the dead children she mourns,

> *for* de *har det så godt, - så godt nu. Nej, det er de* små *tab i livet, som skærer en så ind i hjertet.*
>
> [H, XII, 103]

> *They* are happy where they are - so happy now. No, it's the *small* losses in life that cut deep into the heart.
>
> [O, VII, 425]

By this she means the relics of a childhood never outgrown - the family portraits, the old silk dresses, the jewels and lace and - worst of all to her - the dolls which she has kept by her side, even after her marriage to Solness. It is for them she shows emotion, not for her dead children -

> *Jeg bar dem under mit hjerte. Ligesom små ufødte barn.*
>
> [H, XII, 104]

> I carried them under my heart. Like little unborn children.

[O, VII, 425]

And in a sense the dolls are her children, fit symbols of a lifeless marriage, a fear of emotional and sexual development, an irretrievable failure to live in time and fulfil her potential. Solness may believe - and may even be right in believing - that Aline *havde sine anlæg... til at bygge op små barnesjæle*, 'had a talent... for building children's souls' [H, XII, 83/ O, VII, 406]. But we perceive, as he cannot, that Aline may always have been emotionally crippled by her own childhood - and that this, as much perhaps as his own Faustian ambitions, may be to blame for what has happened.

Yet Solness is determined, for reasons of his own (not all of which he understands, or is even aware of) to shoulder all the burden of guilt himself. He is not really carrying on an affair with Kaja Fosli; and even if he were, it is unlikely that the fact of such an affair would mean nearly as much to his wife as do the true (and usually unspoken) causes of her own unhappiness and resentment. Yet he deliberately fosters the illusion of an affair not (he says) to torment her, but to place himself in the wrong, to inflict on himself

> *... en slags velgørende selvpinsel for mig i* det *at la' Aline få gøre mig uret.*
>
> [H, XII, 48]

> a kind of beneficial self-torment for me, just in letting Aline do me an injustice.
>
> [O*, VII, 372]

Irony undercuts irony. Solness brings down on himself unjustified anger, assumes an unmerited appearance of guilt. Yet he does so as a means of paying off *en smule afdrag på en bundløs, umådelig gæld*, 'a tiny instalment on a huge immeasurable debt'.

Characteristically, a false, assumed guilt masks a real one. But what is the nature of this 'immeasurable debt'? In a strictly *causal* sense, Solness is as innocent of the death of his children as is Aline - perhaps more so. Though he has been aware of a dangerous crack in the chimney of Aline's family home, which *might* have caused the fire which (indirectly) killed his children and (more directly) enabled him to make his fortune - in *fact* the fire started elsewhere. But guilt is seldom a matter of pure fact. Inner truth (the Ibsen of the 1890s had come to realize) is always more potent than historical fact. Or rather - the kind of historical fact which is most relevant in this case is that Solness is a 'late man' with an over-sickly conscience, who has (imaginatively at least) defied the moral pieties, the enforced humility of his own childhood background, yet is haunted by the notion that he is in some sense a criminal.

For the point about irrational guilt is not so much that it is based upon imaginings (however oblique a relationship those imaginings may bear to historical 'reality') as that it distorts *present* behaviour, creating new pain and guilt as it goes. Solness believes that he has entered into some kind of Faustian bargain with Nature, a bargain by which artistic and worldly success (*min kunstnerplads*, 'my status as an artist') has been paid for, not in money, but in human happiness. *Og ikke med min egen lykke alene*, 'And not with my own happiness alone' [H, XII, 83/ O, VII, 406]. How this bargain has been entered into, and when (before the death of the twins? on the church tower at Lysanger, when Solness declares his independence of God?) is left deliberately unclear. What *is* made clear is the human consequence of the bargain. Solness believes that God (or was it his own inner will?) has taken away his children

> *for at jeg ingenting andet skulde ha' at hæfte mig ved. Ikke sligt noget, som kærlighed og lykke... Jeg skulde bare være bygmester.*
>
> [H, XII, 117]

> so I should have nothing else to distract me. No love or happiness or anything like that... I was to be a master builder, and that was all.

[O*, VII, 439]

But such independence must always be illusory. For Solness to summon up the 'luck' which has enabled him to prosper as master builder has entailed not so much exile from the world of human feelings but a sinister transformation of that world:-

> *den lykken... kendes som et stort, hudløst sted her på brystet. Og så går hjælperne og tjenerne og flår hudstykker af andre mennesker for at lukke* mit *sår! - Men såret heles ikke endda.*
>
> [H, XII, 89]

> that sort of luck... feels as if my breast were a great expanse of raw flesh. And these helpers and servants go flaying off skin from other people's bodies to patch *my* wound. Yet the wound never heals...
>
> [O, VII, 412]

It is almost like an extension of the Philoctetes-myth, an extension in which other people, too, must atone for the isolation of the artist.

Indeed, Solness makes them pay. Obsessed by the notion that youth (implying the young lives he believes himself to have sacrificed, the time against which his whole career has been a kind of blasphemy) will exact retribution, he systematically undermines and exploits the young. Terrified of Ragnar's technical skill and imagination as an architect, Solness makes use of the skill whilst destroying the young man's confidence. Worse, he exploits Kaja's love for himself to keep Ragnar dangling in the office rather than striking out on his own. Solness even thinks of Hilde first of all as his own private weapon against youth - *Ungdom imod ungdom altså - !* 'Youth against youth...!' [H, XII, 66/ O, VII, 389]. He even seems to resent the youth of his clients. There appears to be no limit to the emotional crimes, major or petty-minded, which he is prepared to commit in order to stave off that moment of retribution at which fate will hammer on the door.

But fate has chosen its instrument with more than usual subtlety. What Hilde represents to Solness is not some abstract of youthfulness which will merely supplant him, but a dream of his *own* younger self. Indeed, their first meeting, ten years before, must have been just at the point at which, two or three years after the house-fire and the death of his children, his bargain with time - or God - was struck; at the time, too, at which his youth began to desert him. What may seem like one of Ibsen's more obvious ironies - Hilde's arrival precisely and symbolically on cue - is transformed by the play's *forhistorie* into an incident of quite unexpected resonance and significance.

Interpreted at one level, what may or may not have happened in Doktor Wangel's *stue* ten years before can have been no more (and no less) than a childhood dream - or *trauma.* A strong fit man at the turning-point between youth and middle-age has flirted with and, perhaps, kissed an impressionable young girl who is herself at the turning-point between childhood and adolescence. But on a deeper and more significant level, both for the characters and for the mythic patterns of the play, what has happened is much more complex. For Solness, that day in Lysanger marks several kinds of farewell. It is at the moment on the church-tower at which Hilde has first seen him that he has renounced his career as a builder of churches, and with it the piety of his childhood home [H, XII, 116/ O, VII, 438]. His faith in God has been shaken - either by his despair at the death of his children, or by the feeling that his half-conscious willing of the fire has involved him in some Faustian compact with the forces of Nature which has excluded him from the conventional salvation of religion. It is the decisive moment at which the personality and ambition of the artist become secularized, individualized, no longer an extension of a settled world system but an attempt to stamp a specifically human image of the self on the world:-

> *... da jeg stod helt der øverst oppe og hang kransen over tårnfløjen, så sa' jeg til ham: Hør nu her, du mægtige! Herefterdags vil jeg være fri bygmester, jeg også. På mit område. Ligesom du på dit. Jeg vil aldrig mere bygge kirker for dig. Bare hjem for mennesker.* [H, XII, 117]

> ... as I stood there on high, at the very top, and as I hung the wreath on the weathercock, I spoke to Him: Listen to me, Almighty One! From this day forward, I too will be free. A master builder free in his own field, as you are in yours. Never again will I build churches for you. Only homes for the people. [O, VII, 439]

In one sense, therefore, the figure that Hilde has seen on the steeple *is* a heroic one, at least in his own terms. Yet, ironically, the image of him which Hilde retains, fixed in her adolescent mind, is that of a youthful self who, at the very moment she is shrieking up *Hurra for bygmester Solness*, is about to renounce his romantic youth and settle down, in effect if not in aspiration, to a peaceful middle age of speculative building.

But, in Hilde's imagination, he is fixed at exactly the moment at which he is ceasing to be what she then, and ever afterwards, visualizes him as being. His heroic appearance ushers in for her a new world of feeling, from which, at least until the ten years are up, she cannot escape. Psychologically, and in terms of the play's patterns of imagery, the moment at which Solness kisses her has sealed off an image of them both in Hilde's mind, as impenetrably as the forest of thorns seals off Thornrose from the world of men. Now the magical ten years are up and - to shift the metaphor a little - the maiden has returned, with what an ironic reversal of roles, to claim her troll.

It is clear almost from the first that Hilde is bent on

recreating the childhood image which she has of Solness. He is to be *m i n bygmester*, '*my* master builder' (H, XII, 123/ O*, VII, 445) - and the emphasis on possession, (not always translated into English) is vital.[128] This is not triumphant erotic passion (she never has possessed him in that sense) but the satisfaction of a childish imagination which has contrived to recreate the adult world in terms of its own imagined ideal. Here Hilde comes in various ways unexpectedly close to certain other Ibsen characters - Gregers Werle, with his boyhood adulation of Hjalmar; Hedda, with her yearning to recreate her role as General Gabler's daughter; even Alfred Allmers, in his longing to preserve his Hänsel-and-Grethel relationship with Asta.

But Hilda's *methods* are highly individual. Despite her claims to be the least literary of heroines, she ensnares Solness not by physical allure, but through the manipulation of imagery. It is important to note that there are at least two quite separate kinds of image at work in the play, joined only tenuously (as tenuously as are the different sides of his own character) in Solness himself. The first kind, predominating in the first two acts and recurring ominously thereafter, relates almost exclusively to the Solness marriage - the empty nurseries, the sacrificed children, the ravening young who will replace their parents, the sorcerer's apprentice who knows more than his master (*alt det dævelskab*, literally 'all that devilry', is how Solness describes the Broviks' knowledge [H, XII, 47/ O*, VII, 371]) and will soon displace him, if more magic is not unscrupulously used to prevent it. Many of these images have the bivalency of true symbols - they are both literal facts (the nurseries, the children) and ciphers for inner truths.

None of the images which Hilde herself introduces into the play, however, have any validity outside her own imagination, except in so far as she can impose her ideal of the truth on Solness, and through him on reality. The imaginary kingdoms, the castles in the air, the harps in the wind[129] have been built around and at the same time transfixed by that traumatic moment in Lysanger as imaginative facts which must, someday, be re-enacted in the outside world.

At least Hilde's images, unlike those which Gregers uses to subvert Hedvig, are of her own invention. But she is no less ruthless in her manipulation of them. Immediately, she sets to work on Solness, charming, cajoling, shaming him into playing a part for which he is obviously unfitted. (His *svimmelhed*, 'giddiness' reflects much more than a fear of physical heights - it is, as she goads him into admitting in Act II, concomitant with that *skranten samvittighed*, 'fragile conscience' [H, XII, 89/ O, VII, 412] which inhibits and distorts his personality.) Yet to bring dramatic reality to her own dreams, she must first of all break into the sealed ritualized world of the Solness marriage, for which inner time has stopped with the death of the children. It is one of the dramatic ironies which give the play such force and momentum, that what restores the marriage to truth and time (if only by destroying it) is itself prompted and motivated by a dream of the past. Youth *does* revenge itself on age, but in the most subtle and paradoxical of ways. What breaks down the doors of time and once more, for a brief time, fills the empty barren nurseries is a child who refuses to grow up. To this Hilde, as to the frustrated mutinous child of the same name in *The Lady from the Sea*, adult disaster is *forfærdelig spændende*, 'terribly exciting' [H, XII, 99/ O, VII, 421]. And there can be little doubt that the nature of this excitement derives from the adolescent Hilde's equation of sexual fulfilment with death - one remembers that when the young Hilde, conscious that the sculptor Lyngstrand will die soon, tempts him to imagine painting her dressed in black in the part (as he says) of *en ung, dejlig, sørgende enke*, 'a beautiful young widow in mourning' [H, XI, 150/ O, VII 118] she corrects him:- *Eller en ung sørgende brud*, 'Or a young bride in mourning'. It is this role that the older Hilde now plays (at least in her own imagination) with Solness. As a child that day in Lysanger what thrilled her was the thought *om han nu faldt udover! Han, - bygmesteren selv!* 'Imagine now - if he were to fall! The master builder himself!'

[H, XII, 58/ O, VII, 381]. This ambivalence between ecstatic admiration and the fascination with destruction and death is as intrinsic a part of Hilde now as it had been then.

For Hilde, then, it is an imperative of the will and imagination that Solness shall climb the tower. Whether he falls or not, is not so much a matter of indifference to her, as part of a thrilling jeopardy (in the original sense of the word) in which, at last, imagination will be confronted with reality, and the possible and impossible may become one. What matters is that the attempt should be made, as a living (and perhaps fatal) proof that she, too, like Solness, *hører til de udkårne*, '[is] one of the chosen'[130] who have the power

> *at* ønske *noget,* begære *noget,* ville *noget - så ihærdigt og så - så ubønhørligt - at de* må *få det tilslut.*
>
> [H, XII, 88]

> to *want* something, to *desire* something, to *will* something... so insistently... and so ruthlessly... that they *must* get it in the end.
>
> [O*, VII, 411]

And get it she does, though she has to cajole, entice and even rage in order to do so:-

> *[lidenskabelig] Jeg vil det! Jeg vil det! [bedende] Bare en eneste gang til, bygmester! Gør det* umulige *om igen!*
>
> [H, XII, 119]

> [passionately] I want it! I want it![131] [pleadingly] Just once more, master builder! Do the *impossible* once more!
>
> [O*, VII, 440]

This is the consummation which she has dreamed of for so long; and it is no coincidence that when Solness does reach the top of the tower one more time, Hilde shrieks, beside herself with joy, *nu, nu er det fuldbragt!* [H, XII, 122] - words which translators usually take to mean 'Now, now, he's done it' [O, VII, 444] but which have all sorts of other slightly blasphemous overtones of religious fulfilment.[132]

But in any sense save that of Hilde's private dream-world, there *is* no fulfilment. *The Master Builder* is a play rich in themes and symbols; but its imaginative richness does not conceal the emotional poverty of its characters. Motives which in *Hedda Gabler* were found in static equilibrium - Hedda's blighted blighting childhood in stalemate with Tesman's - become more complex and dynamic in *The Master Builder*, because here three characters in the grip of longing for their past selves intersect. Yet each of these dreams - Solness's longing for the might-have-beens of his lost youth, Aline's for the lost dolls, the children that can never be born, Hilde's frantic, compulsive drive to recreate her ideal Master Builder[133] - is based on illusions which deny life, time, development. They are dreams of lost time which have the power to destroy, but not to create. What Aline might have been - the builder of children's souls - will remain as barren of potential as her dolls, her dead children. Solness, in finally reaching for that world of emotional possibility which lies beyond, and in conflict with his sacrificial bargain with the 'helpers and servants', suffers just that penalty at the hands of youth which he has dreaded for so long. And Hilde herself, at the end of the play, has only managed to create the *illusion* of 'her' master builder. This, too, is 'the impossible' - a moment which cannot last except in an imagination which can summon up harps in the air. But time and gravity will not be gainsaid. From this Doll's House there is no escape.

CHAPTER TEN

Little Eyolf

My primal self from the pure blue sea,
my purer self, how it whispers to me:
How could you part from me, how could you part?
and yet how I yearn for you, yearn in my heart!

Schack Staffeldt, 'By the Sea'.

Of all Ibsen's plays, *Little Eyolf* is the one which deals most explicitly with the sacrifice of a child to the immaturity of its parents. It is not surprising, therefore, that such discussion as there has been of this theme in Ibsen has concentrated on the play, and that some recent criticism has accorded it a more central place in his output.[134] The traditional view of *Little Eyolf* on the other hand saw it as an enigmatic failure, incomprehensible and dramatically ineffective. There is something to be said for both views of the play. It *is* a central work in Ibsen's output. It draws together themes and motives from at least the previous five plays - respectively, the sacrificed child; the influence of heredity on the present; the sea as symbol of unconscious desires; the hostility of a frustrated wife to her husband's scholarship; and the sacrifice of domestic happiness to vanity and ambition. And what gives these themes their dramatic focus in the play is the death of a child.

Even given the thematic interconnectedness of Ibsen's plays, this drawing together of ideas and motives is unusual. Yet such explicit treatment of an issue so central to a writer's creative personality is no guarantee of the work's artistic success. On the contrary, the drafts for the play show how intractable was the struggle between the implications of the play's content and the demands of dramatic form. That the result was not entirely successful could be taken as evidence of how central the issues involved were to Ibsen's creative personality. Whatever the dramatic failings of the play, especially in its inconclusive, dissonant final act, a close study of *Little Eyolf* is essential to an understanding of Ibsen's work as a whole, and gives a specially valuable insight into his creative methods.

Despite the title, and despite the loving care which Ibsen brought to his characterization, Eyolf is not the central character of the play, or even of the first act. He is rather the focus (and, so long as he lives, the suppressant) of the unused and distorted feelings which are destroying his parents' marriage.[135] When the play opens, his father has just returned from a lengthy tour in the mountains. Alfred is not a Tesman (he has not the latter's honesty, nor his love of fact, nor his humility) but he has Tesman-like features distorted into a much more threatening and insidious form. What has driven him to take a holiday in the mountains is a near-breakdown caused by his inability to get on with writing his *magnum opus*, the book on Human Responsibility. Now he has returned, the book still unwritten, determined instead to devote himself to cultivating the happiness of his crippled son. What Alfred seems to have realized during his wanderings is what Brand has half-learned before he is brought to the test:-

> *Ej nogen Sjæl kan* alle *favne,*
> *hvis ikke først han elsked* en.
>
> [H, V, 235]

> ... A man cannot love all men unless
> He has first loved *one.*
>
> [O, III, 130]

Now Alfred will devote all his care and attention to that *'one'* - Eyolf.

But all is not as it seems. Alfred's half-sister, Asta, is delighted at his new-found devotion to family life. But Rita, his wife, is sceptical. Will Alfred really be able to live up to those ideals *her hjemme*, 'here at home'? Alfred takes her hand:-

> *I forbund med* dig *kan jeg det. [rækker den anden hånd frem.] Og i forbund med dig også, Asta.*
>
> [H, XII, 215]

> In company with you I can. [Holds out his other hand.] And in company with you, too, Asta.
>
> [O, VIII, 54]

Rita abruptly withdraws her hand:-

> *Med to altså. Du kan altså* dog *dele dig.*

> With two people. So you *can* in fact divide yourself.

Her reaction seems, on the face of it, incomprehensibly petty and jealous. And Rita *is* frantically, obsessively jealous of his work, of their child, of Asta, of anyone or anything that could come between herself and total possession of her husband.

This jealous possessiveness and the erotic demands she has placed on the unwilling Alfred were taken by many people at the time of the play's first performance, and for long afterwards, as a sign that Rita is in some sense the villain of the whole piece, and that Alfred is merely the unhappy, at worst the inadequate victim. Even in the 1890s, though, some more perceptive critics saw past the outward unpleasantness of her behaviour to the character within. The Swedish novelist, Hjalmar Söderberg, who was amongst the first to grasp the significance of the play as a whole, spoke of Rita in a review of 1895 as 'a warm and good woman, entirely straightforward... a little bit vulgar... but with, above all, an impulsive open nature'.[136] In any final analysis of the play, Söderberg was probably right. But a play is a structure in time; dramatic truth develops sequentially, and any attempt to ignore this does violence to what makes plays dramatic at all. To make too many allowances for Rita too soon courts the danger of missing what Ibsen is trying to achieve in this first act. Psychologically, it is essential that we first be made aware of the human ugliness which repression of unpleasant truths can bring - that we do sense, even before Eyolf's death, that there *is* something which *gnaver her i huset*, '[is] gnawing in this house' [H, XII, 206/ O, VIII, 46]. And because Rita is a vital, open personality, it is natural that it is she who should display most openly the symptoms of this suppressed crisis.

Indeed it is essential to an understanding of the play that, before we realize the full measure of Alfred's inner crisis, we should already be aware of what has been gnawing away inside Rita. For the one is mirror or echo of the other. Rita is (presumably) an only child, the daughter of rich parents. She has married - at 19 or 20 - an impoverished teacher (*timelærer*) without private means or even a permanent post. She is vivid, passionate, highly-sexed; and she is also spoilt. When she cries out to Alfred,

> *... jeg bry'r mig ikke en smule om at være fornuftig! Jeg bry'r mig bare om dig! Om dig alene i hele verden!... Om dig, om dig, om dig!* [H, XII, 219]
>
> I don't care a damn about being reasonable! All I care about is you! Nothing in the whole wide world but you!... You! You! You! [O, VIII, 58]

we see the frustrated young wife flinging herself at the husband who has always been frightened of her sexuality. But we also catch an echo of that other, younger Rita, the rich, spoilt, bored only child, who has (without knowing it) bought her young husband, has discovered sex, love, romance with him (or has imposed them on the marriage by force of personality) only to watch them slowly taken away from her by time and change. Rita's jealous, possessive rage is the product of frustration; but it also stems from her determination to preserve for ever the moment of new-married ecstasy, to seal their relationship against the possibility of change. The half-expressed wish to be without Eyolf, so crucial to the symbolic pattern of the play, is not really connected with Eyolf himself. It is, as much as anything, nostalgia for the passions of her own youth. She, as much as Alfred, has sought to deny the principle of growth in favour of an idealized (and, as it turns out, an illusory) past; and it is appropriate that her great declaration of passion for Alfred should be couched in the terms of a childish tantrum.

To ignore this side of Rita's character is to destroy the symmetry of emotional forces which Ibsen has so carefully built up in the play. But, even more important, to overlook the more unpleasant aspects of her character in foreknowledge of what is to come is to violate the play's dramatic and moral structure, which pivots on the moment of Eyolf's drowning. Until that moment, what we are made most aware of is Rita's frustrated rage and jealousy, pent up within a situation which seems unalterable, and which shuts off any examination of the past. What the Rat-wife has done in luring Eyolf to his death is not to exorcize directly what is gnawing away at the Allmers' marriage, but to remove the unhappy crippled obstacle to that exorcism. For the events after Eyolf's drowning constitute one of the most remarkable *volte-face* in all Ibsen's drama. Into the second act of *Little Eyolf* is concentrated the highly structured yet apparently uncontrollable momentum of catastrophe, one of those plunges backwards into time which are amongst the most consummate achievements of Ibsen's dramatic method. What distinguishes this effect in *Little Eyolf* from the comparable explorations in *Rosmersholm*, *The Lady from the Sea* and *The Master Builder* is the catastrophic suddenness and swiftness of the revelations which it brings, and the dramatic revaluation of the play's structure which they impose.

The act begins quietly enough. Allmers sits gazing out over the fjord, despairing and alone. Asta comes to him. For a few moments they talk, desolately and seemingly at random. Alfred can find no meaning in what has happened, no grudge against Eyolf which could have led the Rat-wife to revenge herself on him - *Der er ingen gengældelse bagved. Ingenting at sone, mener jeg*, 'It can't be retribution that's behind it. There's nothing to atone for, I mean' [H, XII, 229/ O, VIII, 68]. Yet the ensuing conversation suggests that there is only too much pattern (of a symbolic, if not of an immediately causative nature) in what has happened. Asta's immediate response - to ask if he has discussed these things with Rita - goes close to the root of the matter. Alfred can talk more easily to his half-sister about these things - and about everything else. As they talk, they relive (as so often before) their past together, before Alfred's marriage - *en dejlig tid for os igrunden*, 'really... a happy timc' [H, XII, 231/ O, VIII, 70] says Asta. And Alfred, moved by the memory, calls her, as he had used to when they were children, *du, min kære, trofaste - Eyolf*, 'my dear, loyal... Eyolf'.

It seems a moment's regression, no more - a harking-back, in a time of despair, to other, happier days. But whilst Asta would rather forget *det dumme vås med navnet*, 'that silly business about the name', Alfred dwells longingly, lovingly on the memory of how, if she had been a boy she *would* have been called Eyolf, of how Alfred, longing for a brother, a mirror-image, made of her that dream brother/sister dressed in his own old shirt and knickerbockers. For Asta, this has been a childhood game, a fantasy which has half-persisted but which she knows she must break free from, if she is ever to grow up. For Alfred, the initiator of the maskerade, older and more conscious at the time the game was being played, it is the dream of an ideal past which has distorted all his own relationships. Asta is disturbed by this new revelation of the abiding depth of his feelings for her. It suddenly occurs to her to ask: he has surely not told Rita of this game of infantile transference? For the first time, Alfred is flustered, tries too hard to appear casual:-

> *Jo, jeg tror jeg har fortalt hende det en gang.*
> [H, XII, 232]

> Yes, I think I did tell her about it once.
> [O, VIII, 71]

As we shall soon learn, he remembers only too well the occasion of his confession; and, with hindsight, we shall see why his next reaction is one of guilt and horror at forgetting what has just happened to the real Eyolf:-

> *Her sad jeg og leved i minderne. Og han var ikke med.* [H, XII, 233]

> I sat here living in my memories. And he wasn't there. [O, VIII, 71]

The subconscious source of his distress, as we can surmise from later events, is not *that* he had forgotten the child but *why* he had done so, and even more to the point, what had brought Eyolf's fate back to his mind.

It is worth noting at this point that almost the whole of this conversation, together with many of the undertones and hidden meanings which it implies, is absent from the first draft of the play.[137] In that version, from the first act onwards the relationship between Alfred and Asta is much less close and obsessive because or in spite of the fact that in the very earliest drafts they *are* full brother and sister; no mention is made of the transference of names between Eyolf and Asta, nor of her dressing up as a boy. Even more crucially to the dramatic and metaphoric structure of the final version, Eyolf was not originally conceived as a cripple; and the traumatic moment (for all the characters) at which his injury had taken place could therefore form no part of the play's original scheme. In Ibsen's first conception, therefore, the root of the tragedy was to lie in Alfred's and Rita's inability to relate to each other or to their sickly, unwanted child. The tone of that initial draft is curiously distant and unengaged. Yet the natural momentum of Ibsen's revisions, the need to delve deeper into the nature of, especially, Alfred's feelings and motives, transformed the central act of the play from a succession of mutual complaints and reproaches to one of the most powerful and frightening dramatic structures he had ever devised. That the tensions set up by these revisions proved too great to allow of convincing resolution at the end of the play is a kind of unwished-for tribute to the imaginative power (and perhaps the personal involvement) which Ibsen brought to the reworking of the second act.

In the final version, the confrontation between Alfred and Rita which forms the second half and climax of the central act becomes the turning point of the whole play. Although Alfred has sought to evade the meeting for as long as possible, Asta sees to it that he and Rita are left alone together. For a moment or two, the conversation is subdued, as Rita tells of her nightmare visions, of seeing in her mind's eye Eyolf's eyes, open (in reproach?) as he is swept along the sea bed by the current. Then Alfred turns on her, taunts her with the phrase she had used at the moment of Eyolf's drowning:-

> *Var det onde øjne, som stirred opad?... Var det onde barneøjne?... Nu har vi fået det, - slig, som du ønsked, Rita... At Eyolf ikke var her.* [H, XII, 239]
>
> Were they evil eyes staring up from the depths?... Were the child's eyes evil?... Now we've got things... the way you wanted, Rita... Eyolf out of the way. [O, VIII, 77]

And now the storm breaks loose.

In moments, the inhibitions set up by a decade of ritual conflict and evasion are broken down. In answer to Alfred's accusation that she had never whole-heartedly loved the boy, Rita answers that this is because Asta had stolen Eyolf, *lige fra det hændte, - det ulykkelige faldet*, 'right from the time it happened... the accident' [H, XII, 240/ O, VIII, 78]. For the moment, the significance of this is not spelled out. Instead, Rita counter-attacks, accusing Alfred of neglecting the child in favour of the book on human responsibility. In answer to Alfred's claim that he had sacrificed (*ofred*) the book for Eyolf's sake (a revealingly dishonest attempt to turn truth back to front - a mirror-image of itself) she retorts that this 'sacrifice' was really a confession that there is no great book to be written. But this is not all - indeed, in the play's final version this is only the beginning of the descent, as Rita hints:-

> *Gå i dig selv! [med skyhed i udtrykket.] Og gransk alt det, som ligger under - og bakved.* [H, XI, 241]
>
> Look inside yourself! [choosing her words warily.] And delve into all that lies under... and behind... the surface. [O*, VIII, 79]

For what lies behind the surface of the original version, what Ibsen, in revising the play, decided to make explicit, is the issue of Alfred's sexuality. And this is where the transformation of Eyolf from sickly little boy into cripple became, not just a (rather obvious) symbol of a crippled marriage, but a vital and dynamic element in the structure of the play. It is Rita's fault, says Alfred, that Eyolf could not rescue himself, for it is her fault that he was crippled when a baby. When the accident happened, Alfred should have been looking after the infant:-

> *Men så kom du, du, du, - og lokked mig ind til dig.* [H, XI, 241]

> But then you came - you! you! - and tempted me to come to you. [O*, VIII, 80]

Both the phrase that he uses, and the suppressed fury (*undertrykt raseri*) with which he speaks, reveal much more than he can intend. For they suggest how far, subconsciously, Alfred fears and hates sexuality. When he says that ... *Jeg glemte barnet - i dine arme! ...I den stund dødsdømte du lille Eyolf*, 'I forgot the child - in your arms... In that moment you condemned little Eyolf to death', he is no longer talking about the accident of nine years before, but rather of his horror, now, always, at giving himself completely to another human being. The real 'sacrifice' of that moment, in Alfred's eyes, is himself. And trying (like so many of Ibsen's self-deceivers) to convict himself of a lesser crime in order to prevent investigation of a greater, *derfor* var *der gengældelse i Eyolfs død alligevel*, 'so there *was* retribution in Eyolf's death, after all' - retribution, not so much for a moment's carelessness, but for the very fact of adult sexuality.

For a little while, the quarrel seems to have burned itself out. But the difference in their temperaments is too great to allow of any resolution. Whereas Rita talks tentatively of forgetting their guilt in the attempt to go on living, for Alfred their love has been *som en fortærende brand*, 'like a consuming fire' [H, XI, 245/ O*, VIII, 83] which must now be *sluknet*, 'extinguished'. In other words (one can hear the relief in his voice) the marriage will become even more of a formality - a monument to Eyolf's memory. The vision of a marriage on those terms fills Rita with horror. Is this what has become of *slig en mødende kærlighed*, 'such a deep love'? [H, XII, 245/ O, VIII, 84].

But, as Alfred now admits, his first feelings for her were *not* love, or even infatuation. They were *Skræk*, 'Terror' - terror of her beauty, her sexuality, her power therefore to break into the enclosed world of the orphan pair, even as her wealth, her 'gold and green forests' could offer them security and a kind of freedom. He tries to lessen the impact of this admission by once again misrepresenting a part for the whole;- *Du var så fortærende dejlig*, 'You were so devastatingly[138] lovely' [H, XII, 245/ O, VIII, 84]. But he cannot conceal that it was Rita's wealth, not in itself but as security for *Asta*, which attracted him to her. This is, to her, the real crime which so many false and lesser ones have conspired to conceal. Now, in the shock of this revelation, Rita is reminded of another - in an epiphany of symbols and motives which is the crux of the whole play:-

> *Det var altså i grunden Asta, som førte os to sammen... ... Eller nej, - lille Eyolf var det. Lille Eyolf, du!* [H, XII, 246]

> So it was Asta who brought us together... ... No, it was little Eyolf. Little Eyolf, Alfred!
> [O, VIII, 84]

At last she has remembered. Alfred's confession of his childhood relationship with his sister was made at exactly that moment, that *fortærende dejlige*, 'devastatingly lovely' moment, at which Eyolf was crippled.

It is here that the particular difficulty of the kind of symbolic truth which Ibsen is dealing with becomes apparent. In the real world of cause and effect, there is no *reason* why Eyolf should be crippled at precisely the moment that a confession which will eventually go near to destroying his parents' marriage is being made. It is, at best, a coincidence which is rather too appropriate to be entirely credible. If we apply to the play the tests of verisimilitude which overly Naturalistic interpretations of Ibsen have encouraged, then the drama of this central act may well seem preposterous. But if we take the symbolic plan as the reality, if we accept that the notion of *Gengældelsen*, 'Retribution' is at the heart of the play - then what had been a *merely* causative (and therefore in some ways rather disputable) concept in *Ghosts* and *The Wild Duck*, takes on in *Little Eyolf* the momentum of ritual poetic justice. Considered only naturalistically, the play would have to be seen as a farrago of immature sexuality and bad parenthood, of improbable coincidences complicating a relationship which has subsisted for years on evasions and suppression of guilt and which now, more or less by accident, faces a test it has not been designed to bear. But if we accept that the sequence of revelations which make up the second act of *Little Eyolf* are psychologically true precisely because they do *not* refer to a causal sequence of events, but to a complex of irrational feelings more real in their way than the symbolic events which are used to convey them, then this act forms a convincing modern counterpart to the drama of Aeschylus and Sophocles.

An overly detailed and specific Freudian interpretation, on the other hand, such as that by James Kerans, can impose on the play a kind of rigid patterning very far from what can be deduced of Ibsen's conscious intentions, and alien to his methods of work or his ways of seeing the world. Ibsen was not a conscious formulator of patterns of human behaviour. He rather observed the world with close and unrelenting rigour, then internalised his observations and formed and re-formed them in his dramatic imagination. That Freud made rich and fruitful use of Ibsen's observations does not prove that Ibsen saw patterns of human behaviour in an explicitly Freudian way, any more than did Sophocles or Shakespeare. On the contrary, one might even wonder whether the insights into human nature suggested by *Oedipus Rex*, *Hamlet* or *Rosmersholm* were not all the more powerful and suggestive because they did *not* spring from a universal systematic view of behaviour, but rather from instinctive individual insight.

Moreover, the point about Alfred Allmers's turning away from human relationships, his fascination with his own image and its imagined extensions in the outer world, his fatal confusion between Narcissism and moral rectitude - is that it is precisely congruent with a line of development in Ibsen's work which stretches from *Love's Comedy*, *'Paa Vidderne'* and *Brand* all the way to *When We Dead Awaken*. When Falk declares his intention to desert the world of human relationships, and to depart, *Tilfjelds, i Guds Natur*, 'To the mountains, to God's natural world' [H, IV, 247/ O*, II, 200] he is articulating a longing for the limitless freedom, the icy serenity of the mountain wastes which haunts both the works of Ibsen's first maturity and those of his final period. When the narrator of *'Paa Vidderne'* turns away from the life of the valley, when Brand comes face to face with his own coldness of heart in the Ice-church, and when Peer Gynt encounters the monstrous self-images of the Troll-kingdom and the Bøjg, all are metaphors for just that kind of escape from human commitment which Alfred has sought in his mountain wanderings. The difference between him and his predecessors lies in his attitude to this process. Not for him the apparently carefree self-abandonment of Falk and Peer, nor Brand's terrible single-minded infatuation with his own will. Like them, Alfred is always looking for images of himself - mountains, fjords, sisters, children - in which, a Narcissus in search of any pool, he can lose himself in the vastness of his self-absorption and self-esteem.[139] But Alfred is a 'late man'. He has lost that *rigtig frodig, struttende sund samvittighed*, 'truly vigorous, glowing healthy conscience' [H, XII, 90/ O*, VII, 413] which earlier generations had taken for granted. Instead, troubled by guilt, he uses that guilt to torment others.

Yet in stating Alfred's bad faith so explicitly and uncompromisingly, Ibsen presented himself with both an ethical and an artistic problem, neither of which could be solved satisfactorily. Alfred is precluded by the central assumptions of the play from finding solace or posthumous justification in a tragic conclusion. More self-admiring and self-willed than Rosmer, less naturally self-destructive than Hedda or Solness (because, in the end, less aware of other people) his natural mode of being is insularity, total self-isolation. Yet isolation is (almost by definition) not a dramatic mode. 'After such knowledge, what forgiveness?' How should Ibsen end the play?

The difficulties he experienced in finding any answer to these problems can be seen by examining the two quite separate versions of the final act. The first draft is as undramatic as the second, but a great deal more perfunctory. Much of it reads like a summary of the final version, though most of the dialogue is entirely different. If one reads this first version carefully, however, it becomes clear that the mood of the second act was to be sustained for much longer - as it could be, given that in this version the conflicts are nowhere near as irreconcilable and destructive as they were later to become. More than half way through the first draft of the final act, Allmers reads to Rita a poem which Ibsen was to publish a few years later as the 'first preliminary study' (*første forarbejde*) for *The Master Builder*.[140] It tells of a house (like the family home of Mrs Solness) which burns to the ground, leaving the couple who have lived there to hunt through the ashes for a lost, but indestructible jewel. But they will never find it:-

aldrig hun finder sin brændte ro, -
han aldrig sin brændte lykke.

[H, XII, 314]

She will never find her burnt peace -
He never his burnt happiness.

[O, VIII, 147]

It is an enigmatic little poem. But its point in this context is to emphasize that nothing in Alfred has really changed; as Rita says,

Om dig og Asta har du skrevet dem.

[H, XII, 314]

You wrote these lines about yourself and Asta.

[O*, VIII, 147]

And for all Alfred's attempts to fudge the issue, it is obvious that Rita is right. In this context, if the poem means anything, it must be a lament for his lost love for Asta, a love which, in this first version, preoccupies him until a couple of pages from the end of the play. It follows that, in Ibsen's first conception of the play, the Allmers' marriage is effectively dead, and that their plan to rescue the beggar-children down by the shore is at best an inadequate substitute for adult relationships, a resurrection, not of a marriage which has never really been alive, but of *tantekærlighed*, 'aunty-love'.

The final scene between Alfred and Rita - after Asta has at last fled with her road-builder - is a dialogue of ghosts, very difficult to bring off in performance and anything but a resolution to the problems of the play. Each character is haunted by images of guilt - the staring eyes of the drowned child, the floating crutch. Yet, as Alfred's parable of wandering lost in the mountains suggests, behind all his protestations of care and love for Eyolf and Asta lies, still, always, that greater longing for the inhuman purity of the sea and the mountain wastes. When he was lost, he says, he ceased to think of his family, and instead

> *nød dødsfornemmelsens fred og velbehag... Jeg syntes, at der gik jeg og døden som to gode rejsekammerater.* [H, XII, 263]

> enjoyed the peace and serenity that comes from the nearness of death... I felt that Death and I walked side by side like two good travelling companions. [O, VIII, 101]

The affinity between this 'companion' and the tutelary stranger in *'Paa Vidderne'* is unmistakable. His reappearance at this stage of *Little Eyolf* indicates how wide is the abyss which separates Alfred from the *jordmennesker*, 'creatures of the earth', like Rita. In previous works, in the early poetry, in *Love's Comedy*, in *Brand*, Ibsen had been content to emphasize the distance between the cold-heartedness of aesthetic or idealistic existence and humanity's craving for warmth and love. Now, at the end of *Little Eyolf*, he seeks to reconcile the two.

Yet all the changes which Ibsen had introduced into the final version of the earlier acts make it more, not less difficult to accept the validity (human or dramatic) of Rita's 'solution' in the play's final pages. When she suggests that, unable to love each other in any full or satisfying sense, the bereaved couple should instead hold open house for the poor children from the village, what disturbs us is not just the Allmers' total unsuitability for the role, nor the echo of that other children's home with which Mrs Alving seeks to assuage her conscience and conceal her mixed motives. It is also the sense that the dramatist has manoeuvered himself into an impasse from which no satisfactory outcome is possible. In purely structural terms, Ibsen could not end the play with some tragic denouement leading directly from the revelations of the second act, without lending to Alfred that tragic stature which everything in the play, especially in its revised version, denies him. Nor, by the same token, could Ibsen allow an unambiguously positive ending, for that, equally, would outrage both credibility and natural justice. Nothing can erase the impression of self-deception and bad faith left by the rest of the play; which means in turn that this final attempt to fill the void of emotion with social concern can only be seen as a further act of self-deception. As the play ends, Alfred is still looking

> *Opad, - imod tinderne. Mod stjernerne. Og imod den store stilhed.* [H, XII, 268]
>
> Up... towards the mountains. Towards the stars. Towards the vast silence. [O, VIII, 106]

Eyolf's sacrifice remains in vain, for nothing in the final act can persuade us that his parents will escape from the ice-palace which Alfred's self-love has created, back to life.

CHAPTER ELEVEN

John Gabriel Borkman

John Gabriel Borkman seems to offer a complete contrast to its predecessor in the cycle. *Little Eyolf* is a fragmented play about fragmented personalities - and is for that reason, and because of its very inconclusiveness, amongst the most 'modern' of Ibsen's works. Certainly, Alfred Allmers, with his rationalized guilt, his perpetual self-deception disguised as self-analysis, is the most recognizably contemporary[141] of Ibsen's major characters. John Gabriel Borkman is incapable of such doubts and questionings. There is no trace here of the *svimmel samvittighed*, the 'conscience which can't stand heights'[142] [H, XII, 110/ O*, VII, 432] that afflicts so many of the characters in the later plays. And whereas the structure of *Little Eyolf* is unusually complex and episodic, requiring meticulous production and a great range of pace and tone to bring it off in performance, that of *John Gabriel Borkman*, though not simple, is as monumental, as monolithically sure of itself, as the character of John Gabriel himself.

Yet despite these obvious differences in structure and tone, there are important similarities between the two plays. Indeed, it is one of the most striking indications of how important the theme is to an understanding of Ibsen's work as a whole, that such apparently dissimilar plays as these should each be built around a child who has become the focus of such entrenched bitterness between his parents that he must leave home or die. In both plays, the principal action consists of the rediscovery and exploration of the past - that past which imprisons the parents and to which they are determined to sacrifice their children. In *John Gabriel Borkman*, this will to sacrifice is conscious and deliberate; if the child escapes, the parents are entombed. *Jeg kom nu netop op fra en gravkælder*, 'I've just emerged from a tomb', says Hilde in *The Master Builder* [H, XII, 105/ O, VII, 426]. No phrase could better describe the experience of watching or reading *John Gabriel Borkman*.

The tomb is not Borkman's alone, however; and any reading of the play which attempts to make him too exclusively the central character must do violence to the structure which Ibsen so carefully builds up. It is of the essence of the play, both structurally and thematically, that for the first three acts the focus of the action is not John Gabriel, but *Erhart* Borkman. In the final version of the play[143], the first words spoken are Fru Borkman's *Erhart! Endelig!*, 'Erhart! At last!' [H, XIII, 41/ O, VIII, 155]. Virtually the whole of the first act, and much of the second and third, are taken up by the struggle between the twin sisters, Gunhild and Ella, for possession of their son/nephew. That, in a deeper sense, poor Erhart is *not* a kind of trapped, living symbol for the whole history of hatreds and rivalries between his elders, serves to make the conflict more not less horrible, a distorted intensification of the human tendency to try to live through one's children. In this play, anticipating its successor, the older characters are already dead shadows seeking resurrection through a child - thus simultaneously recalling Alfred Allmers's exploitative dreams for Eyolf, and anticipating Rubek's fantasies of 'Resurrection' in *When We Dead Awaken*.

What makes *John Gabriel Borkman* a greater play than either - indeed, one of Ibsen's supreme achievements - is the way in which these motives are absorbed and embodied in the structure of the play. The conversation between Gunhild and Ella which takes up most of the first act, for example, may seem to be a conventional, even an obvious piece of stagecraft - an exposition of themes, a rehearsal of information about the past for the benefit of the audience. But Ibsen turns this traditional device into a dramatic event of great intensity. We do learn, unobtrusively, if in the space of improbably few moments, that the sisters have been estranged for at least eight years; that Fru Borkman's husband is a former bank director, imprisoned for fraud and released, also eight years ago; that the sisters' family considers itself to be *fornem*, 'distinguished'; that Fru Borkman has cut herself off completely from *Bankchefen*, 'The Director', as she refers to him; and that their son, Erhart, has spent part of his childhood living with his Aunt Ella. But, essential though it is to the play that we learn these things, they are perceived in the context of this dialogue, not as mere facts, but as *weapons*, used by two unhappy, desperate women to belabour each other. The most potent weapon of all is the living human being, Erhart, over whom the sisters struggle for mastery.

For Gunhild Borkman, Erhart is an instrument to recover the lost family (*her* family) honour, to achieve *Oprejsning for navn og ære og velfærd! Oprejsning for hele min forkludrede livsskæbne*, 'Restitution of name, of honour, of fortune. Restitution for the whole of my ruined life!' He is the *en i baghånden*, the 'someone up my sleeve', who will *tvætte* rent *alt det, som - som bankchefen har tilsmudset*, 'cleanse, make *pure* everything which - which the director has defiled' [H, XIII, 45-6/ O*, VIII, 159]. The mixture of metaphors[144] - the language of the card-table mingling with that of the Bible - is revealing. Gunhild feels that she and her family honour have been soiled. Yet these noble sentiments are undercut by her passion for intrigue and manipulation, for game-playing. She is Nora Helmer grown old and married to a Torvald who has not managed to survive the scandal.[145] Like Nora, like Hedda, she is struggling to repossess the outward trappings of a childhood she has never outgrown. And like both of them, Gunhild uses other people to live out her own fantasies. It is her will Erhart is to live out in the sacred task, *at oprejse slægten, huset, navnet. Alt det, som* kan *oprejses. - Og kanske mere til*, 'to restore the family, the house, the name. All that *can* be restored. And more besides, perhaps'. The meaningless rhetorical flourish at the end reveals how far humiliation has bred vague, obsessive dreams. And the fulfilment of Erhart's mission, as she will later tell her husband, is to efface the memory of John Gabriel Borkman from the world, to plant, as it were, *en klynge af levende hegn, af trær og busker tæt, tæt omkring dit gravliv*, 'an impenetrable clump of trees and bushes about your tomb' [H, XIII, 101/ O, VIII, 210]. For her, the sole purpose of posterity is to obliterate the immediate past - that is, her own adult life - in favour of that wealth and position which seems to be all she remembers of her own childhood. As for Erhart's chances of finding happiness, Gunhild rejects them with uncomprehending scorn:-

> *Pyh, - folk i vore kår har nok andet at gøre, end at tænke på lykke.* [H, VIII, 47]
>
> Pah! People in our position have better things to do than think about happiness. [O, VIII, 161]

It might be the spirit of the House of Rosmer, where children neither cry nor laugh. But the Rentheims are too much a part of the commercial world of Eastern Norway to maintain the outwardly disinterested nobility of an aristocratic tradition. All that is left of Gunhild's heritage is self-destruction, anger, pride and greed.

Ella, on the other hand, does seem to remember their house as a place of childhood and happiness. She is moved to think that the hat and cloak which John Gabriel has not used for the eight years of his self-imposed isolation hang in the hall cupboard - *det skabet, vi legte i da vi var små* - 'The cupboard we used to hide in when we were little'[146] [H, XIII, 51/ O, VIII, 163], for she alone of the three has retained any conception of that instinct for happiness which is in almost every child. It is Ella who has given Erhart whatever childhood he may have had; and though he later dismisses it as a time of *roser og lavendler, - stueluft, der som her!* 'roses and lavender - stuffy rooms, there as here!' [H, XIII, 104/ O*, VIII,

213], it seems not to have prevented him growing into a relatively healthy, straightforward young man. Ella is the only character of the three who shows any tenderness towards him, or even mentions her feelings for him. It may or may not be true that the boy was *lidt svagelig i opvæksten*, 'rather weakly as a child' [H, XIII, 47/ O, VIII, 160] - after all, this is her reason (or excuse) for taking him off to the west coast. But it is evident that Gunhild would not have allowed herself to recognize the fact even if it were true. Ella has enough imagination (as well as self-interest) to see how outrageous are the demands which Gunhild imposes upon Erhart:-

> *Tror du at et ungt menneske, i Erharts alder, - sund og glad, - tror du, at* han *går hen og ofrer sig for - for sligt noget som en 'mission'!*
>
> [H, XIII, 55]

> Do you think any young man of Erhart's age ... sound in body and mind ... is going to go off and sacrifice himself on some 'mission'!
>
> [O, VIII, 167]

And Ella has a wide enough knowledge of human nature - roses and lavender or no - to see what is likely to happen between Erhart and Fanny Wilton, whereas Gunhild cannot even imagine that anything - let alone an affair with an older woman - could deflect her son from the destiny she has planned for him.

Yet even Ella's motives are not pure. As the play progresses, one becomes more and more aware that her feelings for Erhart have been distorted by her frustrated love for his father. Whilst it seems to be true that she has wished to make Erhart happy, her reasons for wishing this are not disinterested. By the end of Act I, when she finally declares her intentions:-

> *Jeg vil fri ham ud af din magt, - din vold, - dit herredømme.* [H, XIII, 55]

> I want to free him from your power ... your tyranny ... your domination. [O, VIII, 168]

we scarcely need to be told that old rivalries are at work which have nothing directly to do with Erhart:-

> *ELLA: ... Vi to, vi har kæmpet på liv og død om et menneske før, vi, Gunhild!*
> *FRU BORKMAN: [sér hoverende på hende] Ja, og* jeg *vandt sejr.*

> ELLA: ... We two have fought over a man before, Gunhild!
> MRS BORKMAN [looks at her in triumph] Yes, and I won.

One might even feel that Ella's longing for Erhart to be a sort of proxy child by the man she loved - even as a proxy for John Gabriel himself - is more dangerous, in its way, because more insidiously possessive, than Gunhild's hunger for power. Gunhild merely wishes to dominate the lad, says Ella, but

> *Jeg vil ha' hans kærlige sind, - hans sjæl, - hans hele hjerte - !*

> I want his affection ... his soul ... his loving heart!

Ella speaks *varmt*, 'warmly', and what she is talking about, at least consciously, is the love of a mother for a child, (though, one might add, a child whom she has made no attempt to see in the past eight years). But the obsessional intensity of her language must already make us suspect what she refuses to admit to Gunhild, yet will declare to John Gabriel - that her feelings for Erhart represent not pity for a lost child (as she has claimed to Gunhild [H, XIII, 47-8/ O, VIII, 160-1]) but a re-channelling of frustrated desire. If some beggar child had come to her door, she tells John Gabriel, she would not have cared for it herself, but handed it over to the kitchen maid to care for. It was because he was John Gabriel's child that she overwhelmed Erhart with love,

> *Vandt ham helt. Vandt hele hans varme, tillidsfulde barnehjerte for mig, - indtil -*
>
> [H, XIII, 89-90]

> Won his love. Won all his childish confidence ... until ...
>
> [O, VIII, 200]

That this passion (as her last word implies) has been powerless to defend itself against Gunhild's straightforward, ruthless determination, must not deflect us from the suspicion that Ella's feelings in their distorted intensity are both compromised and, in a special sense, untrue.

From the struggle between the sisters for possession of the child, John Gabriel has kept grandly aloof. He is so obsessed with his own 'mission' - the resurrection of his industrial empire, the waterfalls to be tamed, the endless web of mine-workings to be constructed so as to free *guldets slumrende ånder*, 'the slumbering spirits of gold' [H, XIII, 87/ O, VIII, 198] - that all merely human feelings have come to seem annoying and irrelevant. He may complain to Foldal that *both* sisters have set Erhart against him [H, XIII, 78/ O, VIII, 189], and to Ella, only a few moments later, that it is Gunhild who keeps his son away from him. But in truth Borkman has been and is indifferent to his son. *Jeg har aldrig blandet mig ind i disse huslige spørgsmål*, 'I never got mixed up in these domestic matters', he says [H, XIII, 83/ O, VIII, 194], dismissing in a single lordly phrase the nomadic childhood of his only son. When Ella tries to talk to him of her feelings for the boy, he is impatient and evasive, unwilling to discuss *følelser og sligt noget*, 'feelings and that sort of thing'.

And well he might be. Years before, he has sacrificed his love for Ella to placate a rival and smooth his own career. Now he even blames Ella for not consenting to marry his rival, so as to avoid his own prosecution for fraud [H, XIII, 85; 82/ O, VIII, 196; 194]. He himself is *helt igennem forgiftet og forpestet*, 'poisoned and infected, through and through', with precisely that *overskurkens moral*, 'morality of the super-scoundrel'[147] which (with grimly comic unconscious irony) he attributes to Hinkel, the rival [H, XIII, 75/ O*, VIII, 187]. To Borkman, human emotions are no more than convenient (but unreliable) levers to move the world of material affairs. It is not surprising that he half-encourages Ella to take Erhart back - for, as he himself says, it is no great sacrifice (*ikke noget så stort offer*) to give up what you do not own and, by implication, don't value much either [H, XIII, 92/ O, VIII, 203]. Emotionally, John Gabriel is already dead; his long conversation with Ella is a dialogue of ghosts. Only Gunhild is real enough to him to move him just a little, we may suspect, for she is *Hård, som den malm, jeg engang drømte om at bryde ud af fjeldene*, 'Hard as the iron I once dreamed of quarrying from the rock' [H, XIII, 94/ O, VIII, 204]. And it is *this* dream - the dream of the boy, taken down into the mines by his father, who seems to hear the ore singing, as it is cut free by *midnatsklokken*, the midnight-bell of fate - which has the power still to rouse him, not feelings of thwarted passion or thwarted paternity. 'O Mensch! Gib acht!'

These are the powers which meet to confront each other and struggle for possession in the third act of *John Gabriel Borkman*. Not one of the three is interested in Erhart for himself alone, as he is now. Even Ella still wants him to be once again the loving boy with which she comforted herself through a decade of spinsterhood. Indeed, none of the three can admit to themselves that he is now grown up. How could they, since what he represents for each of them is a dream of lost happiness which will, precisely, annihilate time, revoke the consequences of change, give them back the twenty years wasted in frustrated ambition, fruitless passion, sterile resentment? Father, mother, aunt - each of them projects on to Erhart a vision of time regained, a resurrection of their own childhood selves which the world of experience has blighted. And the form of each vision is an exact reflection of the ways in which, in a corrupt world, the limitations of childhood personality become further distorted and intensified in adulthood. John Gabriel is still haunted by his boyhood dream of power and glory to be found, not in the world of men, but by will alone, in some half-material, half-abstract private world of his own making. Like the miner in Ibsen's early poem, he has

> *glemte liens sus og sange*
> *i min grubes tempelgange.*
>
> [H, XIV, 333]

> forgot the hillside's whispering song
> in the cloisters of my mine.
>
> [O*, VIII, 340]

Mentally, he still wanders those mineshaft-cloisters, denouncing the daylight, adult world which has destroyed his dreams:-

> *Å, de kvinder! De fordærver og forvansker livet for os! Forkvakler hele vor skæbne, - hele vor sejers-gang.*
>
> [H, XIII, 78]

> Oh, women! How they distort and corrupt our lives! Tamper with our destinies! Rob us of our victories!
>
> [O, VIII, 189]

Yet the women in his life - Gunhild and Ella - are equally limited, not just by a sibling rivalry stretching far back into childhood, but also by everything which the house - their childhood home, the stage for all this drama - represents for them. Gunhild's stiff, blind, crippling devotion to family honour; Ella's over-protective longing for domestic cosiness, that sweet-smelling, cloying, stifling *stueluft* of which Erhart complains; - each is a reflection of the way in which human beings who fail to mature or develop do not merely stand still but regress into an increasingly damaging, distorted version of their childhood.

But Erhart, somehow, has survived all this - which must in itself make him the most impressive witness in any case against too determinist an interpretation of Ibsen's work. Indeed, Ella's protective anxiety that Erhart *kommer til at gå til grunde i dette uvejr*, 'will be destroyed in this storm' [H, XIII, 94/ O*, VIII, 204] turns out to be quite unnecessary. When he eventually returns to face the by now hysterical trio (*Der er han, - der er han! Erhart!* 'Here he is! Here he is! Erhart!' [H, XIII, 101/ O, VIII, 210]) his plans for escape from this bear-garden are already worked out. *Jeg kan ikke ofre mig for dig nu*, 'I cannot sacrifice myself to you now', he says to Ella; and to Gunhild:- *Jeg kan ikke vie mit liv til soning for nogen anden*, 'I can't dedicate my life to making atonement for somebody else' [H, XIII, 103, 104/ O, VIII, 212, 213]. Escape from his own family, even into the arms of the rich, divorced and (ominously?) older Fanny Wilton has restored to him the knowledge that he is living in time, in a world in which others mature and develop:-

> *For jeg er* ung! *Aldrig har jeg vidst af, at jeg var det før ... Jeg* vil *ikke arbejde! Bare leve, leve, leve!*
> [H, XIII, 106]
>
> I'm young! I never realized it before ... I don't want to work. I just want to live, live, live!
> [O, VIII, 215]

And Fru Wilton, older though she may be, is at least aware, as the Borkmans and Rentheims are not, of the human need for joy, and of the need to come to terms with change and human weakness. Just how flexible she is prepared to be, is shown when Gunhild asks her 'with a malicious smile', whether she doesn't think it unwise to take the fifteen year old Freda with them to the south? Fanny returns the smile, 'half ironically, half seriously'. Men are so unreliable, and women too:-

> *Når Erhart er færdig med* mig, - *og* jeg *med* ham, - *så er det godt for os begge at han, stakker, har nogen at falde tilbage på.*
>
> [H, XIII, 111]

> When Erhart is finished with *me* ... and *I* with *him* ... then it'll be good for both of us if he, poor boy, has somebody else to fall back on.
>
> [O*, VIII, 219]

It is one of those startling moments in Ibsen's dramas at which any too-confident interpretation must pause and take stock. Is there not an implication here that the patterns of the past may be repeated, that Fanny may someday be used as Ella and Erhart himself have been used? The question remains open-ended, in suspense, rather like the doubts raised (for rather different reasons) by Bolette's engagement to Arnholm in *The Lady from the Sea*. With this last salute to moral realism, the lovers disappear into the night.

This, and not Borkman's death at the end of the fourth act, is the true climax of the play, in terms both of dramatic tension and of thematic content. In the blank, desolate silence which follows Erhart's going, each of the remaining characters begins to take in the implications of what has happened. Because the real focus of their passion is not Erhart himself but the last frustrated ambitions or blighted hopes which they have used him to represent, his going represents for each of them a coming to terms with the false perspectives, the 'life-lies' by which, alone, they have lived. When Borkman goes to seize his hat and cloak, and - for the first time in sixteen years - goes *Ud i livets uvejr*, 'out into the storm of life' [H, XIII, 111/ O, VIII, 220], he is acknowledging the hermetic nature of the existence which each of them has lived, cut off not only from fresh air, but from time itself.

The shift of scene between the third and fourth acts (which, like the rest of the play takes place in - to all intents and purposes - continuous time[148]) is symbolic of the moment of revelation which Erhart's departure brings. Now all the seals are broken. Out in the winter night, as the sound of sleigh-bells recedes, Borkman comes face to face with his opposite, his 'mask' (in the Yeatsian sense), the old clerk Vilhelm Foldal, who comes in, limping and battered, covered in snow, having just been knocked down by the lovers' sleigh. His reappearance is comic and touching - but it is also of great importance for the play's moral structure. Foldal has sacrificed his career to the vain dream of becoming a poet. He is old now, and despised by most of his family. But he is still capable of unselfish (and perhaps naive) rejoicing at what he takes to be his daughter's good fortune:-

> *Det er min - min smule digtergave, som har omsat sig til musik hos Frida. Og så har jeg altså ikke forgæves været digter alligevel da.*
>
> [H, XIII, 119]

> There's my ... my modest talent for poetry been transformed into music in Frida. So after all's said and done I haven't been a poet for nothing.
>
> [O, VIII, 227]

Now she will journey into the great wide world he has dreamed of seeing; and with that, bowled over, knocked aside by the future though he has been, Foldal can be content. It is as brilliant and daring a stroke as any Ibsen devised for a final act - indeed, the only moment it can directly be compared with is Ulrik Brendel's reappearance in the last act of *Rosmersholm.* Foldal, naive and pathetic though he is, retains a pathos and human dignity in comparison with which the hysterical squabblings of the Borkmans can only seem tawdry and mean-spirited.

But it is too late for John Gabriel to change or to learn. He talks of becoming a free man again, yet cannot - dare not - go back into the house:-

> *Gik jeg op på salen* nu, - *loft og vægge vilde skrumpe sig sammen. Knuge mig. Klemme mig flad som en flue.*
>
> [H, XIII, 121]

> If I went up to that room now ... the walls and the ceiling would shrink and crush me ... crush me like a fly.
>
> [O, VIII, 228]

It is the language of inner collapse, of one who now recognizes and fears the emptiness of his inner self - acknowledges, what we also sense, that already he is 'a dead man'.

From this death, there can be no awakening for Borkman, only a further retreat into dream. With a stage-direction which (given the play's strict time-scheme, the place-centredness and claustrophobia of the first three acts) seems uncanny, even surreal, the scenery begins to dissolve and change:-

> *Huset og gårdspladsen tabes af sigte. Landskabet, med lier og højdedrag, forandrer sig stadig langsomt og bliver vildere og vildere.*
>
> [H, XIII, 122]

> The house and the courtyard disappear. The landscape, with slopes and ridges, slowly changes and grows wilder and wilder.
>
> [O, VIII, 229]

It is as if the extraordinary pressures built up in the first three acts, now released, dissolve and annihilate the dimensions of space and time.[149] As the landscape grows wilder, Borkman seems to hear the unborn children of his imagination, those unbuilt factories and undelved mines, *Alle de, som* jeg *vilde skabt!* 'All those factories *I* would have created' [H, XIII, 123/ O*, VIII, 230]. And, even now, it is to these and not to Ella that his love goes out:-

> *Jeg elsker eder, der I ligger skindøde i dybet og i mørket! Jeg elsker eder, I livkrævende værdier - med alt eders lysende følge af magt og ære! Jeg elsker, elsker, elsker eder!*
>
> [H, XIII, 124]

> I love you: you who lie in a trance of death in the darkness and the deep. I love you! You and your life-seeking treasures and all your bright retinue of power and glory. I love you, love you, love you.
>
> [O, VIII, 231]

It is, as Durbach says,[150] the most impassioned declaration of love in all of Ibsen's work; and it is spoken by a man to his lost dreams, spoken whilst the woman he loved, used and betrayed stands by his side. For Borkman, it is only the children of his imagination who are *livkrævende*, 'life-seeking'. But these are 'absence, darknesse, death; things which are not' - they are not just *skindøde* ('apparently dead') but the stillborn offspring of his own fascinated, obsessive self-regard.

In this final scene, Ibsen combined two of the most powerful images which had haunted his work for forty years; - that of *Bergmanden*, 'the miner' who hopes to find, underground, *fred fra evighed*, 'peace from eternity', through the exercise of the hammer-blows of the individual will; and that of the isolated soul wandering on the icy heights, whilst the rest of the world fumbles below. It is perhaps the most terrible of all the variations which from *Brand* onwards, Ibsen was to compose on the theme of *hjertekulden*, 'the coldness of the heart'.

CHAPTER TWELVE

When We Dead Awaken

> To write is to carve in granite and to make irrevocable ... a protest against life, against its protean richness, its inconstancy.
>
> R. R. Eklund

Ibsen's last play, his 'dramatic epilogue', forms a conclusion not only to the final group of plays, but to his whole life's work, from the poetry of the 1850s onwards.[151] Though not as formally perfect or as powerful as some of its predecessors, lacking the monumental energy of *John Gabriel Borkman*, it develops nevertheless an enormous imaginative momentum of its own. Much of this momentum derives from the play's final transformation of those themes of regression and sacrifice which have been traced throughout Ibsen's work. But in *When We Dead Awaken* there is a crucial difference, which simultaneously takes the argument on to its logical conclusion and back to its original premise in the early poetry and plays. Whereas, in the major phase of his work - between, say, *Brand* and *John Gabriel Borkman* - Ibsen imposes a distance between the inner life of his characters and the experience of writing about them, *When We Dead Awaken* (like the final version of Rubek's statue) contains its own, intensely personal criticism of the relationship *at leve - at digte*, between writing and life.

In *When We Dead Awaken*, the central character is, for the first time in Ibsen's dramatic work since *Love's Comedy*, a true creative artist. Arnold Rubek is a successful sculptor - in the mould, perhaps, of Rodin or of Ibsen's much younger contemporary, Vigeland[152] - who has come north to revisit his native land. With him he brings the young wife whom he had married (or *forskaffe[t]*, 'acquire[d]', as she later puts it [H, XIII, 252/ O, VIII, 270]) on a previous visit. Maja is restless and dissatisfied; neither the beautiful new villa on the Taunitzer See - a house not a home, she says, echoing Aline Solness [H, XIII, 216/ O, VIII, 240] - nor her husband's fame as a sculptor can compensate for a marriage to which neither is really committed. Their dialogue in the first act glowers with that irascibility and exhausted resignation which signifies a relationship on the point of explosion or collapse, as pent-up unsatisfied desires seek new directions for fulfilment. It is around the irreconcilable nature of their different desires for life - Maja's craving for physical excitement, even in the raw and brutal form offered by Ulfhejm; Rubek's longing to recapture the innocence he has petrified or killed by transforming it into art - that the play is built.

As Maja is tempted back to the life of unreflective instinct by Ulfhejm, with his noisy contempt for the spa, its *halvdøde fluer og mennesker*, 'half-dead flies and ... people' [H, XIII, 228/ O, VIII, 250], Rubek is drawn to a figure - perhaps only a spectre - from his own past. Irene has been the original model for the sculpture *Opstandelsens dag*, 'Resurrection Day', which has been hailed as his masterpiece. But she has been much more than just a physical model. They have enjoyed an intense relationship, the more so for remaining unconsummated. Irene was, Rubek tells her, *min skabnings ophav*, 'the source of my creation'[153] [H, XIII, 239/ O, VIII, 260]. Yet all the intensity of their love has been diverted - and distorted - into Rubek's art, into the statue which has become a surrogate for the loving relationship they should have enjoyed. From the first moments of their conversation in Act One, Irene refers to the statue as *Barnet*, 'the child' [H, XIII, 232/ O, VIII, 254]. Since both the statue and its metaphoric implications play a central role in the dramatic structure, any reading of *When We Dead Awaken* must examine closely all that is said about this 'child', and the lives which have been sacrificed to it.

'Resurrection Day' has *gjort sin far berømt*, 'made its father famous', as Irene says; *Det var din drøm*, 'That was your dream'.[154] But her feelings for the statue are not in any conventional sense motherly:-

> *Jeg skulde ha' dræbt det barn ... Bagefter har jeg dræbt det utallige gange ... Dræbt det i had - og i hævn - og i kval.*
>
> [H, XIII, 232-3]

> I should have killed that child ... Since then I've killed it countless times ... Killed it in hatred, in vengeance, in torment.
>
> [O, VIII, 254]

In some terrible and as yet unexplained sense, as Irene has poured her ardent young soul into the statue, into the service of Rubek's art, her own spirit has been used up and displaced. At the point at which she believed the statue to be completed, therefore, she has disappeared suddenly from Rubek's life, from *én, som ikke havde brug for min kærlighed. Ikke brug for mit liv længer*, 'someone who had no use for my love. No use any longer for my life'. Only the child has been left *i forklarelsens lys*, 'transfigured in light' [H, XIII, 233/ O, VIII, 255]. Irene believes herself to have been destroyed by her experience with Rubek. Whether what she says about her life after she left him is literally true, or a metaphor for mental breakdown, the crazed delusions of a woman who believes herself to have died, or whether these are the dark dreams of someone who really has in some sense died and been resurrected - all this is the more powerfully suggestive because it remains unclear.[155] The men she claims to have murdered or driven mad, the children she talks of having killed or aborted or just not conceived [H, XIII, 234-5/ O, VIII, 256] are all symbolic illustrations of the charge she makes against Rubek - that by transforming her spirit into timeless art, he has destroyed it.

Yet it would be unwise to accept her reproaches at face value. The question remains - sharpened rather than answered both by Ibsen's revisions to this scene and by what happens later in the play - *why* did Irene give up her precious youth, the beauty of her naked body, and most precious of all, *min unge, levende sjæl*, 'my young, living soul' [H, XIII, 241/ O, VIII, 262] to someone whose demands must have been so different from, so much greater than those which other artists make on their models? The simplest and most obvious explanation - that she was an impressionable young woman in love for the first time with a creative artist - may be part of the truth; but it scarcely accounts for the nature of her sacrifice, the fury of her later hatred. Irene herself hints at a further explanation, however, when she and Rubek remember the original conception of the statue. As originally planned, it was to depict

> *en ung kvinde, som vågner af dødssøvnen - ... Det skulde være jordens ædleste, reneste, idealeste kvinde ... Så fandt jeg* dig.
>
> [H, XIII, 237-8]

> a young woman waking from the sleep of death ... the world's noblest, purest, most perfect woman. Then I found *you...*
>
> [O, VIII, 259]

The younger Rubek has chosen, as a symbol of resurrection, an idealized young maiden who has died, presumably, before she has had time to be corrupted by adult experience and desire. And since she is to be *ren*, 'pure' (Rubek harps upon this point), this day of resurrection can be in no sense a day of judgement. On the contrary, he specifies that she is to be

> *Ikke undrende over noget nyt og ukendt og uanet.*

> *Men fyldt af en helligdoms glæde over at genfinde sig selv uforvandlet, - hun, jordkvinden...*
>
> [H, XIII, 238]

> Not wondering at things new and unfamiliar and unimagined, but filled with a holy joy at finding herself unchanged - a mortal woman...[156]
>
> [O, VIII, 259]

Rubek's dream of resurrection is thus, in its essential nature, *uforvandlet*, unchanged and changeless, sealed in by death from the transformation and developments which time can bring - so that his Last Day will be, not the occasion for the final examination of souls, an inquisition into the uses which human beings have made of their time on earth, but the apotheosis of that timelessness which only death - or art - can confer.

Hence the curious and very revealing phrase which in the play's final version Irene uses of the statue. It is to be *min barnealders opstandelse*, 'my childhood's resurrection' - and the phrase suggests the extent to which the statue is the result of a collusive vision, a common longing for regression to childish purity.[157] Rubek's fantasizing about the untouchable child-woman,

> *en høj-hellig skabning, som bare måtte røres ved i tilbedende tanker.*
>
> [H, XIII, 238]

> a sacred being, untouchable, a thing to worship in thought alone.
>
> [O, VIII, 259]

his superstition that if he has a carnal affair with her, the work of art will in some way be destroyed, is paralleled by Irene's vision of the statue as the resurrection of her childhood self. No less than Rubek, she has sought refuge from experience in the timeless reflection of her own image. Yet this willed turning-away from maturity has brought its own conflicts. At various points in the play, she claims to have hated Rubek, *fordi du kunde stå der så uberørt*, 'because you could stand there so unmoved' [H, XIII, 259/ O, VIII, 276]. Yet she also says that if he *had* touched her, she would have killed him on the spot, with the blade or needle which she always carries with her, and with which (so she now claims) she has killed her second husband.[158] Especially in the play's final version, the keynote of Irene's character is not some gentle longing for idyllic childhood, but an embattled, indeed enraged fear and hatred of maturity.[159]

Indeed, the girl whom young Rubek has idealized as a Solvejg, a pure innocent girl, seems on close examination to have something in common with Rita Allmers, but far more with Hedda Gabler and Hilde Wangel. Ibsen, when in revising the play he accentuated the daemonic side of her character, sought to emphasize that, far from being a passive victim of Rubek's egotism, she has brought to their relationship qualities which form a dangerous parallel to Rubek's own. Yet whereas for Irene, time has stopped, so that she regards her life after she has left Rubek as dream or nightmare, thinks of herself as dead - Rubek has gone on developing as an artist, though not perhaps as a human being. She has seen the statue as a monument to her pure childhood self and to her 'pure' relationship with Rubek. His view of it is much more impersonal. On the one hand he seeks to excuse the immature view of womanhood which the first conception of 'Resurrection Day' implies:- *Jeg var jo endnu ung den gang*, 'I was still young then' [H, XIII, 238/ O, VIII, 259]. On the other, even then, he was *Først og fremst kunstner*, 'Above all else an artist'; like John Gabriel Borkman, he has always seen his highest duty and commitment as being to something other and higher than human beings and their relationships. Yet his attitude is by no means as remorselessly consistent as Borkman's. On the contrary, it is torn by inconsistencies which seem to reflect both a fundamental opposition between art and life and also the awareness that the creative artist needs both, yet must frequently and self-defeatingly deny himself one to secure the other. Hence, perhaps, the despair which he expresses both to Maja and to Irene, and his mixture of contempt and malevolent amusement at the success of his recent works - these portrait-busts which, unbeknown to their subjects, reveal the domesticated beast in man, *Alle de dyr, som menneskene har forkvaklet i sit billede. Og som har forkvaklet menneskene til gengæld*, 'All those animals that man has corrupted in his own image. And which have corrupted man in return' [H, XIII, 220-1/ O, VIII, 244]. Yet Rubek, at least, knows that this is not true imaginative creation. *Intet har jeg digtet efter den dag*, 'I have created[160] nothing since that day', he tells Irene - and 'that day' is the moment at which, his masterpiece seemingly finished, she has disappeared from his life.

But of course the statue has *not* been finished at that point; and the account of its subsequent development, wrested by Irene from Rubek in Act II, shows how complex and intractable are the problems implicit in the confrontation between inspiration and experience. Initially, 'Resurrection Day' was to show the triumph of a pure ideal over the corruptions of time. As Rubek says, *Jeg var ung dengang*, 'I was young then' [H, XIII, 261/ O, VIII, 278] and by 'young' he implies artistically and spiritually immature, *uden al livserfaring*, 'with no experience of life'. The private vision of the statue in its earlier form assumes validity precisely by virtue of its distance from the experienced (in Rubek's case, the still-to-be-experienced) world. It would therefore follow that such a vision could not withstand, indeed would have by definition to exclude 'all experience of life'. But, *Jeg blev verdensklog i de årene, som fulgte efter*, 'I gained worldly wisdom in the years that followed' - and knowledge of the world implies knowledge of its complexity and its nastiness:

> *'Opstandelsens dag' blev noget mere og noget - noget mere mangfoldigt i min forestilling.*
>
> [H, XIII, 262]

> 'Resurrection Day' became something more, and something ... something more multifarious, as I imagined it.
>
> [O*, VIII, 278]

The plinth of the statue has widened, as the basis of Rubek's experience of life has widened. What he now seeks to transform into art is *d e t ... som jeg rundt omkring mig i verden så med mine øjne*, 'Things I saw with my own eyes in the world around me'. Art was no longer to be the stage for a private dream, but *et stykke af den buede, bristende jord*, 'a part of the heaving, cracking vault of the earth itself '. Out of the earth on Resurrection Day will swarm

> *mennesker med dulgte dyreansigter. Kvinder og mænd, - slig som jeg kendte dem ude fra livet.*
>
> people with animal faces under the skin. Women and men ... as I knew them from life.

representing all those animal passions of whose existence Rubek's earlier idealism has been a denial. As for Irene, the untouchable, virginal muse-goddess of his youth, she has been moved sideways and backwards, *For helhedsvirkningens skyld*, 'For the sake of the total effect'. Even the radiant, transfigured joy of her expression has been *lidt afdæmpet kanské. Således, som min ændrede tanke kræved det*, 'A little subdued, perhaps. As was demanded by my changed conception' [H, XIII, 262/ O, VIII, 279].

Irene's reaction to the news is less subdued. She is beside herself with fury that, in the work of art to which she has sacrificed life, children, the prospect of happiness - indeed, which she has treated as a surrogate for all these, 'our child' - she should now be reduced to *en baggrundsfigur - i en gruppe*, 'a background figure ... in a group'. But the scene reveals more than just the pathos of Irene's hurt feelings, the comedy of her affronted vanity. What has happened to Rubek's sculpture is a kind of paradigm of the process by which the creative artist comes to realize that, like Andersen's little mermaid, he is doomed to be a citizen of two worlds, at peace in neither. This is the knowledge from which Falk and Peer Gynt and the young artist in *'Paa Vidderne'* manage to shy away, the necessary process of self-revaluation which Ibsen himself described - and then revalued - in the different versions of 'Building Plans'. To become truly a *digter*, a creative artist, one needs both an aesthetic genius for falsehood (the power 'to tell beautiful lies', in Gunnar Ekelöf's formulation) *and* the ethical capacity to tell the truth, to show the world as it is, to make moral discriminations, to 'hold judgement-day over oneself'. This, surely, is the significance of the way in which Rubek has introduced his own image into the sculpture;-

> *en skyldbetynget mand ... Jeg kalder ham angeren over et forbrudt liv... Han når i al evighed ikke fri op til opstandelsens liv. Blir evindelig siddende igen i sit helvede.*
>
> [H, XIII, 263]

> a man weighed down with guilt ... I call him remorse for a forfeit life ... Never in all eternity will he win free to achieve the life of the resurrection. He must remain forever captive in his hell.
>
> [O, VIII, 279]

Significantly, it is at this point that Irene calls him by the name which so often in Ibsen's work cuts two ways, undercuts the position of the artist himself:- *Digter!* The ambivalence of the writer who must tell lies if he is to achieve artistic truth, which has for so long underlain Ibsen's work, now, like Rubek's image of himself, breaks through the surface, *Foran*, centre-stage.[161] The idea that Rubek, *slap og sløv og fuld af synds-*

forladelse, 'soft and spineless and full of excuses' [H, XIII, 263/ O, VIII, 279] can simply excuse and forgive himself by showing himself in his art-work in an attitude of guilty penitence - thus attempting to bridge, in his own image, the moral gulf between creation and responsibility - seems to Irene to be outrageous. But it is an outrageousness which, paradoxically, is mitigated for her by the terms of her own condemnation. *Digter er du, Arnold... Du kære, store, aldrende barn, - at du ikke kan sé* det! 'A poet[162] is what you are, Arnold... You dear great ageing child - that you can't see *that*!' [H, XIII, 264/ O*, VIII, 280]. For the excusing quality which lies in the word *Digter* and which draws a cloak over human weakness, suggests the immunity of creative artists from the commandments which for other people are paramount:- to live, to be happy, to bear children and lead a full life. But whereas his failure to live is (like the fate of Coleridge's Ancient Mariner) both privilege and curse, Irene's failure to do so is *et selvmord. En dødsens brøde imod mig selv*, 'suicide. A mortal sin against myself'.

When Rubek says, defiantly, that he is *f ø d t til kunstner*, '*born* to be an artist', he is claiming both immunity from the moral judgement of others, and citizenship of his own private hell. His is the Romantic conception, familiar from Coleridge, Baudelaire and others, of the artist as a self-sufficient isolated being, simultaneously of the damned and the elect. Yet all of Ibsen's mature work represents a protest, implied or explicit, against so Troll-like an interpretation of the artist's role. For what it ignores is any account of the artist's relationships with other human beings. In Irene, who has longed in her naive vanity to become part of the creative process, yet now realizes that she has committed an unforgivable crime against herself, Ibsen seeks to show what may happen when the private truths of artistic creation are translated into the terms of ordinary human existence. Irene realizes, too late, that for those who have *en menneskeskæbne at fuldbyrde*, 'a human destiny to fulfil' and are *not* born to be artists, to flirt with the ideal of a timeless absolute is not even a mixed blessing, but merely a curse. To her, 'Resurrection Day' has become no more than an idol to which her own children have been sacrificed,

> *Jeg skulde født børn til verden. Mange børn. Rigtige børn. Ikke af dem, som gemmes i gravkælderne. Det havde været mit kald. Skulde aldrig ha' tjent dig, - digter.*
>
> [H, XIII, 264]

> I should have borne children. Many children. Real children. Not the kind that are preserved in tombs. That should have been my calling. I should never have served you - poet!
>
> [O, VIII, 280]

Yet although Irene may posit different sets of ethical rules for the artist and for the rest of humanity, all the evidence of this play, and of the rest of Ibsen's mature work, suggests that so absolute a distinction cannot be made. The pure aestheticism of the tutelary 'friend' in *'Paa Vidderne'*, the exclusive emphasis on form suggested by the eighth poem in the cycle 'In the Picture Gallery' (*Hvis Du vil dømme Skaldens Tonestige,/Saa hør* hvorledes, *ikke* hvad *han sang*, 'if you would judge the flight of a poet's song/listen to *how* he sings, not *what* he says' [H, XIV, 243]) must never be taken as straightforward, unambiguous statements of Ibsen's own beliefs. On the contrary, these are positions taken up in an inner argument which has its origins both in the intellectual controversies of the 'Golden Age' of Danish literature and in Ibsen's own inner conflicts. *When We Dead Awaken* revives and makes explicit a problem which, unspoken, underlies all his plays from *Brand* to *John Gabriel Borkman*. In all his major plays, the readiness to sacrifice oneself or (more usually) others in the name of some ideal is condemned as a distortion of human nature. Yet that is precisely what Rubek has done to Irene, what all artists seek to do (in some sense or other) to the living human beings who are their raw material. When Irene calls Rubek an 'ageing child' she is defining the paradox implicit in all creation, that element of irresponsible play and of manipulation which is how the shaping imagination transforms life into art, yet makes the artist so dangerous to those around him. By refusing to subscribe wholeheartedly either to a purely aesthetic Heibergian view of the artist's role or to a Tolstoyan moralism which denies that the problem exists, Ibsen made his last play into a confrontation to which - given the terms in which the problems are stated - there could be no satisfactory resolution.

Something of the difficulty of the problem, and of Ibsen's ambivalent attitude towards it, can be seen in the revisions which he made to the draft of the final act. In the first version, to be entitled *Opstandelsens dag*, 'Resurrection Day', the play is allowed to end on a note of ambiguous, qualified optimism. The two pairs of lovers separate on terms which are civilized and even amiable - they take time to bolt down a glass of champagne together before parting [H, XIII, 337-9/ O, VIII, 304-5]. Afterwards, they take their separate ways, Rubek and Irene through thickening fog towards the mountain peak. Irene begs him to save her from a second death; Rubek points in reply to the mountain peak:-

> *Ovenover tågerne skimter jeg fjeldtinden. Den står der og glittrer i solopgangen - did må vi op - gennem nattetågen op i morgenlyset.*
>
> [H, XIII, 340]

> Above the mists I glimpse the mountain peak. There it stands glittering in the sunrise. We must go up there ... through the mists of night up into the light of morning.
>
> [O, VIII, 307]

They are lost in the mists. Only a glimpse of Irene's doppelgänger, the Nun, peering through the fog, adds a note of menace. There is in the earlier version no storm, no avalanche. The final image left by the stage directions is that of the mountain peak, shining above the mist.

Resurrection Day ends with an image of concord, with the implication that creative artists (and their models) can find happiness, and that there *are* other, perhaps higher forms of freedom to be found than those allowed for by Maja's vulgar, instinctive humanity. But in revising the play, Ibsen also revised the terms of the problem in such a way as to preclude the (even in its context) rather facile optimism of that original conclusion. By emphasizing, through the accumulation of dozens of incidental changes and additions, the daemonic side of Irene's nature (the threatening gestures with the knife, the hoarse cries and much of her abuse of Rubek are all later additions to the draft) Ibsen also underlined the death-obsessed violence of Rubek's own longing for the past. Yet, as if to balance the equation, Ulfhejm's nature is also made much more brutal, more animal and violent - thus suggesting that Maja, too, is compromised by a quality which is *dyriskt*, full of mindless, amoral high-spirits. In the final version of the play, therefore, *both* sides of Rubek's existence - life and death, humanity and art - are shown to have become, as a result of the tragic act of separation which the life of the artist demands, unattractive and dangerous. In the final judgement, the distance between Maja's triumphant assertion of the body's independence of spirit,[163]

> *Jeg er fri! Jeg er fri! Jeg er fri!*
> *Mit fangenskabs liv er forbi!*
> [H, XIII, 283]

> I am free! I am free! I am free!
> No longer this prison for me!
> [O, VIII, 297]

and the burial of the dead souls, Rubek and Irene, in the avalanche with which the play concludes, signifies that for those who have sacrificed love to their own timeless image, there can be no resurrection:-

> *IRENE. Den kærlighed, som er jordlivets, - det dejlige, vidunderlige jordlivs, - det gådefulde jordlivs, - den er død i os begge.*
>
> [H, XIII, 282]

> IRENE. That love which is of our earthly life - the glorious, marvellous mysterious life on earth - that love is dead in us both.
>
> [O, VIII, 295].

The echoes of the ending of *Brand* are resounding and deliberate. What Rubek has sacrificed to his art, Brand destroys in the name of his God; and the judgement of the invisible choir, sighing in the wind, is reinforced by everything Ibsen had written since:-

> *Arv og Odel har du tabt;*
> *alt dit Offer gjør ej rig ham;-*
> *for dit Jordliv er du skabt!*
>
> [H, V, 355]

> Your heritage is cast away
> Your sacrifice will never make Him rich...
> It was for life on earth you were created
>
> [O, III, 242]

Conclusively, and with all the resources of the imagination, Ibsen seeks to demonstrate that creative imagination is no substitute for life. That, in this 'dramatic epilogue', the 'child' which is at the heart of the play's symbolism is an idol to which real human lives, even real children, are sacrificed, is an irony which can only properly be understood in the context of the symbol's gestation from *Brand* onwards. In retrospect,the trolls with which Ibsen's characters do battle, trolls in the world, in each other, in themselves, are all precursors of the final judgement day which must always be, finally and irrevocably, *dommedag over sig selv*, 'Judgement Day over one's self'. In *When We Dead Awaken*, a play which proclaims the incompatibility of life and art, *at leve* and *at digte*, which shows an artistic masterpiece as, humanly, the petrified child of dead illusions, Ibsen confronted the warring halves of his own nature - of art as a criticism of the impurity of life, of life as a standing reproach to the sterility of art - and out of this double negation made his own final masterpiece, the last, strangest and most personal child of his art.

Epilogue

With *When We Dead Awaken*, the Ibsen cycle returns, after how long and circuitous a journey, to what is recognizably its starting point. Throughout the sequence, certain themes appear with such insistent regularity that they cannot be ignored by the critic without doing violence to the nature of the individual plays. To trace such a theme through the plays is to become more aware of them as rich and complex works of art; it is also to understand why the experience of seeing Ibsen's dramatic work as a whole is greater than studying its individual parts. His world may be more austere, less various, than Shakespeare's. But in its coherence and cumulative power it offers a sense of completeness which no other dramatist since the Renaissance can match.

What, though, is the *significance* of Ibsen's constant engagement with childhood, regression and sacrifice? Aspects of Ibsen's treatment of children do have much in common with the sort of nostalgia for Paradisal innocence so common amongst the English Romantics - and even more obsessively present in the Danish tradition from Jens Baggesen to H. C. Andersen and H. E. Schack. But nostalgia as such has no place amongst the moral positives of Ibsen's world. On the contrary, a longing for the past is almost always associated in these plays with a refusal to live fully in the present - a refusal which, time and again, leads to the destruction of childhood, of the human capacity for development. The advice of the Devil in Blake's *Marriage of Heaven and Hell*, 'Sooner murder an infant in its cradle than nurse unacted desires', expresses only too exactly the view of life which impels so many of Ibsen's major characters, as they sacrifice other people to preserve their own childish dreams and desires.

It is not a view which Ibsen shares. A careful reading of the work shows how insistently he exposes the egocentric romanticism of his central characters, by denying it that freedom from context and consequence which it demands. Blake's maxim, 'One Law for the Lion & Ox is Oppression' may accord exactly with Borkman's declaration (speaking for all such characters) that legal precedent and moral law 'aren't necessary for exceptional people'. Yet a central concern of Ibsen's drama is to show, not just that such views are morally wrong and humanly damaging, but that they are also concomitant with a failure to give or receive love, a failure almost invariably associated with personalities damaged in childhood. That 'the child is father to the man' is axiomatic in Ibsen's plays; but the moral and psychological corollaries of this are insistently spelt out. That such characters are prepared to sacrifice others, especially children, to their own sense of uniqueness, to that selfhood which suspends or pre-empts moral value in the name of mission or duty or artistic calling, constitutes in itself a devastating attack on a certain kind of Romantic individualism.

But to what extent can this be interpreted (as both the early and the final plays seem to imply) as a self-criticism, either of the author personally, or of the whole business of being a creative artist? Much in Ibsen's work seems to pre-figure that almost obsessive interest in the psychological and spiritual development of the creative personality which was to characterize so much European writing in the first decade of this century, from James Joyce to Rilke to Hermann Hesse to Robert Musil. Perhaps the greatest of these writers to explore such themes, and the most interesting parallel with Ibsen is Thomas Mann, most truly Ibsen's successor in his exploration of the relationship between the traditional moral rectitude of the merchant classes and the 'dubious' nature of the creative impulse.

Yet what is most striking - given the closeness of their subject-matter - is how different morally and psychologically, Ibsen's world is from Thomas Mann's. What Mann proclaims as self-evident, unalterable fact, that 'good work comes from a bad life ...', that 'one must die to life in order to be completely a creator' is certainly implied by *The Master Builder* and *When We Dead Awaken*, as it had been in *'Paa Vidderne'* and *Love's Comedy*. But in Ibsen's drama, such a recognition is always tempered by the aspiration, through 'warring with trolls', through some 'judgement-day over the self' to transcend the origins of the creative impulse, to restore the writer, in spite of his crippled nature, to a full and useful life amongst his fellow-men. In the fallen world of the plays, these disinherited children do die in vain. But what preserves the moral dignity of Ibsen's imaginative world is the refusal to accept that this must always be so. In his last poem, a couplet dedicated, with a copy of *Brand*, to Hildur Andersen's niece, the one year old Eldrid Arstal, he wrote

> *Gid dit liv må føje sig som et digt*
> *om den store forsoning mellem lykke og pligt.*

> May your life achieve a concord, like a song
> reconciling duty and human joy.

For all their recognition of the dark side of the world, Ibsen's plays, too, seek such a reconciliation.

NOTES

Preface

1 M. Bradbrook, *Ibsen the Norwegian*, London, 1946, p. 10.
2 J. Kerans, '*Kindermord* and Will in *Little Eyolf*' in *Modern Drama: Essays in Criticism*, ed. Bogard and Oliver, New York, 1965, pp. 192-208.
3 E. Durbach, '*Ibsen the Romantic*', London, 1982.
4 Ibid., p. 87.
5 For a useful survey of the differing ways in which other critics have treated this theme in Ibsen, see Durbach, Op. Cit., p. 74 and note.

Introduction

6 The main sources seem to have been the *Volsung saga*, the *Laxdale saga* and *Njal's saga*; see H. Koht, *Henrik Ibsen; Eit Diktarliv*, 1st ed., Oslo, 1928-9, I, ch.X, and F. Bull, *N. L. H.*, IV, 316.
7 For a useful discussion of differing schools of thought on the poem, see H. Dahl's *Bergmannen og Byggmesteren*, Oslo, 1958, pp. 133-137. Dahl's own discussion of the poem (pp. 137-146) seems to me rather less satisfactory.
8 A striking anticipation of ideas and images in this poem, and in corresponding passages in *Peer Gynt* (Peer's Rondane-speech) and, especially, in *Brand*, is to be found in Wergeland's poem, '*Paa Skakastølstinden*'. There, too, the speaker flees to the high mountains, to a world of peaks and glaciers, of eagle, falcon and hawk;-

Hid steg kun over Fannens Vold
en Ørn en Storm og Jeg...
Her er jeg nærmest Gud; thi fra
den Slægt jeg fjernest er,
som bander i Halelujah...

('Here only reach, beyond the Devil's might,/ an eagle, a storm and I....Here I am nearest God, for here/ I am furthest from that race/ who blaspheme against God in singing hymns of praise....')

But Wergeland's poem is notable for the absence of any trace of self-irony - indeed it could serve as an illustration of just that tradition of Romantic self-affirmation which Ibsen so often attacks. (The poem is reprinted in *Wergeland for hvermann*, ed. H. Beyer, Oslo, 1947, pp. 135-8, from which edition these extracts are taken.)

9 In later versions this was altered to *fløje*, 'wings' [of the dream-castle].

10 The later, more pessimistic version of the last line, *storfløjen blev for liden, den lille fløj forfaldt*, 'the great wing grew too tiny, the lesser in ruin fell', dates from 1870, and another stage in his career [c.f. H, XIV, 325].

11 The quoted edition is *En Sjæl efter Døden*, ed. M. Borup, Dansklærerforeningen, 6th ed, 1963.

12 Durbach mentions another, less specific instance of *Kindermord*-symbolism in *The Pretenders*, only to doubt that it can be linked with other appearances of the motive in Ibsen's plays, or that *any* 'comprehensive or monolithic theory' could account for its frequent recurrence (Op. cit., p. 74).

13 A character to whom Skule is much more obviously a forerunner than is Hjørdis in *The Warriors at Helgeland*.

I Brand

14 *Offervillighed* means, more literally, 'willingness to sacrifice'; *uvæsentlig* is the word that the reformed Ejnar uses to discomfit Brand [H, V, 330/ O, III, 219].

15 In the *Epic Brand* the memories are much more traumatic still. There his mother strikes his father's corpse crying, *Det er, fordi du har forspildt mit Liv* [H, V, 376. See also Larsen, *Den episke Brand*, pp. 63-73] - '*This* is because you spoilt my life' [O, III, 43]. The impact on the young Brand is so deep that, a few weeks later, he attacks a favourite dog with a sledge-hammer and, when his mother protests, replies 'This is because it spoilt my life'.

16 For a full and very interesting discussion of the significance of family relationships in *Brand*, see Clara Stuyver, *Ibsens dramatische Gestalten*, Amsterdam, 1952, esp. pp. 156-79.

17 Literally, this means, as O translates it, 'Fight for the inheritors of Heaven' [III, 99]; but the term *Odelsmænd* has a resonance untranslatable into English. An *Odel* implies property, land, and the right of the oldest son, the *Odelsgutt*, to inherit that land.

18 Consider, for example, the number of times the word *Billed* - 'image' - and its compounds appears in the text.

19 It is notable - and one of the untranslatable features of the play - how often the word *Offer*, 'sacrifice', and compound nouns derived from it, are used in the play. The *Ibsen*

Ordbok lists 13 different such compounds used in the play: *Offerbrøde, offerdag, offerdrift, offerdød, offerdåb, offerkalk, offerlam, offerlydighed, offerløn, offerpil, offerskræk, offersten, offersvøbe* -- 'Sacrificial sin', ' - day', ' - urge', ' - death', ' - baptism', ' - cup', ' - lamb', ' - obedience', ' - reward', ' - arrow', ' - terror', ' - stone', ' - scourge'. The list is not exhaustive [cf. H, XXI, 651-2].

20 See B. Hemmer, *Brand - Kongs-emnerne - Peer Gynt*, Oslo, Universtitetsforlaget, 1972, pp. 50-1.

21 There can surely be no doubt that, for all Ibsen's later disavowals, he was familiar with at least some of Kierkegaard's work, perhaps as early as the Grimstad years, that he would have heard much about the work in the Thoresen household in Bergen, and that later, in Christiania, he would have heard much discussion of it in the reading-and-discussion circle, *Det Lærde Holland*.

22 S. Kierkegaard, *Fear and Trembling* (*Frygt og Bæven*) tr. W. Lowrie, N.Y., Doubleday-Anchor, 1954, p. 67. Original in S.K., *Samlede Værker*, V, Kbhvn, 1962, p.53.

23 In an earlier draft for this speech, the line reads *han er en evig Herkules*, 'He is an eternal Hercules' [H, V, 455/ O, III, 436]. In the later version, this God is younger, more immediate, less like a classical statue - and even more like his apostle, Brand.

24 Perhaps it is not after all such a coincidence that it was in St Peter's that the overall plan for *Brand* first came to him?

25 Compare also the irony of J. P. Jacobsen's hero, Niels Lyhne - *Der er ingen Gud, og Mennesket er hans Profet!* - 'There is no God, and Mankind is his prophet!'

26 The revivalist preacher and aesthete who became known in Ibsen's boyhood for his 'restoration' of Bamble church, a few miles from Skien, and who a few years after Ibsen left home, started a sectarian movement in Skien against the established church. Larsen, (*Den episke Brand*, p. 246) notes many similarities with *both* Brand and Ejnar...

27 From the second part of Kierkegaard's *Enten/Eller* (*Either/Or*), in *S. V.*, III, pp. 158-9.

28 The Norwegian here is ambiguous: the word *Slægt* means, primarily, 'family', 'kindred', 'tribe', or 'generation' - only secondarily does it imply 'mankind'. Thus it *could* be read: 'Each family's son must die/ For the family's sins...'

29 *Frygt og Bæven, S. V.*, V, pp.61-2; English translation, *Fear and Trembling*, Anchor ed., p. 77.

II Peer Gynt

30 In an earlier draft, Peer is given an older brother, Niels, who has gone to the wars and been killed [H, VI, 249/ O, III, 460]. Ibsen later rewrote the passage, omitting all reference to the brother - perhaps to strengthen the bond between Aase and Peer.

31 The more piquantly and fascinatingly so since so much of the actual *material* of the play, including the semi-mythical Peer Gynt-figure is so distinctively Norwegian. A part at least of the play's vibrancy and charm derives from this yoking-together of dissimilar cultural traditions.

32 Or even, by extension, to lie. 'Story-teller' [O] comes close to translating Ibsen's *Digter*; 'Liar', on the other hand (Archer, Meyer) translates only one extreme meaning and ignores the ambiguity.

33 It is amusing to note in this context that the Peer Gynt story underwent a similar transformation from its original version - really a blending of two or three separate stories, not even about the same characters, cobbled together by a 15 year old goat-boy to oblige the folk-tale collector Asbjørnsen. Ironically, the goat-boy was, later, to become a writer - the dialect-poet and educationist Engebret Hougen. In the meantime the story had been extensively reworked, with an entirely new fictive narrator, by Asbjørnsen, then seized on by Ibsen as the raw material (together, perhaps, with other material from his friend Botten-Hansen, who came from the same village as Hougen) for his own *Peer Gynt*. *Digtet ihob*, indeed! (See F. Hougen, 'Omkring Asbjørnsens Reise til Gudbrandsdalen 1842', *Edda*, 35, pp. 433-62, esp. 444-55.)

34 Notably W. H. Auden, in a brilliantly suggestive, but on this point misleading essay; see 'Genius and Apostle' in *The Dyer's Hand*, London, 1963, pp. 433-55.

35 Auden, Op. cit., p. 440.

36 Translated from Kierkegaard, *Enten/Eller* (*Either/Or*), *S.V.*, II, p. 23.

37 Heiberg considers that such a limbo *is* the true Hell.

38 One of Ibsen's contemporaries, at least, saw the significance of this passage. In Grieg's setting (No. 21 in the posthumously published complete score) the accusing voices make of the scene a little judgment day (in harmonies which echo the Wolf's Glen scene from *Der Freischütz*) with a dramatic menace far beyond anything which Peer experiences 'under the Mountain'.

39 See H. Logeman's commentary on the play (The Hague, 1917), p. 309.

40 Ibsen seems to have added all Peer's interjections after the composition of the original songs - see H, VII, 323-4 and the manuscript facsimile in Larsen, Op. cit., p. 34.

41 Much of the symbolism in Andersen's story - the ice-palace, signifying coldness of heart; the tears which Kay at last sheds, melting the ice - is of direct relevance to *Brand* and *Peer Gynt*. It is also worth noting, and very relevant to both plays, that the shaft of ice which enters Kay's heart is a *Spejlkorn* - the fragment of a *mirror*. Compare also a modern variant on the same theme - Tarjei Vesaas's great novel *Is-slottet*, (*The Ice Palace*), 1963.

42 *Det gyntske selv*. Ibsen often uses this rather old-fashioned Danish construction - making a family name into an adjective - to indicate high-flown self-admiring nonsense. c.f. *ekdalsk* in *The Wild Duck*, *allmersk* in *Little Eyolf*.

43 By a beautiful - and entirely appropriate - irony, Jarry took part in Lugné-Poë's French premiere of *Peer Gynt* in 1896. He played the Troll-King (M. Meyer, *Henrik Ibsen*, III, 264).

44 Compare, again, the accusation of the unborn children's voices, 'half-way to song'...

III A Doll's House

45 Even her name is a childhood foreshortening.

46 For very different readings of the drafts, see H. Weigand, *The Modern Ibsen*, pp.71-4 (a view close to my own), M. Rosenberg, 'Ibsen v. Ibsen', *Modern Drama*, (1969), pp.187-97, and J. Northam, *Ibsen's Dramatic Method*.

47 In *The League of Youth* of 1869, Ibsen had created, but found as yet no way of using dramatically, a character, Selma Bratsberg, who clearly prefigures Nora:-

> *I klædte mig paa som en Dukke; I legte med mig, som man leger med et Barn...* [H, VI, 433]
> You dressed me up like a doll. You played with me as you might play with a child... [O, IV, 93]

The appearance of such a character, in what was taken to be Ibsen's most conservative and anti-idealist play, written a full decade before *A Doll's House*, should serve as a warning against any too-easy assumptions about a 'revolutionary change' in his thought in the mid-1870s, and against any automatic equation between scepticism about conventional marriage and other forms of radical thought.

48 The effect is the more striking since the real-life model for Nora, Laura Kieler, was much more harshly treated - she was even at one stage confined to an asylum for her 'crime' - and her husband much more unstable and difficult

in temperament than Ibsen's play would suggest. Either he did not realise this or - more probably - he *chose* to remove from Nora's character and situation all those elements which would make her a convincing martyr. (See B. M. Kinck, 'Henrik Ibsen og Laura Kieler', *Edda*, 35, 498-543.)

49 The last phrase and the whole of the next quotation are missing from the first draft [H, VIII, 375/ O, V, 290-1].

50 This passage is included, almost *verbatim*, in the first draft of Act III, suggesting that by the time that stage had been reached (late July, 1879) the later, more ambiguous version of Nora's character was beginning to take shape [H, VIII, 436/ O, V, 337].

51 In one of the drafts, Nora complains that her father has encouraged/compelled her to learn French and write poetry [H, VIII, 441/ O, V, 339]. The high-water mark of Torvald's cultural aspirations seems to be the mildly lascivious posturing of the musical theatre.

52 There is thus a revealing parallel between Torvald and Krogstad, the man he seeks to have dismissed from the Bank. Krogstad, too, has had to resign his post because of a professional scandal; and, like Torvald, has had to work his way back to respectability. One might feel that Torvald's treatment of him is as worthy of blame as any injustice which has been done to Nora.

53 *Der er to slags åndelige love, to slags samvittigheder, en i manden og en ganske anden i kvinden...* [H, VIII, 368] 'There are two kinds of moral law, two kinds of conscience, one in man and a completely different one in woman...' [O, V, 436]

54 *Fornøjeligt* could also be translated 'enjoyable' or 'pleasurable'.

55 The scene is missing from the first draft, and included in a less suggestive form at an intermediate stage in composition. (Compare H, VIII, 412-13 and 456/ O, V, 316-7 and 445.)

56 *Stygt* here surely suggests something less indulgent than O's 'horrid'; it is a word which can imply both genuine evil and (physical or moral) ugliness. Gerd in *Brand* uses it of the church, Solvejg in *Peer Gynt* of Peer's behaviour at the wedding.

57 As so many of Ibsen's major characters seem to be:- Brand, Peer, Nora, Osvald, Hjalmar, Gregers, Rebekka West, Ellida, Hedda, Tesman, Rita...

58 Rather too much has been made of Nora's tarantella at the end of Act II, as signifying the end of childishness; one can accept D. Haakonsen's argument ('Tarantella-motivet i *Et Dukkehjem*', *Edda*, 1948, pp. 263-74 (266)) that the dance represents the terror of an immature person faced with adult experience, without necessarily seeing the dance

as a sign of inner *growth*. A frightened child is a child, nonetheless; Nora dances because she is (understandably) scared and because she wishes to distract Torvald. To argue on the basis of 'visual pointers' that this scene represents the birth of a 'new Nora' seems to me to ignore all the evidence later in the play that the old Nora is still very much alive.

59 Ibsen to Erik af Edholm, 3. 1. 1880; *Brev, N. S.*, 247-8 (248).

60 Though - as will have been obvious to anyone familiar with the history of Ibsen-criticism - some aspects of my approach to *A Doll's House* are in broad agreement with Weigand's classic account of the play (*The Modern Ibsen*, 1925), I cannot agree at all with his assessment that the situation it describes is 'fundamentally comic'. On the contrary, the dangers of a damaged childhood not outgrown seem to me as menacing here as in any other Ibsen play. In my view, an ideal performance would be built around the tension between Nora's aspirations to freedom and the real, probably incurable limitations of her personality - a tension which seems to me essentially tragic in its implications.

IV Ghosts

61 Ibsen had read the novel a few weeks after its first appearance, in December 1880; and had been enraptured by it. 'It belongs amongst the finest things of its sort which present-day literature has produced', he wrote to his publisher on 16 January 1881 [H, XVII, 416/ *Br.*, II, 85]. According to John Paulsen, 'Ibsen has devoted four weeks to reading the novel, talks of it every day and reads selected passages aloud at his *soirées*' [quoted, *Br.*, I, 233].

62 Compare also another tale of spiritual passivity and biological decline, the novel *Haabløse Slægter* (*Hopeless Families* - or *Generations* - the title is appropriately ambivalent) by another Dane, Herman Bang, also published in 1880.

63 D. Russell Davis, 'A Reappraisal of Ibsen's *Ghosts*', reprinted in *Henrik Ibsen: A Critical Anthology*, ed. J.W.McFarlane, London, 1970, pp. 369-83.

64 Drafts for the earlier play show Ibsen searching for a way of suggesting within the proprieties that Rank has *tabes dorsalis*. Nora says [H, VIII, 312/ O, V, 237] that he has *tæring i rygmarven*, 'consumption of the spine'. But she garbles her terms: *tæring* usually implied tuberculosis, but *rygmarvstæring* meant locomotor ataxis, or dorsal syphilis. Verbal ambiguity allowed Rank's illness to pass misunderstood or unnoticed. There is no such ambiguity in *Ghosts*.

65 Compare the relationships between Brand and Gerd, between

Gregers and Hedvig and even, in one sense, that between Alfred and Asta.

66 Compare Aline Solness in *The Master Builder* - another dutiful wife who has failed or refused to grow up.

67 Ibsen had been preoccupied with this theme in the period before *Ghosts* was written. In March 1880, he had written to the novelist Kristian Elster of the necessity for Northern artists to experience a wider world: 'I often think with fellow-feeling of the many gifted people back at home, hemmed in by the narrowness of their circumstances (*snevre forhold*) [*Br*., II, 75-6; 25. 3. 80]. Elster, a major, long-neglected writer, never did get his travel grant. News of his death (from consumption) came as Ibsen was drafting *Ghosts*. It may well be that this event, like some of Elster's own writing, especially his fine essay on landscape and society in Western Norway, found its way into Ibsen's subconscious as he was writing the play.

V The Wild Duck

68 Even more so in the first draft of the play in which Gregers's long interrogation of Hjalmar in the first act [H, X, 48-53/ O, VI, 134-8] is almost entirely absent [H, X, 181-2/ O, VI, 246-7].

69 *Overspændt* is a difficult word to translate into English. The standard German translation, 'überspannt', comes close [G, IV, 320]. It can mean both 'neurotic' [O] and 'romantic'. Ibsen plays on the ambivalence.

70 This passage was a late insertion - after the second draft [c.f. H, X, 258, 298/ O, VI, 279] and was only fully worked into the text later still.

71 As distinct, of course, from the 'real' secrets - those in which Gregers is really interested.

72 *Fornem* is a difficult word to translate. It does have the sense of 'important' [O] but also carries with it the implication of some sort of aristocratic or personal distinction. The duck, Gregers implies, is a Werle, not an Ekdal.

73 It is no coincidence in the play's design that at this point the malapropisms which Gina has been dropping throughout now come closer and closer to the bone: *Mandfolk ... skal altid ha' noget at dividere sig med* ('Men ... always need to have something to divide [i.e. divert] themselves with' [H, X, 100/ O*, VI, 185]). And, with an even grimmer resonance, speaking of the wild duck, *Den gjøres der da krusifikser nok for*. What she means is, 'A lot of fuss is made of it' (*gjøres krus af*). But what she says (roughly, 'they make a crucifixion of it'), is much closer to the

point [H, X, 101/ O*, VI, 185]. See also the useful note in T, 405.

74 Gina, surely, is one of the great exceptions (there are others) to Durbach's comment that, 'no-one in Ibsen ever looks at the *child*. They see only symbols and emblems and analogies' (Op. cit., p. 92).

75 Mention of the 'maiden' was not included until the final draft. (The word *jomfru* also implies virginity.)

76 In the draft version, Gregers puts the question more blatantly still: *Han sa' det jo selv før han gik; hverken De eller den gamle gad bringe sligt offer for hans skyld*, 'He said it himself before he left. Neither you nor the old man would make such a sacrifice for his sake' [H, X, 254-5/ O, VI, 278].

77 Gregers, like Brand, is an industrious inventor of compound words built on *offer* ('sacrifice'). The *Ibsen Ordbok* credits him with *offerhandling* ('sacrificial deed'), *offersind* (roughly, 'mind ready to sacrifice'), *offerstemning* (see above) and *offervillig* ('willing to sacrifice').

78 *Aldrig skal nogen binde mig på næsen, at dette her var et vådeskud*, 'Nobody's ever going to persuade me this was an accident' [H, X, 160/ O, VI, 241].

79 At one point in her monograph on the play (*Vildanden av Henrik Ibsen*, Oslo, 1967, p. 197) Else Høst, who otherwise sees Gregers as a misguided idealist, permits herself to wonder whether he *can* be aware of the implications of his suggestion, given 'the mysterious identification (*mystiske identitet*) between the wild duck and Hedvig? Her grounds for dismissing the suggestion - that a desire (even an unconscious one?) for Hedvig's death would be totally out of character - seem to me logically circular, and especially unconvincing in view of all the evidence in the play that Gregers does not understand his own motives, or even wish to.

VI Rosmersholm

80 In the earliest sketches Rosmer has two children; a slightly later draft names two characters, presumably his dead wife and child, who like Beate *hører endnu ligesom huset til*, 'still seem to belong to the house' [H, X, 454/ O, VI, 389].

81 The apparent discrepancy between these two realistic political characters and the rest has been a problem for producers from the play's first production onwards. See K. Nygaard, *Gunnar Heiberg, Teatermannen*, Bergen, 1975, p. 159 f.

82 Not in previous drafts, however. There, Brendel is merely a passing acquaintance, someone whom Rosmer *har kendt lidt til... i hans velmagts dage*, 'knew... slightly in better days'

[H, X, 460/ O, VI, 393]. In this as in other ways, Ibsen's transformation of Brendel's character played a vital part in establishing the dramatic structure of the final version.

83 Ironically, it is Kroll's telling her of Brendel's former influence over Rosmer that has attracted Rebekka to Rosmersholm in the first place [H, X, 416/ O, VI, 360].

84 Ibsen twice revised this passage, first emphasizing Rosmer's fear (*skræk*, 'fear' - *rædsel*, 'terror') [H, X, 471/ O*, VI, 403] then the wild uncontrollable nature of Beate's passion.

85 The exceptions to this are few but fascinating - notably Julian's consort Helena in *Emperor and Galilean* [c.f. H, VII, 132/ O, IV, 290-1] and Hjørdis in *The Warriors at Helgeland* [H, IV, 54/ O, II, 52].

86 Compare Jonas Lie's *Den Fremsynte* and *Trold*, and Knut Hamsun's *Pan* and *Benoni*; also the extraordinary, spectral, almost monochrome Nordland landscapes by Peder Balke, some of which seem like visual correlatives to scenes in Ibsen.

87 It is commonly assumed that *Rosmersholm* and *The Lady from the Sea* are set in the same area of Norway - i.e. the region around Molde which Ibsen had visited in 1885. But he specifically indicates that *Rosmersholm* is set in 'Western', *The Lady from the Sea* in 'Northern' Norway.

88 The *draug* has two quite separate forms in Norwegian folk-lore. The more general one is that of a ghost or 'barrow-wight'. This is the sense in which Gerd uses it in *Brand* [H, V, 259/ O, III, 152]. But in *The Warriors at Helgeland*, *draugen* is used in the specifically North-Norwegian sense of the spirit of a drowned man, who appears to the doomed as an omen of approaching ill-luck. On his appearance, see the introduction to Jonas Lie's *Trold* [Lie, *S.V.*, IV, 344].

89 As if to emphasise this, Ibsen took great pains to ensure that Laura Gundersen, the great interpreter of Hjørdis (whom Ibsen had seen acting in Bergen in 1885, just before he began work on *Rosmersholm*) should *not* play Rebekka [*Br. Chr. T.*, 47].

90 See Freud's essay, reprinted in McFarlane, *H. I.: A Critical Anthology*, London, 1970, pp. 392-9.

91 In the final draft, Rebekka's confession of her *fortid*, her (guilty) past, comes at the climax of Act III; and the words which in the final version she uses to describe West, *Doktoren havde lært mig både løst og fast*, 'The doctor taught me most things...' [H, X, 416/ O, VI, 360], are used in the draft of her seducer [H, X, 527/ O, VI, 419].

92 In provincial Norway, doctors were very much reckoned as *kondisjonerte* - members of the gentry. See, besides the doctors in Ibsen's plays, those in the novels and stories of Hans Kinck.

93 The expression she uses is more vivid in Norwegian - literally

'fight over the keel of the capsized boat'. Compare the scene in *Peer Gynt*, Act V, in which Peer struggles with the Cook [H, VI, 196/ O, III, 383].

94 ... *jeg kan da ikke bli stående udenfor evig og altid*, he says in the second draft of *White Horses*. ... *Jeg må dog begynde at leve engang, jeg også*: 'I cannot for ever stand looking on as an outsider... I too must begin to live' [H, X, 477/ O, VI, 408].

95 In all but the final version, this is all it is. None of the lines quoted from this scene appear in any of the drafts [c.f. H, X, 536-40/ O, VI, 419-22].

96 Rebekka's words [H, X, 369/ O, VI, 316] spoken lightly, but bearing a greater charge of irony than she can possibly be aware of.

97 The contrast between Brendel and Mortensgård is strikingly reminiscent of that between the revolutionaries of Ibsen's youth (Thrane, Harring, Abildgaard) and the new politicians of the parliamentary left. Thrane had also been a teacher (of, amongst others, Ibsen's friend Paul Botten-Hansen) and an actor. After imprisonment in Norway and exile in America (where he had made a living as travelling photographer) he returned to Norway on a visit in 1883-4, alarming old friends and delighting old enemies (amongst them Ibsen's friends from the *Lærde Holland* days) by declaring his new-found belief that the people were not yet fit to rule. On Thrane's 1883 visit, see O. Bjørklund, *Marcus Thrane*, 2nd ed., 1970, pp. 326-32.

VII The Lady from the Sea

98 Did Thomas Mann perhaps have this phrase at the back of his mind when he made Gerda Buddenbrook say of little Hanno that, 'Er hat Heimweh nach der See'?

99 [H, XI, 112]. An untranslatable word - O's 'undertow' [VII, 84] is probably as close as we can come in English - which suggests both a physical pull and a psychological fascination.

100 In the draft Ellida does not know where he comes from; in the final version she says that he is a *Kvæn*, a Finnish immigrant, brought to Northern Norway as a child. (A sketch for this exchange was added to the MS of the draft.) In the draft he is merely *jungmanden*, 'the able seaman'; in the final version he is specifically *understyrmanden*, 'the second mate' [H, XI, 196/ O*, VII, 140-1; H, XI, 87-8/ O, VII, 61].

101 Did Thomas Mann have this figure - or, even more interestingly, perhaps, some similar archetype? - in mind when he described the red-haired stranger who appears in so many

guises, and with equally telling dramatic effect, in *Der Tod in Venedig*?

102 Compare H, XI, 62/ O, VII, 38 with H, XI, 177/ O, VII, 131; and H, XI, 92/ O, VII, 65 with H, XI, 200-1/ O, VII, 144.

103 = in the final version H, XI, 95/ O, VII, 68; except that *dette her*, 'that thing' becomes *dette gådefulde*, 'that mystery'.

104 A common motive both in Norwegian folklore and in 19th century Scandinavian literature; see Kierkegaard's discussion of the motif in *Fear and Trembling*, quoted at the head of this chapter. For a striking parallel in prose fiction, see H. Kinck's *'Datteren paa Breibø'* in *Flaggermusvinger* (1895).

105 Here Ibsen made a crucial change from the draft. There, Ellida has seen him in her dream as he is now [H, XI, 202/ O, VII, 147]. In the final version, he has appeared, as the ghost of a time-locked past, exactly as she had last seen him [H, XI, 94/ O, VII, 67].

106 Unusually, Ibsen took the trouble to confirm the importance of this trait in Hilde and of its significance to the play as a whole. Writing to the Director of the Christiania Theater he stated that 'the demonic trait [*drag*] running through her has its origin to a considerable extent in her childlike longing, which remains unsatisfied, to win "Ellida's" affection' [to Schrøder, 18. 12. 1888, *Br. Chr. Th.*, 62/ O, VII, 465].

107 A feeling Ibsen much accentuated in the play's final version. See, for example, Hilde's outburst at the end of Act I (*Abekatstreger!* 'Monkey tricks!' [H, XI, 77/ O, VII, 51]) missing in the draft [H, XI, 189/ O, VII, 138].

108 It is worth noting that the general outline of both Hilde's and Bolette's characters is noted in the very first drafts for the play which became *Rosmersholm* [H, X, 444/ O, VI, 444]. But whereas Bolette's character is outlined fairly exactly, Hilde's is merely indicated by *iagttagende; opdukkende lidenskaber*, 'observant; dawning passions'. The daemonic element he only seems to have discovered during the composition of *The Lady from the Sea*.

109 What Wangel says of Ellida, that she *tænker og fornemmer i billeder*, 'thinks in images' [H, XI, 155/ O, VII, 122], is true in a more sinister sense of Hilde, too...

110 In the projected play's first title-sheet, the action was to take place at midsummer (*midtsommertid*) - see H, XI, 171/ O, VII, 125. Compare Ibsen's earlier, equally ambivalent exercises in the genre, *Love's Comedy* and its unpublished forerunner, *St. John's Eve*.

111 In English literature, something approximating to the first genre might be found in *A Midsummer Night's Dream*, to the second in the final act of *Love's Labour's Lost*.

112 Significantly whereas Rebekka carries her own past, her *fortid*, her 'Northernness', within her, as a burden from

which she can escape only in death, Ellida's longing for what the North offers her is externalized in the fantasy-figure of the Stranger, a self-projection who can therefore be exorcized.

113 There is no mention of *ansvar*, 'responsibility' in the drafts. There, as it could never be in life, the choice is entirely free [H, XI, 241-2/ O, VII, 164-5].

VIII Hedda Gabler

114 Both comments are quoted in O, VII, 506 and 510. There *are*, in fact, affinities between the style of this play and the narrative impressionism cultivated by Norwegian and Danish novelists of the later 1880s. See, for example, Jonas Lie's *Livsslaven*, Herman Bang's *Tine* and *Ved Vejen* and Arne Garborg's *Mannfolk*. Ibsen wrote to Bang to congratulate him on *Tine* and *Ved Vejen* shortly before he began work on *Hedda Gabler* [21. 11. 1889; printed in *Brev, N. S.*, 348-9].

115 See T. K. Derry, *A Short History of Norway 1814-1972*, 1973, pp. 139-40. Ibsen would have had every chance to hear about the affair in some detail: the Minister in question was Fru Ibsen's cousin, Ludvig Daae of Solnør.

116 The parallels with the social conflicts described in *Rosmersholm* are strong. It is worth noting that in an early draft, Hedda's unmarried name is 'Rømer' - a name which recalls both 'Rosmer' and its own earlier form, 'Boldt-Rømer' [H, XI, 406/ O, VII, 273].

117 I can see little justification for Halvdan Koht's assertion that Hedda is the 'least Norwegian' character in the play (a comment which seems to cast more light on Koht's social attitudes than it does on Ibsen's); and I find equally unconvincing Else Høst's belief that Hedda's character was closely modelled on that of Emilie Bardach. (See Prof. Høst's 1958 monograph on the play.) Quite apart from the difference in age and (so far as one can tell) in temperament and outlook between the two, so many aspects of Hedda's character can be related to the Norway of her time that it seems wilful to seek a model from so different a background.

118 On Hedda's passion for harking-back, see S. Saari, '*Hedda Gabler*: the past recaptured', *Modern Drama*, 20, pp. 299-316.

119 In an early sketch for the play, Ibsen added a different dimension to these hints of biological and cultural exhaustion. There, he makes Hedda say:- *Husk på jeg er et gammelmandsbarn - og dertil en udlevet mands - eller en affældig da ...*, 'Remember that I'm the child of an old

man - and a decrepit one what's more - or at least past his active life...' [H, XI, 515/ O, VII, 478].

120 It was a technique which had been used before by Scandinavian writers to indicate aristocratic decline. The Danish novelist J. P. Jacobsen describes a similar disproportion between the form of a face and its texture in the first chapter of his *Niels Lyhne* (1880):- 'She had her ancestors' black shining eyes with their fine straight brows, their well-formed nose, their powerful chin.. but her cheek was pale, her hair was soft as silk and clung limp and smooth to the shape of her head...'

121 This line is missing from the draft versions [H, XI, 412/ O, VII, 278] as is all reference to Hedda's and Thea's hair.

122 Again, this final sentence is missing from the draft [H, XI, 460/ O, VII, 319] and Berte does not witness the scene, as she does in the final version but merely calls out from another room.

123 *næsten lydløst* - a direction which Ibsen uses only sparingly, and to great effect. Compare Hilda's *forfærdelig spændende*, 'terribly exciting', whispered at the end of Act II of *The Master Builder* [H, XII, 99/ O, VII, 421].

124 Again, the mention of Thea's hair, with its overtones of childish animosity, is missing from the draft [H, XI, 482/ O, VII, 338-9].

125 The most direct, and perhaps too obvious example of this counterpointing, Ibsen actually omitted from the play's final version. In the draft version of Act III, Brack complains that he is tired of losing 'friends' to *uvedkommende... børn*, 'intruders... children' whom he cannot abide because they supplant him in their mothers' affections [H, XI, 474/ O, VII, 332].

126 The parallel between *A Doll's House* and *Hedda Gabler* must have been a conscious one. That Krogstad is right and Brack wrong is partly a reflection of a shift in Ibsen's artistic ideals (which corresponded to a much wider change in the temper of Scandinavian literature in the late 1880s) but also a fundamental difference in *class*. Nora is unmistakably a *bourgeoise*, a new woman in more senses than one.

IX The Master Builder

127 On the other hand, it should perhaps be pointed out that Ibsen *had* probably met the dedicatee of the play's manuscript, Hildur Andersen, in 1874, when he was 46 and she was a girl of 10; and that there seems a strong probability that she later destroyed early drafts and jottings for the play. (See F. Bull, *Edda*, 57, p. 47f., and

Brev, N. S., Kommentarbind, p.126.)

128 An emphasis which Ibsen strengthened still further in the final version by making Hilde repeat the *min* - [c.f. E, III, 497. The earlier version not noted in H or O].

129 It is worth noting that perhaps the most resonant and evocative image of all, the harps in the air, was added at a very late stage in the play's development. In the one draft version that has been preserved, the whole of the passage in which Hilde describes Solness singing on the tower [H, XII, 58/ O, VII, 382] was inserted later [H, XII, 138/ Not noted in O].

130 These rather sinister words of Hilde's, with their implied threat are again a late addition to the manuscript [H, XII, 151/ O, VII, 525].

131 Again, this outburst of childish petulance was a late addition to the draft [H, XII, 165/ O, VII, 527].

132 They are the traditional translation of Christ's last words on the cross. See Inga-Stina Ewbank, 'Ibsen's Dramatic Language as a link between his "Realism" and his "Symbolism"', in *Contemporary Approaches to Ibsen*, I, pp. 96-123 [104-5].

133 As Clara Stuyver rightly observes (Op. cit., p. 457), 'Trotz ihrer scheinbaren Gesundheit und ihres eingebildeten "robusten Gewissens" ist sie [Hilde] gewiss nicht weniger kränklich als Aline und Kaja, und als Solness selber'.

X Little Eyolf

134 J. Kerans, '*Kindermord* and Will in *Little Eyolf*', in *Modern Drama; Essays in Criticism*, ed. Bogard and Oliver, New York, 1965, pp. 192-208.

135 On the 'plexus of blood ties and family ties' in the play, see J.W.McFarlane, 'The Structured World of Ibsen's Late Dramas', in *Ibsen and the Theatre*, ed. Durbach, 1980, pp. 134-7; and O, VIII, 4-7.

136 The review is reprinted in *Varia*, the fifth volume of Söderberg's reissued *Samlade Skrifter*, Stockholm, Liber Förlag, 1978, pp. 195-202.

137 On the relationship of the draft to the final version, and its significance for the play, see McFarlane, O, VIII, 8-9, 17-24, and 313-5.

138 *Fortærende* carries with it the sense, appropriate to Alfred's view of Rita's sexuality, of that which 'consumes', 'devours' or even 'corrodes'.

139 For a perceptive and extended analysis of Alfred's state of mind and its antecedents in the Romantic (and especially Byronic) obsession with incest, see Durbach, '*Ibsen the Romantic*', pp. 111-127.

140 In the separate version published in F, IV, 436, it is dated 16 March 1892; *ro*, 'peace' is changed to *tro*, 'faith'. For a discussion of the relative appropriateness of the poem to the two plays, see D. A. Seip's introduction, H, XII, 20-1.

XI John Gabriel Borkman

141 In both senses of that ambivalent word. Alfred's bad faith is instantly familiar to us; but it is also characteristic of many of the decadent heroes of mid- and late-19th century fiction, from Turgenev's 'superfluous men' to Hardy's Clym and Jude, Jacobsen's Niels Lyhne, Hamsun's Nagel and Glahn, and the narrator of Garborg's *Weary Men.*

142 Ellis-Fermor's translation.

143 But not, interestingly, in the surviving draft version [c.f. H, XIII, 130/ O, VIII, 330]. The line is a late addition, introduced, perhaps, to strike the key-note for what is to follow.

144 Not usually translated. Nor is the full force of her hesitation (*som - som*) as she struggles (or pretends to) to bring herself to name her husband.

145 Nora, too, talks about having *noget i baghånden*, 'something up my sleeve' [H, VIII, 288/ O*, V, 215].

146 This passage was a late insertion into the draft [H, XII, 135].

147 Although it is not normally translated in this light (even, surprisingly, in the standard German version [G, V, 427]), this phrase surely parodies Nietzsche's concept of the *Übermensch*. (See Archer's note to the original English edition, p.ix, and F. Paul, *Symbol und Mythos. Studien zum Spätwerk Ibsens*, München, 1969, p. 61.) *Overskurk* does not otherwise seem to exist in Norwegian; and Ibsen uses it only here.

148 One of the most remarkable features of the play's structure is the matching of dramatic and experiential time. Few Ibsen plays explore deeper in the characters' past; yet the whole of the play's present action is concentrated into exactly the time it takes to perform.

149 The scene, indeed much of this play as a whole, looks forward and leads on to the later dramas of Strindberg (*A Dream Play*, the chamber-plays) in a more important and substantial sense than the more obviously experimental *When We Dead Awaken*. The significance of this 'transformation scene' has been largely overlooked by critics; but see F. Paul, Op. cit., pp. 124-5.

150 Op.cit.,p.66. Much of Durbach's account of the play seems to me very perceptive; but I think he over-romanticizes, especially, Borkman's worship of these *værdier* (literally, not 'treasures' but just 'large sums of money'). As

McFarlane rightly stresses [O, VIII, 25] Borkman is an embezzler, not a Romantic seer. The gold he has longed to 'liberate' lies in a bank-vault, not a mine (the final version of this speech actually says this, though the draft did not - cf. H, XIII, 179 /O, VIII, 337); and if the literary analogues Durbach adduces suggest anything, it is how far capitalism has debased the currency of the Romantic imagination.

XII When We Dead Awaken

151 For an interesting and suggestive account of the way in which the play *does* function as a recapitulation of past themes and motives, see H. Anker, '*Når Vi Døde Vågner*, Ibsens Dramatiske Epilog', *Edda*, 56, pp. 178-219.

152 Vigeland's later work - the celebrated 'Monolith' in Frognerparken, for example - contains much that is reminiscent of Rubek's masterpiece. But the motif of a human pillar was a common one in the art of this period. Compare Edvard Munch's lithograph, *Funeral March*, of 1897.

153 This line is a later addition to the manuscript of the draft.

154 In the first draft, the line read ... *vor drøm*, '... our dream' [H, XIII, 303].

155 As James Hurt notes (*Catiline's Dream*, p. 28) this uncertainty is a motif which has antecedents in Ibsen's earliest work.

156 The Norwegian *jordkvinden* carries with it a suggestion of vitality which is difficult to render in English. Morgenstern's German translation ('das Weib der Erde' - G, V, 507) comes closer.

157 In the original draft, she speaks instead of *mit eget livs opstandelse*, 'my own life's resurrection' [H, XIII, 308]. For an illuminating discussion of the significance of the phrase's final version, see Durbach, Op. cit., p. 144.

158 It is notable that these lines, and indeed almost all the references to the dagger/needle, with its murderous, demonic associations, were later additions to the draft manuscript (c.f. H, XIII, 305-7; 323-4, etc).

159 Against this, it could be argued that the scene in Act II in which a group of playing children run to Irene and she responds to them [H, XII, 255/ O, VIII, 273] represents a kind of maturity in her which is denied to Rubek and Maja. (See Durbach's interesting treatment of this passage, Op. cit., p. 72.) But Irene's reaction represents an appearance, a might-have-been, not a reality reflected in her present personality. One may note that this scene is carried over directly with little alteration from the play's first version, suggesting an earlier view of Irene's character, elsewhere largely negated by later revisions.

Notes

160 *Digtet* implies imaginative creation - and also (c.f. Ch II, p.61 above) falsification.

161 Literally, 'in the foreground'. Compare (as Irene undoubtedly does) what has become of her own image.

162 As distinct from the title Rubek claims in his own defence, *Kunstner*, 'artist'.

163 Significantly, her song is missing altogether from the original draft.

Select Bibliography

The secondary literature on Ibsen is so extensive that it would have been neither practicable nor profitable to give more than the most selective of bibliographies. Accordingly, reference to secondary sources, here as in the text, has been confined to those books and articles which bear most directly on the subject-matter of the present study, to those more general works on Ibsen with which I agree or disagree in ways which may prove interesting and thought-provoking, and to those which pursue lines of enquiry congruent with mine but outside the scope of this book. I have omitted from the bibliography one or two sources of purely factual information referred to in the footnotes.

PRIMARY TEXTS

Norwegian and Danish

The principal edition of Ibsen's works used has been the *Samlede Verker*, I - XXI, Hundreårsutgave, ed. Bull, Koht & Seip, Oslo, 1928-57. (H)

Other editions consulted:

Samlede Værker, 1st ed. ('Folkeudgave'), I - X, København, 1898-1902. (F)

Efterladte Skrifter, I - III, ed. Koht & Elias, Kristiania & København, 1909. (E)

Henrik Ibsens episke Brand, ed. Larsen, København & Kristiania, 1907.

Ibsens dramatik, (annotated ed. of 5 plays) ed. Törnqvist, Stockholm, 1971. (T)
Breve fra Henrik Ibsen, I - II, ed. Koht & Elias, København & Kristiania, 1904. (*Br.*)
Henrik Ibsens Brevveksling med Christiania Theater, 1878 - 1899, ed. Anker, Oslo, 1964. (*Br. Chr. Th.*)
Henrik Ibsen: Brev 1845-1905, Ny samling, ed. Ø. Anker, Oslo, 1979-80. (*Brev, N.S.*)

Of literary texts by other authors cited or referred to:
those by Kierkegaard are drawn from the *Samlede Værker*, I - XX, København, 1962; those by Jonas Lie from the *Samlede Værker*, I - V, Mindeudgave, Kristiania & København, 1908-9; and those by J. P. Jacobsen from the *Samlede Værker*, I - V, ed. Borup, København, 1924-9.
The edition of J. L. Heiberg's *En Sjæl efter Døden* used is that ed. by Borup, 6th ed., Dansklærerforeningen, 1963.

Translations

The principal English translation of Ibsen's plays and their drafts used is that of *The Oxford Ibsen*, I - VIII, ed. McFarlane, Oxford U.P., 1960-77. (O)
Other English translations consulted include those by Archer, Meyer and Ellis-Fermor.
The German edition of Ibsen's work used is the *Sämtliche Werke*, I - V, (Volksausgabe), ed. Elias & Schlenther, Berlin, 1911. (G)

SECONDARY TEXTS

Anker, H. 'Ibsens Skyggeskikkelser', *Nordisk Tidskrift*, (1956), pp. 185-93.

Anker, H. '*Når Vi Døde Vågner* - Ibsens Dramatiske Epilog', *Edda*, (1956), pp. 178-219.

Arestad, Sv. 'Ibsen's Portrayal of the Artist', *Edda*, (1960), pp. 86-100.

Auden, W. H. 'Genius and Apostle', in *The Dyer's Hand*, London, 1963, pp. 433-55.

Beyer, Edv. 'Henrik Ibsens *Rosmersholm*' in *En ny Ibsen?*, ed. H. Noreng, Oslo, 1979, pp. 74-88.

Beyer, H. *Søren Kierkegaard og Norge*, Kristiania, 1924.

Bradbrook, M. *Ibsen the Norwegian*, London, 1946.

Bull, F., Paasche, F., and Winsnes, A.H. *Norsk Litteraturhistorie*, III - V, 2nd ed., Oslo, 1959-63.

Chamberlain, J. *Ibsen: The Open Vision*, London, 1982.

Dahl, H. *Bergmannen og Byggmesteren*, Oslo, 1958.

Derry, T. K. *A History of Modern Norway, 1814-1972*, Oxford, 1973.

Downs, B. *Ibsen: The Intellectual Background*, Cambridge, 1946.

Durbach, E. '*Ibsen the Romantic*', London, 1982.

Ewbank, I.-S. 'Ibsen's Dramatic Language as a link between his "Realism" and his "Symbolism"', *Contemporary Approaches to Ibsen*, 1, 1965, pp. 96-123.

Freud, S. 'Rosmersholm', (tr. J. Strachey), repr. in *Henrik Ibsen: A Critical Anthology*, ed. McFarlane, London, 1970.

Ganz, A. 'Miracle and Vine leaves: an Ibsen play rewrought', *PMLA*, 94, pp.9-21.

Haakonsen, D. 'Tarantella-motivet i *Et Dukkehjem*', *Edda*, 1948, pp.263-74.

Haakonsen, D. 'The Function of Sacrifice in Ibsen's Realistic Drama', *Contemporary Approaches to Ibsen* [1] (1965), pp. 21-34.

Haaland, A. *Ibsens verden. En studie i kunst som forsking*, Oslo, 1978.

Haugan, J. *Henrik Ibsens metode*, København, 1977.

Hemmer, B. *Brand - Kongs-emnerne - Peer Gynt*, Oslo, 1972.

Holtan, O. *Mythic Patterns in Ibsen's Last Plays*, Minneapolis, 1970.

Hurt, J. *Catiline's Dream*, Urbana, Illinois, 1972.

Høst, E. *Hedda Gabler*, Oslo, 1958.

Høst, E. *Vildanden av Henrik Ibsen*, Oslo, 1967.

Johnson, K. *The Symbolic Child: A study of transformation in Henrik Ibsen's later plays*, unpublished PhD diss., University of California, 1977.

Kerans, J. '*Kindermord* and Will in *Little Eyolf*', in *Modern Drama: Essays in Criticism*, ed. Bogard and Oliver, New York, 1965.

Kinck, B. M. 'Henrik Ibsen og Laura Kieler', *Edda*, 1935, pp. 498-543.

Koht, H. *Henrik Ibsen, Eit Diktarliv*, Oslo, 1st ed., 1928-9 and 2nd revised ed., 1954.

Logeman, H. *A commentary, critical and explanatory, on the Norwegian text of Henrik Ibsen's 'Peer Gynt'*, The Hague, 1917.

Lyons, C. *Henrik Ibsen: The Divided Consciousness*, Carbondale & Edwardsville, Illinois, 1972.

McFarlane, J. *Ibsen and the Temper of Norwegian Literature*, Oxford, 1960.

McFarlane, J. 'Meaning and Evidence in Ibsen's Drama', *Contemporary Approaches to Ibsen*, [1] (1965), pp. 35-50.

McFarlane, J. 'The Structured World of Ibsen's Late Dramas', in *Ibsen and the Theatre*, ed. Durbach, London, 1980, pp. 131-140.

Meyer, M. *Ibsen*, I - III, London, 1967-71.

Mosfjeld, O. *Henrik Ibsen og Skien*, Oslo, 1949.

Munzar, J. 'Henrik Ibsen und die Tradition der Bürger-Künstler-Problematik in der deutschen Literatur', *Contemporary Approaches to Ibsen*, 5, (1985), pp. 183-93.

Noreng, H. 'Henrik Ibsen som komediedikter - med konsentrasjon om 1860-årene', in *En Ny Ibsen?*, ed. Noreng, Oslo, 1979, pp. 9-51.

Northam, J. *Ibsen's Dramatic Method*, London, 1953.

Northam, J. *Ibsen: A Critical Study*, Cambridge, 1973.

Northam, J. 'The Substance of Ibsen's Idealism', *Contemporary Approaches to Ibsen* [1], (1965), pp.9-20.

Nygaard, K. *Gunnar Heiberg: Teatermannen*, Bergen, 1975.

Ording, F. *Henrik Ibsens vennekreds: Det Lærde Holland*, Oslo, 1927.

Paul, F. *Symbol und Mythos. Studien zum Spätwerk Henrik Ibsens*, München, 1969.

Rosenberg, M. 'Ibsen versus Ibsen: Or Two Versions of *A Doll's House*', *Modern Drama*, (1969), pp. 187-97.

Russell Davis, D. 'A Reappraisal of Ibsen's *Ghosts*', repr. in *Henrik Ibsen: A Critical Anthology*, ed. McFarlane, London, 1970.

Saari, S. '*Hedda Gabler*: the past recaptured', *Modern Drama*, (1977), pp. 299-316.

Stuyver, C. *Ibsens dramatische Gestalten*, Amsterdam, 1952.

Weigand, H. *The Modern Ibsen*, New York, 1925.

Østvedt, E. *Henrik Ibsen: Barndom og ungdom*, Skien, 1968.

Index to the Works

[See also under 'drafts and revisions' and 'sources, analogues and models' in the General Index.]

General Index

[Please note:
(1) Where there is an accepted, satisfactory English translation of a Scandinavian title it is listed thus; otherwise titles are given in the original.
(2) For Scandinavian names (only) the order of the Norwegian alphabet is followed: thus æ, ø (+ Swedish ö) and å (+ aa) follow z, throughout.]

SERIES A
SCANDINAVIAN LITERARY HISTORY AND CRITICISM

Series A: No 1

STRINDBERG AND AUTOBIOGRAPHY
Reading and writing a life

MICHAEL ROBINSON
Senior Lecturer in English and Drama
Loughborough University

1 870041 00 3 192 pages £9.50

This is a book of major scholarly importance both about Strindberg as a writer and also about the nature of autobiographical writing. The myth that any writer generates about his own experiences will always leave a distinct stamp on his work. In the case of Strindberg – a consummate creator as well as a player of roles – a sense of the configuration of that myth is of crucial importance for a proper understanding of the author's achievement.

In this sensitive and discerning study, Michael Robinson has turned aside from the more traditional biographical approach to Strindberg. Instead he sets out to explore the highly idiosyncratic way in which Strindberg projected himself in language, looking at the problems which this brought in its trail and laying bare the subterfuges it engendered. He has not limited himself to those works explicitly designated by Strindberg as autobiographical but ranges widely over the dramas, the narratives and other prose works.

Michael Robinson read Comparative Literature at the University of East Anglia, took his doctorate in the Department of Scandinavian Studies in the University of Cambridge, and now teaches at Loughborough University. His much acclaimed critical study of Samuel Beckett, *The Long Sonata of the Dead*, was published in 1969.

Series A: No 2

ASPECTS OF MODERN SWEDISH LITERATURE

Edited by IRENE SCOBBIE

Reader in Scandinavian Studies

University of Edinburgh

1 870041 02 X c.376 pages £10.50
Publication Spring 1988

This book gives a comprehensive account of the main currents in Swedish literature since the 1880's. Among its ten chapters, there are survey accounts of the more important periods and movements (such as the working class literature of the thirties, 20th century lyric poetry, and the modern novel), as well as individual studies in depth of selected writers. Professor Inga-Stina Ewbank (University of Leeds) contributes a penetrating chapter on Strindberg; Karin Petherick (Reader in Swedish at the University of London) writes on Hjalmar Bergman; and Irene Scobbie, in addition to exercising overall control, contributes a chapter on Pär Lagerkvist.

Other contributors to the volume include teachers of Scandinavian Studies at other British universities and other recognised authorities.

The book is designed and written both for the student of Swedish literature (in whose interest the original Swedish of the illustrative quotations has been included) and also for the general reader who will find English translations of the quoted passages.

Irene Scobbie, the editor of the volume, is Reader in Scandinavian Studies at the University of Edinburgh. Her publications include Sweden. Nation of the Modern World (1972), Pär Lagerkvist. An Introduction (1962), Lagerkvist's Gäst hos verkligheten (1974), An Anthology of Swedish Poetry from 1880 to the present day (with P. Holmes, 1980) and numerous articles on modern Swedish authors, especially Lagerkvist, P.C. Jersild and P.O. Sundman.

Series A: No 3

IBSEN AND MEANING

Studies, essays and prefaces 1953-87

JAMES McFARLANE

Emeritus Professor of European Literature,

University of East Anglia

1 870041 07 0 c.396 pages £10.50
Publication Autumn 1988

At the heart of this book is the series of eight critical introductions written by James McFarlane for the successive volumes of *The Oxford Ibsen* as they appeared over a twenty year period in the 1960's and 1970's. Taken individually, these prefaces examine with sensitivity and insight the entire corpus of Ibsen's dramatic authorship in its chronological development – an exercise which Ibsen himself urged on any reader who wished to reach the fullest understanding of his work. Taken together, and published as they now are between the covers of one book, these prefaces constitute a uniquely authoritative account of Ibsen's dramatic achievement.

As a back-up to these chapters, James McFarlane has included six other selected critical pieces on Ibsen, written at various times over the past thirty years: on Ibsenism as a phenomenon; on Ibsen's methods of dramatic composition as revealed by his draft manuscripts; and on various aspects of Ibsen's place in the history of nineteenth century European thought.

The collection is prefaced by a thoughtful examination of the nature of translation, of its modes and problems, which sets out the theoretical framework upon which the translations in *The Oxford Ibsen* are based.

'. . . His linguistic and textual skills, allied to a sharp eye for dramatic structure, built up a standard work' (The Times, reviewing The Oxford Ibsen)
'James Walter McFarlane is the supreme Ibsen editor of our time . . .' (J. C. Trewin in the Birmingham Post)

Series A: No 5

STRINDBERG'S MISS JULIE

A Play and its Transpositions

BARRY JACOBS, Professor of Comparative Literature, Monclair State College, NJ and

EGIL TÖRNQVIST, Professor of Scandinavian Studies, University of Amsterdam

1 870041 08 9 c.296 pages £9.50
Publication Autumn 1988

August Strindberg's one-act drama *Miss Julie* is today one of the most frequently produced plays of all time, written by one of the most seminal playwrights of the modern age. Its remarkable *Preface* is moreover widely regarded as one of the most penetrating pronouncements on the nature of naturalistic drama.

This present volume, written by two of the leading Strindberg scholars of the day, offers the first detailed study of this important work in all its different manifestations: stage play, film, radio and TV drama, opera and ballet. Part One sets the biographical and literary background of the play, illuminates its genre, discusses the *Preface* in relation to the play itself and to the dramatic theories of its day, and gives a structural and thematic analysis of the work. A concluding chapter examines the significance of the play in relation to the development of the drama of today. Part Two considers the problems which attach to its various transformations: into the medium of English; into radio and TV; into opera and ballet. There is an annotated list of major productions of the play world-wide, and a full bibliography.